THE MARSHALL CAVENDISH
ILLUSTRATED ENCYCLOPEDIA OF
WORLD WAR II

Volume 7

**An objective, chronological and comprehensive history
of the Second World War.**

Authoritative text by
Lt. Colonel Eddy Bauer.

Consultant Editor
Brigadier General James L. Collins, Jr., U.S.A., Chief of Military
History, Department of the Army.

Editor-in-Chief
Brigadier Peter Young, D.S.O., M.C., M.A., F.S.A. Formerly head
of Military History Department at the Royal Military Academy,
Sandhurst.

Marshall Cavendish New York & London

Editor-in-Chief Brigadier Peter
   Young, D.S.O., M.C., M.A., F.S.A.
Reader's Guide Christopher Chant, M.A.
Index Richard Humble
Consultant Editor Correlli Barnett,
   Fellow of Churchill College, Cambridge
Editorial Director Brian Innes
Illustrators Malcolm McGregor
   Pierre Turner
Contributors Correlli Barnett, Brigadier Michael Calvert, Richard Humble,
   Henry Shaw, Lt.-Col. Alan Shepperd, Martin Blumenson, Stanley L. Falk,
   Jaques Nobécourt, Colonel Rémy, Brigadier General E. H. Simmons
   U.S.M.C. (ret'd), Captain Donald Macintyre, Jonathan Martin, William
   Fowler, Jenny Shaw, Dr. Frank Futrell, Lawson Nagel, Richard Storry,
   John Major, Andrew Mollo.
Cover Design Tony Pollicino
Production Consultant Robert Paulley
Production Controller Patrick Holloway
Cover illustration The end of war;
   Corporal C. Dunn, U.S.M.C., raises the U.S. Flag over Yokosuka Naval
   Base in Japan.

16341

Reference Edition Published 1981

Published by Marshall Cavendish Corporation
147 West Merrick Road, Freeport, N.Y. 11520
©Orbis Publishing Ltd. 1980, 1979, 1978, 1972
©1966 Jaspard Polus, Monaco

Printed in Great Britain by Jarrold and Sons Ltd.

Bound in Great Britain by Cambridge University Press

Cataloguing in Publication Data

Marshall Cavendish Encyclopedia of World War II.
   1. World War, 1939–1945—Dictionaries
   I. Young, Peter, *1915–*
   940.53'03'21   D740

   ISBN 0-85685-948-6 (set)
   ISBN 0-85685-955-9 (volume 7)

Picture Acknowledgements
1681: Keystone; 1682: Imperial War Museum; 1683: U.S.I.S., Keystone; 1684:
Imperial War Museum, Camera Press; 1684/1685: Imperial War Museum; 1685:
Keystone; 1686/1687: Imperial War Museum; 1687: U.S. Army; 1688: Imperial
War Museum; 1689: Orbis; 1690: U.S.I.S.; 1691: Imperial War Museum; 1692:
U.S. Army; 1693: Keystone; 1694: U.S.I.S.; 1694/1695: Keystone; 1696: Popper-
foto; 1697: Orbis, Popperfoto; 1698/1699: Keystone; 1700: Keystone; 1701:
Magnum, Popperfoto; 1702: Popperfoto; 1703: Documentation Française, Camera
Press; 1704/1705: Orbis; 1706: Popperfoto; 1707: Orbis; 1708: Camera Press;
1709: Bibliothèque Nationale/Dorka; 1710: Weidenfeld & Nicolson; 1711: Bapty;
1712/1713: Weidenfeld & Nicolson; 1714: Weidenfeld & Nicolson; 1715:
Weidenfeld & Nicolson; 1716: Weidenfeld & Nicolson; 1717: By courtesy of Mr.
H. M. Rigby; 1718: Musée de la Radio/Dorka; 1719: Robert Hunt Library; 1720:
Imperial War Museum; 1721: Imperial War Museum; 1722/1723: Imperial War
Museum; 1724: Bapty; 1725: Bapty; 1726: Keystone; 1727: Bapty; 1728/1729:
Musée de la Guerre, Vincennes/Dorka; 1730: Imperial War Museum; 1731: Im-
perial War Museum; 1732: Imperial War Museum; 1733: Musée de la Guerre,
Vincennes/Dorka; 1734: Keystone; 1735: Imperial War Museum; 1736: Imperial
War Museum; 1737: Keystone; 1738: Keystone; 1739: Keystone; 1740:
Keystone; 1741: U.S. Army; 1742/1743: Camera Press; 1743: Camera Press,
Keystone; 1744: U.S. Army; 1744/1745: Camera Press; 1745: Camera Press;
1746/1747: Keystone, U.S. Army; 1747: Camera Press; 1748: Camera Press; 1749:
Orbis/Alan Rees; 1750/1751: Camera Press; 1752: Keystone, Imperial War
Museum; 1753: I.W.M./Keystone; 1754/1755: U.S. Army; 1755: U.S. Army;
1756: Imperial War Museum; 1757: Imperial War Museum; 1758: Imperial War
Museum; 1759: Imperial War Museum; 1760: Imperial War Museum; 1761: Jean
Lemaire; 1762/1763: Imperial War Museum; 1763: Keystone; 1764: Musée de la
Guerre, Vincennes, Popperfoto; 1765: Keystone; 1766/1767: Keystone; 1768:
Keystone; 1769: Keystone; 1770: Imperial War Museum; 1770/1771: Keystone;
1771: Keystone; 1772: Keystone, U.S. Army; 1773: Keystone; 1774: Keystone;
1775: Keystone; 1776: Keystone; 1777: U.S. Air Force; 1778: U.S.I.S.; 1779:
U.S.I.S., Associated Press; 1780: Orbis; 1781: U.S.I.S.; 1782/1783: Popperfoto;
1783: *Punch*/Illingworth; 1784: Popperfoto; 1785: Orbis; 1786: U.S.I.S.; 1787:
Keystone; 1788: Orbis/Alan Rees, Keystone; 1790/1791: Bapty;
1792: Bapty; 1792/1793: Bapty; 1793: Bapty; 1794: Imperial War Museum;
1794/1795: Imperial War Museum; 1795: Imperial War Museum; 1796: Fox
Photos; 1797: Fox Photos; 1798: Blitz; 1798/1799: Blitz; 1799: Blitz; 1800:
I.W.M./Camera Press; 1801: I.W.M./Camera Press; 1802/1803: Orbis; 1804: Imperial War Museum, Popperfoto, I.W.M./Camera Press; 1805: Orbis; 1806:
I.W.M./Camera Press; 1806/1807: I.W.M./Camera Press; 1807: Imperial War
Museum; 1808: I.W.M./Tweedy; 1809: Andreas Feininger/Library of Congress;
1810: Musée de la Guerre, Vincennes; 1811: New York Public Library/Nicole
Marchand, Associated Press; 1812: Orbis; 1813: Imperial War Museum;
1814/1815: Imperial War Museum; 1816: Imperial War Museum, Blitz Publications; 1817: Orbis; 1818: Keystone; 1819: U.S.I.S., Imperial War Museum,
I.W.M./Camera Press; 1820: Imperial War Museum, I.W.M./Camera Press, Imperial War Museum; 1821: Imperial War Museum; 1822/1823: Popperfoto, Imperial War Museum, Popperfoto, Imperial War Museum, Popperfoto, 1824:
I.W.M./Chris Barker, H.M.S.O.; 1825: Popperfoto; 1826/1827: Orbis; 1827: Imperial War Museum; 1828: Imperial War Museum; 1828/1829: Keystone,
Keystone; 1829: Keystone, Keystone; 1830/1831: The Commando Association;
1832: Black Star; 1833: Popperfoto, Black Star; 1834: Bapty; 1835: Popperfoto,
Black Star; 1836/1837: Blitz Publications; 1838: Blitz Publications; 1839: Blitz
Publications; 1840: Blitz Publications; 1841: Imperial War Museum; 1842: S.A.S.;
1842/1843: S.A.S.; 1844/1845: Orbis/Pierre Tilley; 1846: S.A.S.; 1847: S.A.S.;
1848: Orbis; 1849: Signal/Nicole Marchand; 1850: Novosti; 1850/1851: Novosti;
1851: Novosti; 1852: Orbis; 1853: Novosti; 1854/1855: Bundesarchiv, Koblenz;
1856/1857: Novosti; 1857: Keystone, Camera Press; 1858: Keystone; 1859:
Keystone; 1860: Keystone; 1861: Keystone; 1862/1863: Bundesarchiv, Koblenz;
1863: Bundesarchiv, Koblenz; 1864: Camera Press; 1865: Novosti; 1866: Novosti;
1866/1867: Novosti; 1868: Novosti; 1869: Fitzpatrick/*St. Paul Dispatch*,
Simplicissimus, Munich; 1870/1871: Novosti; 1871: Keystone; 1872: Orbis; 1873:
Novosti; 1874: Signal/Dorka; 1874/1875: Signal/Dorka; 1876: Novosti; 1877:
Signal/Nicole Marchand, Novosti; 1878: Novosti; 1878/1879: U.S.I.S.; 1879:
Keystone; 1880: Orbis; 1881: Blitz Publications; 1882/1883: Novosti; 1883:
Novosti; 1884: Novosti; 1885: Novosti; 1886: Novosti; 1886/1887: Novosti; 1887:
Novosti; 1888: Blitz Publications; 1888/1889: Novosti; 1890: Blitz Publications;
1891: International News; 1892: Harrisiadis; 1892/1893: Harrisiadis; 1894:
Keystone; 1895: Bundesarchiv, Koblenz; 1896: Orbis/Alan Rees; 1897: Orbis;
1898/1899: Orbis; 1900: Bundesarchiv, Koblenz; 1901: I.W.M./Tweedy;
1902/1903: Camera Press; 1903: Popperfoto; 1904: Novosti; 1905: *Punch*, London,
Punch, London, *London Star*; 1906: Novosti; 1907: U.S.I.S.; 1908/1909: U.S.
Signal/Corps; 1909: U.S. Signal/Corps; 1910: Orbis; 1911: U.S.I.S.; 1912:
Associated Press, U.S.I.S.; 1912/1913: U.S.I.S.; 1913: I.W.M./Camera Press;
U.S.I.S.; 1914: Etablissement Cinématographique des Armées, U.S.I.S.; 1915: Or-
bis/Alan Rees, U.S.I.S.; 1916: Keystone; 1916/1917: Keystone; 1917: Keystone;
1918: Keystone; 1919: U.S.I.S.; 1920: U.S.I.S.; 1921: Documentation Française,
Robert Hunt Library; 1922: Documentation Française; 1923: Orbis; 1924: New
York Public Library/Nicole Marchand; 1925: Keystone; 1926: Musée de la
Guerre, Vincennes/Dorka, Keystone; 1927: I.W.M./Tweedy, Keystone; 1928:
Keystone; 1929: Keystone; 1930: Keystone; 1931: Keystone; 1932/1933:
Keystone; 1933: Keystone; 1934/1935: Keystone; 1936/1937: Keystone; 1938:
Documentation Française; 1939: U.S.I.S., Documentation Française; 1940: Robert
Hunt Library; 1941: Etablissements Cinématographiques des Armées, Keystone,
Keystone; 1942/1943: Keystone; 1944: Orbis/Alan Rees; 1945: U.S. Army;
1946/1947: U.S. Army; 1947: U.S. Army; 1948: Documentation Française,
Keystone; 1949: Keystone; 1950: Etablissements Cinématographiques des Armées;
1951: Keystone; 1952/1953: Keystone; 1954: U.S.I.S.; 1954/1955: Archives de la
Musée de la Guerre; 1955: U.S.I.S.; 1956: U.S.I.S., Documentation Française;
1957: Orbis; 1958/1959: Keystone; 1959: Keystone; 1960: Keystone,
Etablissements Cinématographiques des Armées.

Contents of Volume Seven

CONTENTS OF VOLUME SEVEN

WORLD
WAR II

CHAPTER 121
Breakout

Major-General Joseph "Lightning Joe" Collins was born in 1896 and graduated from West Point Military Academy in 1917. He was a battalion commander of the 18th Infantry Regiment in Koblenz after World War I. Between the wars he served both as an infantry and artillery instructor. In 1941 Collins was chief-of-staff of VII Corps and then of the Hawaii Department. Early in 1943 he commanded the 25th Division in the last stages of the campaign that drove the Japanese off the island of Guadalcanal. Collins was then transferred to Europe to command VII Corps in the battle for Normandy. Here he captured Cherbourg 20 days after D-Day and then spear-headed the break out at the western side of the Cotentin peninsula. Later his corps broke through the *Westwall*, took Cologne and Aix-la-Chapelle, closed the pincer round the Ruhr from the south, and then pushed on to meet the Russians at Dessau on the Elbe. He had an enviable reputation as a hard, yet flexible, infantry commander.

It is now time to return to the Western Front, where on July 25 General Bradley began Operation "Cobra".

On that day the German forces defending Normandy consisted of:
1. from the coastal battery at Merville to the area of Caumont-l'Eventé: 5th *Panzerarmee* (General Eberbach) comprising LXXXVI Corps, I and II *Waffen-S.S.* Panzer Corps, LXXIV Corps, with between them 11 divisions, including two Panzer and two *Panzergrenadier*, with about 645 tanks (these faced the British and Canadian forces); and
2. from Caumont-l'Eventé to the western coast of the Cotentin peninsula: 7th Army (General Hausser) astride the Vire with three corps of 13 divisions: on the right bank of the river XLVII Panzer Corps and II Parachute Corps with between them six infantry divisions and on the left bank LXXXIV Corps with one *Panzergrenadier* and two Panzer divisions with about 190 tanks (these faced the Americans).

But, we would repeat, there are divisions and divisions. Let us take the case of LXXXIV Corps, which was going to bear the brunt of the attack. Its 91st, 243rd, and 352nd Divisions had only 2,500 rifles between them, after the fierce fighting in the *bocage,* and its three armoured divisions (*"Lehr"* and 2nd S.S. *"Das Reich"* Panzer, and 17th S.S. *"Götz von Berlichingen" Panzergrenadier)* were down to something like half their establishment. The German front twisted and turned along the stretch Bradley was to attack, and the German 7th Army was very weak because Montgomery had drawn the weight of the German forces into the Caen sector. Bradley brought up no less than 12 divisions, including four armoured:
1. on the left the American VII Corps (Major-General J. L. Collins), with its left flank along the Vire, was given the job of making the breakthrough. The 30th, 4th, and 9th Divisions were engaged in first echelon along a four mile front. The breach came in the Marigny area and the 1st Infantry and the 2nd and 3rd Armoured Divisions

poured through south and south-west, not, however, going beyond Coutances on their right, so as to leave the way open for VIII Corps; and

2. VIII Corps (Major-General T. H. Middleton) had the 8th, 79th, 83rd, and 90th Infantry and the 4th and 6th Armoured Divisions and, by a frontal attack, seized Coutances and pressed on to Avranches. When it reached Pontaubault on the Brittany border, it was to come under General George S. Patton's 3rd Army, which was to exploit this success towards the Loire and the Seine.

The 1st Army attacks

The attack of July 25 had the benefit of exceptionally powerful air preparation, the details of which were drawn up by General Bradley and Air Chief Marshal Leigh-Mallory. On July 24 4,000 tons of bombs fell on LXXXIV Corps' positions. During the morning of the following day no fewer than 1,880 four-engined and twin-engined bombers, and 550 fighter-bombers dropped 4,150 tons of bombs opposite the American VII Corps front to a depth of a mile and a half and on the bridges upstream of the Vire from Saint Lô. By special orders from Bradley, who did not want the terrain to be pitted with deep craters, only light bombs and napalm were used.

In spite of precautions, bombing errors caused casualties to the tune of 111 dead and 490 wounded in VII Corps. Amongst the dead was Lieutenant-General McNair, C.-in-C. of the "shadow" army group ostensibly stationed in south-east England to deceive the enemy into expecting a landing across the Straits of Dover. These were tragic losses: on the enemy side the bombing cut a swathe of death through the defences. "Nothing could withstand it," wrote the German historian Paul Carell. "Trenches, gun-emplacements: ploughed up. Petrol-, ammunition- and supply-dumps: set on fire." The Panzer-"*Lehr*" Division, in particular, down to 5,000 men, was heavily knocked about: "at least half its personnel was put out of action: killed, wounded, buried alive or driven out of their minds.

All the tanks and guns in the forward positions were wiped out. Every road in the area was made useless."

Neither Colonel-General Hausser nor Field-Marshal von Kluge expected an attack of such violence from the American 1st Army between the Vire. and the Channel. General von Choltitz, commanding LXXXIV Corps, who had seen it coming and whose warning had not been heeded by his superiors, now had to rely on his own resources to plug the gap created by the annihilation of the Panzer-"Lehr" Division. On July 26 Collins was able to pass his 2nd and 3rd Armoured Divisions (respectively Major Generals Edward H. Brooks and Leroy H. Watson) through his infantry lines. By evening the 3rd had passed through Marigny and was on its way to Coutances and the 2nd was patrolling through Saint Gilles and Canisy, some seven to eight miles from its point of departure.

The 2nd and 116th Panzer Divisions were hastily withdrawn from the 5th *Panzerarmee* in the Caen area but did not get to the breach until July 29, by which time it was widening every hour. There was therefore no alternative for LXXXIV

Corps but to retreat, and do so quickly, as its left flank had been pierced in the area of Périers by the American VIII Corps. The direction this retreat was to take gave rise to a conflict between the LXXXIV Corps and 7th Army commanders. The latter, anxious to retain some coherence in his dispositions, wanted Choltitz to withdraw south-eastwards, whereupon the latter protested vehemently that if he were to do this he would be opening the way for the enemy to get into Brittany. This is what happened, in fact; Kluge wrongly attributed the blame to Choltitz and replaced him by Lieutenant-General Elfeldt. Choltitz had no difficulty in clearing himself and was rewarded with the command of *Gross Paris*.

Coutances and Avranches captured

On July 28 the U.S. 4th Armoured Division (Major-General John S. Wood) took Coutances and that same night got across

△ ◁ *American armour crashes forward along the road and through fields in the lightning advance after the breakthrough at Saint Lô.*
△ *Technician 5th Grade Floyd L. Meyer of Potter Valley, California, examines the aftermath of a strafing run by Allied fighter-bombers: a knocked-out SdKfz 4/1 Opel Type S/SSM "Maultier" (Mule) carrier fitted with a ten-tube 15-cm Panzerwerfer 42. Note the dead crewman in the foreground.*

△ *U.S. infantry take advantage of a bursting white phosphorus grenade to rush across a street in Brest, preparatory to clearing a German-held house.*

the Sienne at Cérences. Twenty-four hours later 6th Armoured Division (Major-General Robert W. Grow), moving on the right flank of the 4th, crossed the See and took Avranches. Facing them there was absolute confusion: continually compelled to move their headquarters by the advancing Americans, the German leaders lost all contact with their men, units got mixed up together and many of them, overtaken by Allied tanks, became moving pockets. At 0100 hours

on July 31 Lieutenant-General Speidel telephoned Kluge: "The left flank has collapsed."

Kluge calls for reinforcements . . .

A few minutes later the C.-in-C. West was again called: this time by General

is in Avranches and possibly also in Villedieu . . . These key positions for future operations must be held at all costs . . . All available strength from Saint Malo has been brought up. Spare naval and air force units, absolutely necessary for decisive struggle which will determine future of bridgehead, . . . impossible to get. General Warlimont agrees to put matter before the Führer.

"C.-in-C. West describes the situation with impressive eloquence. It might even be asked if the enemy can in fact be stopped at this point. His air superiority is terrifying and stifles our every move. On the other hand all his movements are prepared and protected by air strength. Our losses of men and *matériel* are extraordinary. Morale of troops has suffered greatly from the enemy's constant withering fire, especially as all infantry units are now only hastily-assembled groups and can no longer offer solid and coordinated resistance. Behind the front lines the terrorists [resistance] feel the end is at hand and are becoming ever bolder. This, and the destruction of many communication installations, makes an ordered command very difficult."

Kluge therefore demanded reinforcements, and urgently, reminding O.K.W. of the example of the taxis of the Marne.

Faced with the development of Operation "Cobra", Hitler at O.K.W. finally gave up the obsession with a second landing north of the Somme which had dominated all his strategy since dawn on June 6.

. . . and gets them, but too late

Responding to Kluge's call for help, Hitler ordered Salmuth to withdraw LXXXI Corps and 85th and 89th Divisions from the 15th Army and send them at once to 5th *Panzerarmee*. Meanwhile Army Group "G", responsible for the defence of "Fortress Europe" between the Loire estuary and the Franco-Italian frontier, was ordered to send its LVIII Panzer Corps, 708th Infantry, and 9th Panzer Divisions to the 7th Army. The 9th Panzer was stationed in the Avignon area and the army group's commander, Colonel-General Blaskowitz, would have liked to see it replaced by the 11th Panzer, stationed in Montauban, as an Allied landing in Provence was expected.

General George S. Patton Jr. was born in 1885 and served with the American armoured forces in France during 1918. This experience led him to become a fanatical tank enthusiast, an interest he developed and expanded between the wars. In 1942 he was the commander of the American forces in the "Torch" landings, and at beginning of the next year he led U.S. II Corps for a short time. Patton headed the U.S. 7th Army during the invasion of Sicily, during which he led a wide sweeping movement to the west, capturing Palermo, and then drove through to Messina. Early in 1944 he was the commander of the "shadow" Allied army group in southeast England intended to deceive the Germans into thinking that a landing in the Pas-de-Calais was imminent. After the Normandy landings, Patton was given the command of the U.S. 3rd Army, which he led in its superb dash from the breakout at Avranches to Metz. The campaign was notable for Patton's almost total disregard of orders and of orthodox military methods. He raised the siege of Bastogne in the "Battle of the Bulge" and then continued his advance into Germany and Czechoslovakia. Patton, one of the most controversial generals of the last war, was without doubt one of the ablest "cavalry" generals ever. He died after an accident in Germany in 1945.

Farmbacher, commanding XXV Corps, to say that, responsible now for organising the defence of Brittany, he found that the Kriegsmarine and the Luftwaffe, sheltering respectively behind Dönitz and Göring, were being removed from his authority. At 1045 hours the wretched Field-Marshal got in touch with O.K.W. and gave General Warlimont, Chief of Operations, a realistic picture of the situation, according to Milton Shulman:

"C.-in-C. West . . . informs that enemy

△ The crew of an American M8 light armoured car pauses to watch a burning building in Canisy. Known to the British as the Greyhound, the M8 was armed with a 37-mm cannon and a .5-inch machine gun. Over 12,000 were built during the course of the war.

The Führer, as was to be expected, failed to see that this was common sense.

Patton's new objectives

Hitler's decisions, however, came too late. On July 31, General Patton, who now controlled VIII Corps (and was soon to become commander of a new Third Army) was given the welcome information from the corps H.Q. that the 4th Armoured Division had reached its objective at Sélune and that the bridge at Pontaubault was still in good order. He made up his mind at once: "All through military history", he cried, "wars have been lost because rivers weren't crossed." He sent off the 6th Armoured and 79th Infantry Divisions (Major-General Ira T. Wyche) towards Brest and the 4th Armoured and 8th Infantry (Major-General Donald Stroh) towards Rennes. The breach was complete, the German 7th Army was beaten

and LXXXIV Corps, from which most of the 20,000 prisoners taken by the Americans since July 25 had come, was virtually wiped out. On August 1 General Bradley, now commanding 21 divisions, including six armoured, took over the American 12th Army Group in accordance with decisions taken in London on the eve of "Overlord". He handed over his 1st Army to General Courtney H. Hodges, having no qualms about his successor:

"A quiet and methodical commander, he knew his profession well and was recognised in the army as one of our most able trainers of troops. Whereas Patton could seldom be bothered with details, Hodges studied his problems with infinite care and was thus better qualified to execute the more intricate operations. A steady, undramatic, and dependable man with great tenacity and persistence, Hodges became the almost anonymous inside man who smashed the German Seventh Army while Patton skirted around it."

The German *Panzerjäger* IV *"Nashorn"* (Rhinoceros)

Weight: 26.5 tons.
Crew: 5.
Armament: one 8.8-cm Pak 43/1 gun.
Armour: 51-mm front and 30-mm sides.
Engine: one Maybach HL 120 TRM, 300-hp.
Speed: 25 mph on roads, 16 mph cross-country.
Range: 133 miles on roads, 81 miles cross-country.
Length: 20 feet 4 inches.
Height: 9 feet 7¾ inches.
Width: 9 feet 7¼ inches.

Changes in the Allied command structure

The 1st Army at this time included V, VII, and XIX Corps. It had transferred VIII Corps to the 3rd Army, fighting alongside it, and Bradley had also moved over to 3rd Army XII, XV, and XX Corps (respectively Major-Generals R. Cook, Wade H. Haislip, and Walton H. Walker). The new C.-in-C. 12th Army Group, promoted over the head of the impetuous Patton, six years his senior, did not much relish the idea of having to send him directives but acknowledged that "George" was a great-hearted and highly intelligent soldier who, in spite of his celebrated outbursts of temper, served him with "unbounded loyalty and eagerness".

The same occasion brought the formation of the British 21st Army Group, under General Montgomery, with the British 2nd Army, still under Sir Miles Dempsey, and the Canadian 1st Army (Lieutenant-General H. D. G. Crerar). On August 15, 21st Army Group was to have five corps of 16 divisions, including six armoured, and several brigades. This reorganisation of the land forces ought to have brought General Eisenhower to their head as previously agreed. Thinking that his presence was more necessary in England, he postponed taking over command until September 1. Montgomery, therefore, continued to act as Eisenhower's representative, sending orders to Bradley under his authority, whilst at the same time retaining the command of his own army group.

Hitler envisages withdrawal

In the afternoon of July 31 Colonel-General Jodl, having informed Hitler of his concern at the capture of Avranches, noted in his diary: "The Führer reacted favourably to the idea of an order for eventual withdrawal in France. This confirms that he thinks such an order is necessary at the present time.

"1615 hours: called Blumentritt (chief-of-staff to C.-in-C. West). Advised him in guarded terms to be ready for such an order, adding that certain actions had to be taken straight away within G.H.Q. and that he should put a small working party on to it from among the general staff."

The matter of withdrawal seemed virtually settled and Lieutenant-General Warlimont was designated as liaison officer with C.-in-C. West. But on the following morning, when the O.K.W. delegate was leaving, the Führer said: "Tell Field-Marshal von Kluge that his job is to look forwards to the enemy, not backwards!"

Warlimont was thus in an embarrassing situation, caught between the "yes" of July 31 and the "no" of August 1. On August 3, the expected order from O.K.W. reached Kluge in the morning, but instead of confirming the withdrawal intimated by Jodl, it ordered a counter-attack. By driving towards Avranches Hitler hoped the 7th Army would trap those American forces which had ventured into Brittany. And, doing half Kluge's job for him, O.K.W. issued an order giving details for the operation. According to General Blumentritt:

"O.K.W. settled the precise divisions which were to be used and which were therefore to be taken out of the line as soon as possible. The exact limits of the sector in which the attack was to take place were laid down, as well as the routes to be taken and even the villages the troops were to pass through. These plans were all made in Berlin on large-scale maps and the opinions of the commanding generals in France were neither asked for nor encouraged."

The plan was to assemble an armoured mass on the left flank of the 7th Army under General von Funck, C.-in-C. XLVII Panzer Corps, attack towards Avranches through Mortain, and cut the communications of the American 3rd Army. But Hitler would not stop there. Funck was then to press on to Saint Lô and overwhelm the American 1st Army by an outflanking attack. This would give Germany an eleventh-hour game and match in the West.

More time needed

Kluge was dumbfounded when he read Hitler's directive. He wrote to Hitler on August 18, before he took poison, to say that, except for the one single division,

△ *A French resistance fighter poses in front of some of the evidence of the late German occupation of Rennes.*

the 2nd Panzer, "the armoured units, after all the fighting they had done, were so weakened that they were incapable of any shock tactics . . . Your order was based on a completely erroneous supposition. When I first learned of it I immediately had the impression that I was being asked to do something which would go down in history as a grandiose and supremely daring operation but which, unfortunately, it was virtually impossible to carry out so that, logically, the blame would fall on the military commander responsible . . .

"On the basis of these facts I am still convinced that there was no possible chance of success. On the contrary: the attacks laid down for me could only make the situation of the Army Group decidedly worse. And that is what happened."

Kluge was in no position to claim freedom of action in face of this order, as stupid as it was absolute. He was aware that Hitler knew of the part he had played in the July 20 plot and that the slightest disobedience would cost him his life.

The discussion therefore centred less on the principles involved than on the date of the operation, which was to be called *"Lüttich"* (Liège). Hitler wanted to hold back until as many American divisions as possible had been drawn into the net; Kluge urged the threat to the left flank and even to the rear of the 7th Army and asked for a start on August 7, to which Hitler agreed.

Allied aircraft beat the Panzers

At dawn on D-day, helped by fog, XLVII Corps (116th and 2nd Panzer Divisions, 1st *"Leibstandarte"* and 2nd *"Das Reich"* S.S. Panzer Divisions) attacked between the See and the Sélune towards Avranches. Mortain fell fairly easily. But neither the American 30th Division (Major-General Leland S. Hobbs), though it had one battalion surrounded, nor the American VII Corps (Major-General J. L. Collins)

△ △ *The American advance under a smoke-blackened sky.* △ *American troops round up a motley assortment of German prisoners-of-war.*

were thrown off their stride, and towards mid-day *"Das Reich"* was stopped less than two miles from Saint Hilaire-du-Harcouët, over 14 miles from its objective of Pontaubault.

The fog had lifted by now, and the Panzers were caught by British Typhoon fighter-bombers, whose armour-piercing rockets again proved their deadly efficiency. The previous day General Bülowius thought he could guarantee the C.-in-C. 7th Army that 300 Luftwaffe fighters would be continuously sweeping the skies above the battlefield. These had been intercepted by Anglo-American fighters as soon as they took off from the Paris area.

Faced with this lack of success, Kluge gave it as his opinion that the German forces should hold on to what they had got, or even let go. The answer was an order to throw in II S.S. Panzer Corps (General Bittrich: 9th *"Hohenstaufen"* and 10th *"Frundsberg"* Panzer Divisions), to be withdrawn from the already depleted 5th *Panzerarmee*. Once more C.-in-C. West had to give in, in spite of vehement protests from General Eberbach, who was expecting a strong Anglo-Canadian attack southwards along the Caen–Falaise axis.

The Americans hesitate in Brittany

In spite of appearances, the first engagements of the American 3rd Army in Brittany betrayed a certain lack of initiative. This is not attributable in any way to lack of enthusiasm on Patton's part, but seems rather to have sprung from the inadequacy of his means of communication, which prevented his driving spirit from reaching down to his men. At the speed with which the armoured formations advanced, the supply of telephone cable within VIII Corps turned out to be insufficient, with a consequential overloading of the radio network and the use of squadrons of message-carrying jeeps to make up for it.

There were also interferences in the chain of command. The 4th Armoured Division received the order from VIII Corps, confirmed by General Bradley, not to go beyond Dinan until Saint Malo was cleared, whereas Patton had ordered it to drive on towards Brest (150

miles west of Rennes) with no intermediate objective. This left a gap in the enemy lines once Rennes had been passed, which 6th Armoured Division exploited along the axis Chartres–Paris, turning then towards Chateaubriant instead of Lorient. It was recalled to its original objective and found, when it got to Lorient, the German 265th Division in a defensive position around this large base. The 4th Armoured Division did manage to destroy the 266th Division, which had tried to take refuge inside Brest, but the German 2nd Parachute Division got there first and its commander, Lieutenant-General Ramcke, was not the sort of man to be impressed by cavalier raids, even ones made in considerable force, such as Patton's.

The responsibility for this Allied mix-up must belong to the Anglo-American high command, which had given two objectives to the forces breaking out of the Avranches bottleneck: the Breton ports and the rear areas of Army Group "B". This was how Eisenhower saw it when on August 5 he ordered only the minimum indispensable forces to be engaged in Brittany.

Patton sweeps on through the breach

This directive from Eisenhower gave Patton the chance to streak out through the enormous gap (65 miles) between Rennes and Nantes, which he did with XV Corps on the left, XX Corps in the centre, and XII Corps on the right with its right flank along the Loire. By August 7, XV Corps was in Laval and Château-Gontier whilst XII Corps liberated Nantes and Angers, ignoring enemy resistance in Saint Nazaire.

Thus Operation *"Lüttich"* did not deflect Montgomery and Bradley from their initial plan. On D-day the German XLVII Corps lost some 50 tanks out of the 120 with which it had started out at dawn. The American VII Corps, strengthened to five divisions, including one armoured, immediately went over to the counter-attack. This was the last chance for Army Group "B" to break out of the ring now beginning to take shape as Patton pushed ahead towards Le Mans. But Hitler obstinately refused to consider any withdrawal.

◁ *An American 57-mm anti-tank gun in action against a German bunker in the little Brittany port of Saint Malo.*
△ *Mixed British and American forces in the Caen area. While the American forces to the west were fanning out to the south, through Brittany, and also towards Paris, the British and Canadian troops in the Caen area were fighting a slow and remorseless battle on the northern edge of what was to become the "Falaise pocket".*

△ *Allied air power triumphs: a burnt-out German column in Normandy.*

Montgomery now had a chance to start a pincer movement which was to bring about the defeat of Army Group "B" between the Orne and the Dives on August 18 and the disgrace and suicide of the wretched Kluge. At 2330 hours on August 7 the Canadian 1st Army attacked south of Caen with its II Corps of four divisions, including two armoured. It was the beginning of Operation "Totalize", which was to capture Falaise.

At zero hour four mechanised columns, consisting of one armoured brigade on each flank and two motorised infantry brigades in the centre, crossed the first German line. When they had covered

CHAPTER 122
Slaughter at Falaise

between two and three miles in the dark, the Canadian and Scottish infantry, from the 2nd Canadian and 51st (Highland) Divisions, left their vehicles to attack the strongpoints of the German line, illuminated for them by green tracer shells. At dawn it was clear that the H.Q. of I S.S. Panzer Corps had been overrun,

the 89th Division, recently arrived on the scene, had collapsed, and the 272nd looked like giving way.

Once more the famous Panzer-Meyer (Brigadier Kurt Meyer) and his 12th *"Hitlerjugend"* Panzer Division saved the situation with the help of 80 assault guns and the 8.8-cm guns sent to them as

△ *British armoured cars on the move in the Falaise area. Note the ruins, the result of Allied bombing.*

△ *A British column pushes south from Caen. With the aid of the Americans, sweeping up north towards Argentan, Montgomery hoped to trap the 5th* Panzerarmee *at Falaise and wipe it out.*

reinforcement. These young veterans, who had been in the line since June 8, were pitted against the Canadian 4th Armoured Division (Major-General G. Kitching) and the Polish 1st Armoured Division (Major-General S. Maczek), both of which were in action for the first time. The military cemeteries in the area bear witness to the valiant fighting of the Allied forces, but they did not succeed in breaking though and "Totalize" ground to a halt some ten miles short of Falaise on August 9.

General Leclerc's charge

On the same day the American XV Corps, having captured Le Mans, turned north. On its left the French 2nd Armoured Division (General Leclerc) was moving down to Alençon with the 79th Division in its wake. On the right the American 5th Armoured Division (Major-General

Lundsford E. Oliver) was on the road to Argentan, followed by the 90th Division which, newly commanded by Major-General Raymond S. MacLain, was to recover from the unfortunate reputation it had acquired in the *bocage*. Conscious of the threat to his rear areas, Kluge attempted to ward it off by improvising a *Panzergruppe* "Eberbach" consisting of LXXXI Corps (General Kuntzen), 708th Division (Lieutenant-General Wilck), and 9th Panzer Division (Lieutenant-General Jolasse) brought up from the south.

The French 2nd Armoured Division, vigorously led by General Leclerc, ran into the 9th Panzer Division on August 11, just as the Germans were moving into their positions. As night fell the French took the bridges at Alençon whilst they were still intact. On their right, the American 5th Armoured Division had crossed the Sarthe and captured Sées, having overcome the feeble resistance of the German 708th Division. On the following day Leclerc had to fight

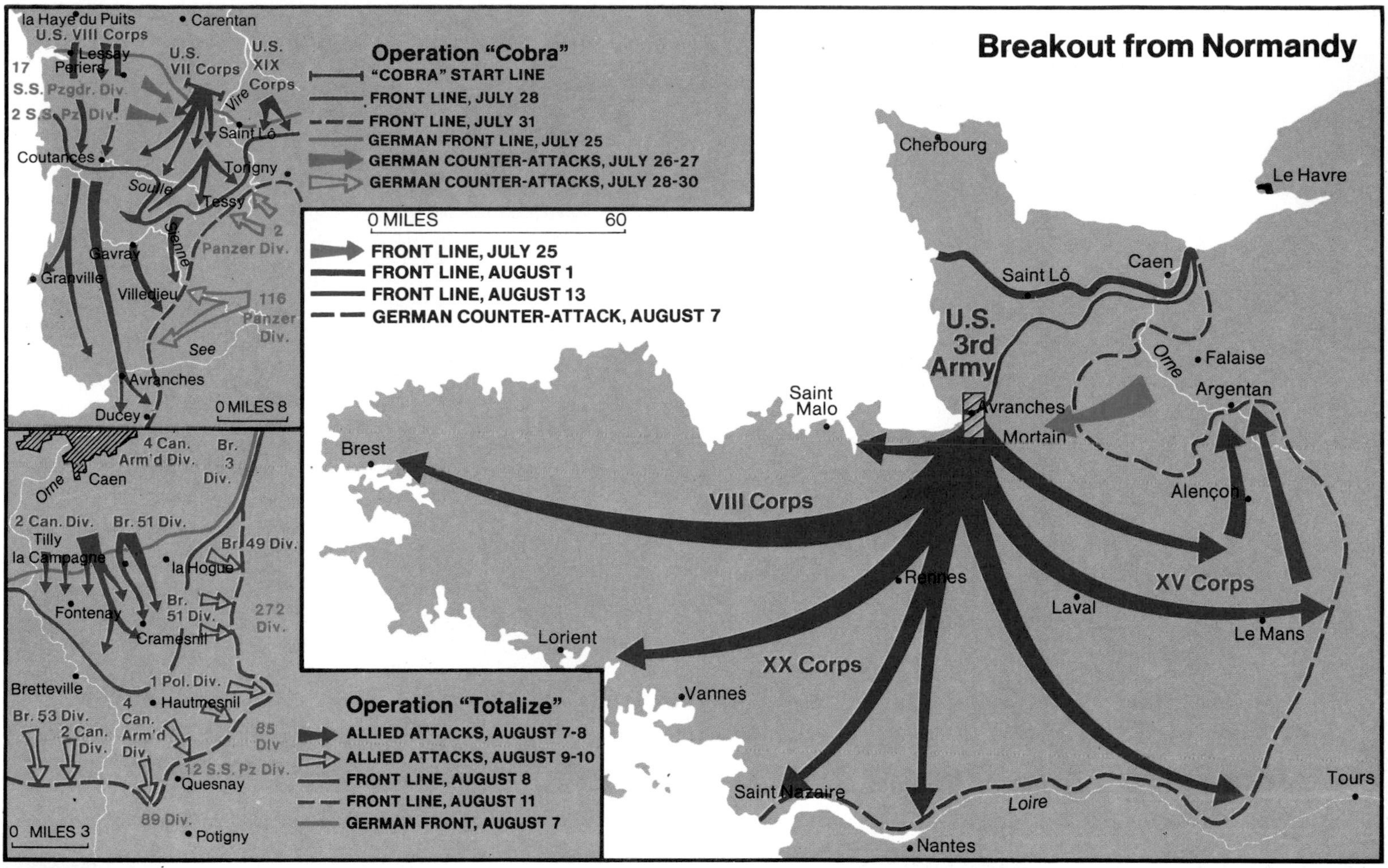
Breakout from Normandy
Operation "Cobra"
"COBRA" START LINE
FRONT LINE, JULY 28
FRONT LINE, JULY 31
GERMAN FRONT LINE, JULY 25
GERMAN COUNTER-ATTACKS, JULY 26-27
GERMAN COUNTER-ATTACKS, JULY 28-30
la Haye du Puits
Carentan
U.S. VIII Corps
U.S. VII Corps
U.S. XIX Corps
Lessay
Periers
17 S.S. Pzgdr. Div.
2 S.S. Pz. Div.
Vire
Saint Lô
Coutances
Torigny
Soulle
Tessy
2 Panzer Div.
Gavray
Granville
Sienne
Villedieu
116 Panzer Div.
See
Avranches
Ducey
0 MILES 8
0 MILES 60
FRONT LINE, JULY 25
FRONT LINE, AUGUST 1
FRONT LINE, AUGUST 13
GERMAN COUNTER-ATTACK, AUGUST 7
Cherbourg
Le Havre
Caen
Saint Lô
U.S. 3rd Army
Orne
Falaise
Argentan
Saint Malo
Avranches
Mortain
Brest
VIII Corps
Alençon
Rennes
Laval
XV Corps
Le Mans
Lorient
XX Corps
Vannes
Tours
Saint Nazaire
Loire
Nantes
4 Can. Arm'd Div.
Br. 3 Div.
Orne
Caen
2 Can. Div.
Br. 51 Div.
Tilly
la Campagne
Br. 49 Div.
la Hogue
Fontenay
Br. 51 Div.
272 Div.
Cramesnil
1 Pol. Div.
Bretteville
4 Can. Arm'd Div.
Hautmesnil
Br. 53 Div.
2 Can. Div.
85 Div
12 S.S. Pz Div.
Quesnay
89 Div.
Potigny
0 MILES 3
Operation "Totalize"
ALLIED ATTACKS, AUGUST 7-8
ALLIED ATTACKS, AUGUST 9-10
FRONT LINE, AUGUST 8
FRONT LINE, AUGUST 11
GERMAN FRONT, AUGUST 7

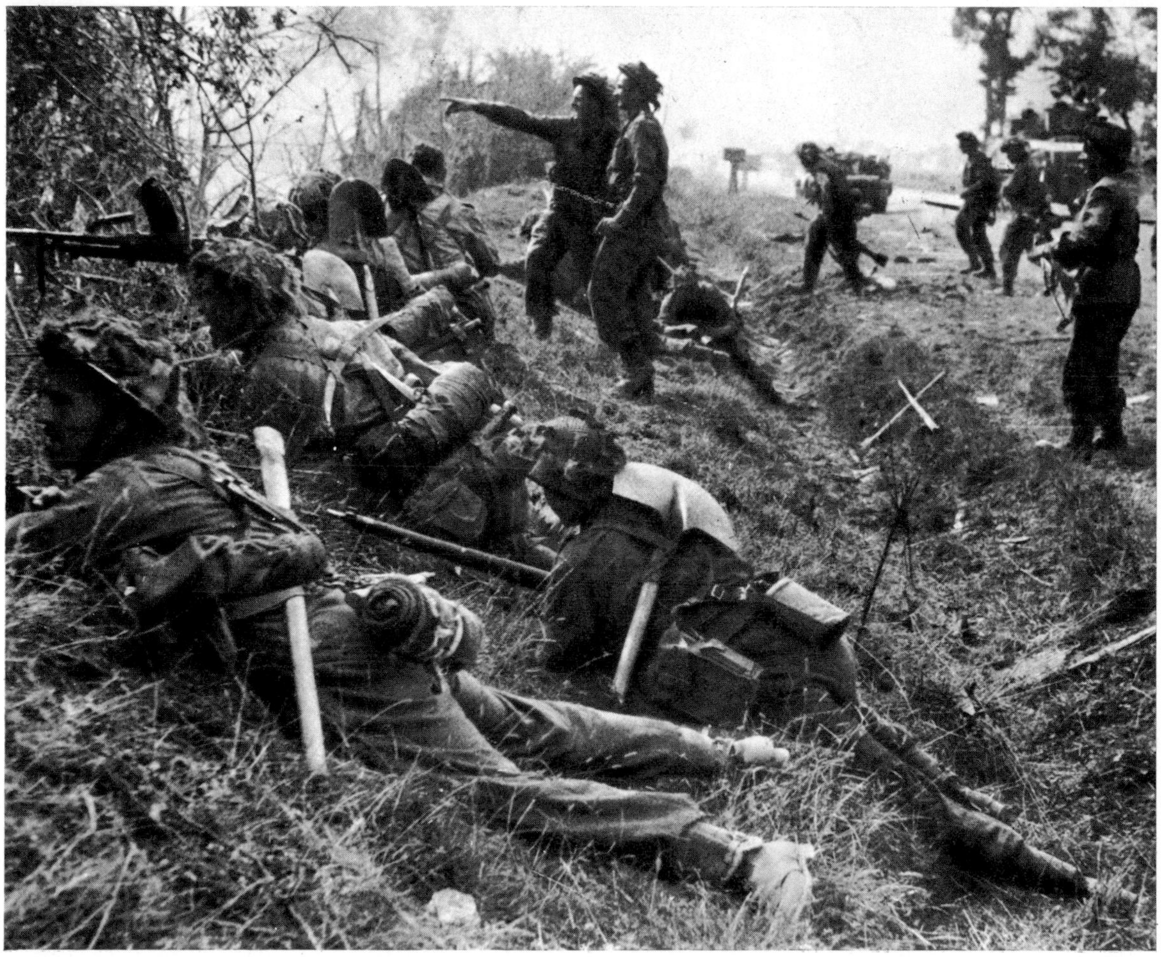

△ The Allied breakout from Normandy and the beginning of the Falaise pocket.
◁ British infantry prepare for an assault near Cagny.

it out with the 2nd *"Das Reich"* S.S. Panzer Division's forward units and the 116th Panzer Division, both of which Kluge had thrown into XV Corps' sector without any further regard for O.K.W.'s orders. The French nevertheless pushed their left flank as far as Carrouges and their right to the outskirts of Argentan.

At dawn on August 13 the American XV Corps was within 16 miles of Falaise, whilst the German 7th Army, caught up in the Condé-sur-Noireau–Tinchebray–Domfront area, had between 34 and 37 miles to go under enemy-controlled skies before it broke out of the pocket. In the afternoon, however, Haislip was ordered by Patton to stop and even to pull back the units "in the neighbourhood of Falaise or north of Argentan".

Why Bradley, via Patton, should have forbidden XV Corps to close the ring round Army Group "B" in the Falaise area has often been discussed, and the reasons given by the two generals in their memoirs do not carry conviction. No more do the arguments of General Eisen-

hower, who takes up Bradley's argument in his *Crusade in Europe,* saying:

"Mix-ups on the front occurred, and there was no way to halt them except by stopping troops in place, even at the cost of allowing some Germans to escape. In the aggregate considerable numbers of Germans succeeded in getting away. Their escape, however, meant an almost complete abandonment of their heavy equipment and was accomplished only by terrific sacrifices.

"I was in Bradley's headquarters when messages began to arrive from commanders of the advancing American columns, complaining that the limits placed upon them by their orders were allowing Germans to escape. I completely supported Bradley in his decision that it was necessary to obey the orders, prescribing the boundary between the army groups, exactly as written; otherwise a calamitous battle between friends could have resulted."

Certainly by exploiting his success on August 12 north of Argentan Haislip had

△ *A Sherman tank stands guard at the cross-roads in St. Martin-des-Besares as a carrier, towing a 57-mm anti-tank gun, and infantry pass through the village.*

△ R.A.F. pilots burst from the "ready" tent after a call for fighter support from an R.A.F. Visual Control Point in the front line.

overstepped the boundary between 12th and 21st Army Groups and risked running into the bombing destined for the Germans opposite the Canadian 1st Army. Was this boundary so vague, though, that the Anglo-American strategic air force, which was admittedly sometimes not very accurate, could not have been given clear orders? And the juncture between the Polish 1st Armoured Division and the American 90th did in fact take place without incident in the area of Chambois-sur-Dives on August 19.

This is why one is inclined to believe, like Jacques Mordal, that Eisenhower and Bradley, under the influence of Montgomery, were unwilling to content themselves with a "little" pincer around Falaise, as they were sure that they could bring about a much bigger one on the left bank of the Seine. They ignored the proverb of the bird in hand and when they said "stop" to Haislip they were intend-

ing to give him a new and bigger task.

Kluge orders retreat

From August 15, Army Group "B" was on the retreat. Kluge did not wait for O.K.W. to confirm, but went ahead, setting in motion an operation involving two armies, seven corps, and no fewer than 23 divisions of all types. On August 17 General Dietrich, who had succeeded Eberbach as C.-in-C. 5th *Panzerarmee*, got I S.S. Panzer Corps out of the net and re-assembled the bits at Vimoutiers. But the Canadians took Falaise and the Polish 1st Armoured Division, advancing up the right bank of the Dives, established contact with the American V Corps (1st Army) which at that moment formed the southern arm of the pincer which was remorselessly closing in.

A German disaster

On August 20, according to Martin Blumenson, the author of the volume devoted to this episode in the official history of the U.S. Army, there occurred the "artillery-man's dream":

"Five battalions pulverized columns driving towards the Dives. American soldiers cheered when German horses, carts, trucks, volkswagens, tanks, vehicles, and weapons went flying into the air, disintegrating in flashes of fire and puffs of smoke."

Nevertheless I S.S. Panzer Corps, which had got out of this attack, collected together some 20,000 Germans from all units and, refusing to be dismayed, managed to find a crack in the Allied lines, through which they got 25 tanks and 60 guns. Included in these forces was General Hausser, C.-in-C. 7th Army, who was seriously wounded in the face. On the following day, however, all firing ceased in the Argentan–Nécy–Brieux–Chambois area. Here the Allies took 50,000 prisoners; there were 10,000 dead. The unhappy decision of August 13 thus left the Germans now with only 40,000 men. Fifteen divisions of Army Group "B" were wiped out in the course of this pitiless battle. According to Blumenson, one American officer, a veteran of the 1918 battles in the area of Soissons, Saint Mihiel, and the Argonne in 1918 and the terrible bombing of London in 1940, said:

"None of these compared in the effect upon the imagination with what I saw yesterday south west of Trun . . . The grass and trees were vividly green as in all Normandy and a surprising number of houses (were) . . . untouched. That rather peaceful setting framed a picture of destruction so great that it cannot be described. It was as if an avenging angel had swept the area bent on destroying all things German.

"I stood on a lane, surrounded by 20 or 30 dead horses or parts of horses, most of them still hitched to their wagons and carts . . . As far as my eye could reach (about 200 yards) on every line of sight there were . . . vehicles, wagons, tanks, guns, prime movers, sedans, rolling kitchens, etc., in various stages of destruction.

"I stepped over hundreds of rifles in the mud and saw hundreds more stacked along sheds . . . I walked through a mile or more of lanes where the vehicles had been caught closely packed . . . I saw probably 300 field pieces and tanks, mounting large caliber guns, that were apparently undamaged.

"I saw no foxholes or any other type of shelter or field fortifications. The Germans were trying to run and had no place to run. They were probably too

◁ △ *Happy soldiers of the French Forces of the Interior escort a German officer prisoner captured near Chartres.*
▽ *The British advance continues towards the east.*

△ *French civilians welcome their liberators. Note the Panther on the right.*

tired even to surrender.

"I left this area rather regretting I'd seen it . . . Under such conditions there are no supermen—all men become rabbits looking for a hole."

Most of the German *matériel* was lost. The French 2nd Armoured Division alone took 100 guns and 700 vehicles and the 90th Division 380 armoured vehicles, 700 guns, and more than 5,000 lorries.

Model succeeds Kluge

This was the situation which Field-Marshal Model inherited when he took over from Kluge at his H.Q. at Saint Germain-en-Laye on August 17. Two days previously a fortuitous incident had, if not provoked, at least hastened, the disgrace of Kluge. Whilst he was up at the front an aircraft bomb had demolished the radio truck which gave him permanent contact with O.K.W., and the ensuing prolonged silence caused Hitler

to conclude that C.-in-C. West had finally betrayed him and gone to see Montgomery about surrender terms.

Kluge's farewell to Hitler

When he said goodbye to his successor, Kluge assured him that he would speak to Hitler with all the clarity which the situation demanded. But in the car taking him back to Germany he rightly persuaded himself that the dictator would give him, not an audience at O.K.W., but a criminal trial and an ignominious death. Potassium cyanide removed him from the Führer's vengeance, but before he committed suicide on August 18, 1944 he sent a letter to Hitler, the conclusion of which is worth recalling:

"I do not know if Field-Marshal Model, who has proved himself in all respects, will be capable of mastering the situation. I hope so with all my heart. If that is not to be the case and if the new· weapons—

especially air weapons, which you are so eagerly awaiting, are not to bring you success, then *mein Führer,* make up your mind to finish the war. The German people have endured such unspeakable sufferings that the time has come to put an end to their terrors. There must be ways to arrive at this conclusion and, above all, to prevent the Reich from being condemned to the hell of Bolshevism ... *Mein Führer,* I have always admired your greatness and your iron will to assert your authority and uphold National Socialism. If your destiny overcomes your will and your genius, it will be because Providence has willed it so. You have fought a good and honourable fight. History will bear witness to this. If it ever becomes necessary, show yourself great enough to put an end to a struggle which has become hopeless."

We know what became of this advice from a man about to die: if it had been accepted Germany would have been spared, not the rigours of occupation (this had been decided at Teheran), but at least the appalling horrors of invasion.

Churchill again opposes a landing in Provence . . .

On the same August 15 when Army Group "B" was trying to escape from the Normandy net, the landing of an Allied force in Provence compelled O.K.W. for the first time to impose on the C.-in-C. West a withdrawal of considerable strategic importance. Right up to the last minute Churchill had tried to urge his American allies to abandon this operation, which was called first "Anvil" then "Dragoon", in favour of his projected offensive towards Vienna and the Danube across the Apennines, the Giulian Alps, and the Ljubljana gap.

In a letter dated August 6 to his friend Harry Hopkins, Churchill expressed his conviction that as the ports of Brest, Lorient, Saint Nazaire, and Nantes might fall into Allied hands "at any time", there was no logistic value left in Toulon or Marseilles. On the other hand, why not take the bull by the horns? "Dragoon", he wrote, would have to be carried out against an enemy who "at the outset [would] be much stronger than we are, and where our advance runs cross-grained

to the country, which abounds in most formidable rocky positions, ridges, and gullies."

"But", he noted in particular, "after taking the two fortresses of Toulon and Marseilles we have before us the lengthy advance up the Rhône valley before we even get to Lyons. None of this operation can influence Eisenhower's battle for probably ninety days after the landings."

. . . in favour of a campaign in the Balkans

On the next day he went to Portsmouth and saw Eisenhower about it, speaking his mind more openly than he had done to Hopkins, and not concealing his interest in a campaign in the Balkans, a subject which he had not broached in his letter. Eisenhower soon realised that the Prime Minister, in his opposition to "Dragoon", was putting forward reasons of strategy so as not to have to declare the political reasons which had made him take up this attitude.

Eisenhower's reserve

As a good American soldier General Eisenhower reckoned that he should not interfere in matters which were the responsibility of the White House and the State Department. He was to react the same way over Berlin later. He makes this perfectly clear in his memoirs when he says:

"Although I never heard him say so, I felt that the Prime Minister's real concern was possibly of a political rather than a military nature. He may have thought that a post-war situation which would see the western Allies posted in great strength in the Balkans would be far more effective in producing a stable post-hostilities world than if the Russian armies should be the ones to occupy that region. I told him that if this were his reason for advocating the campaign into the Balkans he should go instantly to the President and lay the facts, as well as his own conclusions on the table. I well understood that strategy can be affected by political considerations, and if the President and the Prime Minister should decide that it was worth while to prolong

△ △ *General Leclerc, holding the map board, follows the progress of his armoured division.*
△ *Lieutenant-General Omar N. Bradley, commander of the U.S. 12th Army Group.*

The American M3 armoured personnel carrier

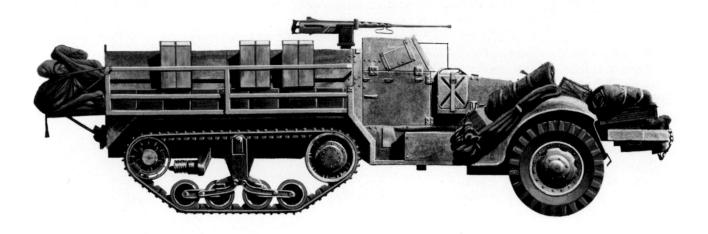

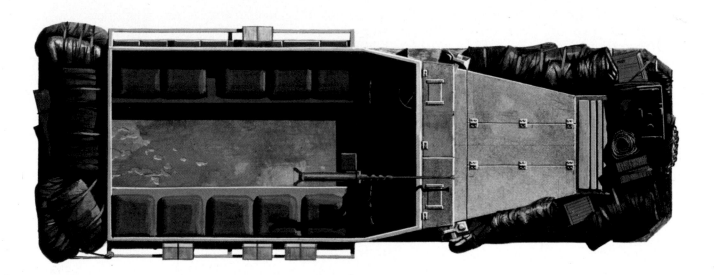

Weight: 10 tons.
Crew: 13.
Armament: one .5-inch Browning M2 machine gun.
Armour: hull front 13-mm, sides and rear 6-mm.
Engine: one White 160 AX inline, 147-hp.
Speed: 47 mph on roads, 35 mph cross-country.
Range: 220 miles on roads.
Length: 20 feet 9⅝ inches.
Width: 7 feet 3½ inches.
Height: 7 feet 5 inches.

The German *Jagdpanzer* 38(t) *"Hetzer"* (Baiter)

Weight: 17.6 tons.
Crew: 4.
Armament: one 7.5-cm PaK 39 L/48 gun with 41 rounds and one 7.92-mm MG 34 machine gun with 600 rounds.
Armour: front 60-mm, sides 20-mm, and rear 8-mm.
Engine: one EPA T2 inline, 158-hp.
Speed: 24 mph on roads, 10 mph cross-country.
Range: 111 miles on roads, 60 miles cross-country.
Length: 16 feet.
Height: 7 feet.
Width: 8 feet 4¾ inches.

△ *The scene that was to greet the Allies when they reached the Seine: wholesale destruction, plus great dumps of ruined* matériel *such as this one at Rouen.*

the war, thereby increasing its cost in men and money, in order to secure the political objectives they deemed necessary, then I would instantly and loyally adjust my plans accordingly. But I did insist that as long as he argued the matter on military grounds alone I could not concede validity to his arguments."

And he was clearly right. The supreme commander may lay down strategic objectives, but it is the political leaders who set the aims of warfare. Moreover Churchill was too late. The drive for Vienna may have been conceivable on June 5 so long as everything was done to annihilate Kesselring south of the line Rimini–La Spezia, but it was not now, on August 7, by which time the enemy, whose

losses in retreat had not been overwhelming, was re-establishing his line along the ridges of the Apennines. At best the Allies would have been caught in late autumn on the narrow hemmed-in roads in the area of Klagenfurt or Ljubljana and have had to fight for peaks between 3,000 and 4,000 feet high. The mountainous terrain and the weather, to say nothing of enemy action, would have severely restricted all movement. As Michael Howard has explained in *The Mediterranean Strategy in the Second World War*: "a pursuit to Vienna through terrain where even comparatively small units could have imposed repeated delays would have been a very difficult matter indeed." Churchill's plans were hopelessly unrealistic.

The American Gun Motor Carriage M18 "Hellcat"

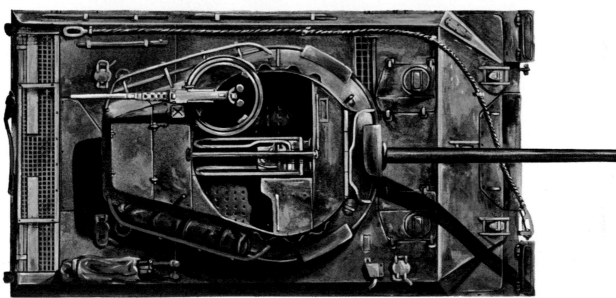

Weight: 19.5 tons.
Crew: 5.
Armament: one 76-mm M1A1 gun with 45 rounds and one .5-inch Browning M2 machine gun with 1,000 rounds.
Armour: hull front and sides 13-mm; turret front 19-mm, sides 13-mm, and mantlet 13-mm.
Engine: one Continental R-975 radial, 400-hp.
Speed: 45 mph.
Range: 150 miles.
Length: 17 feet 6 inches.
Height: 8 feet 4¾ inches.
Width: 9 feet 1¼ inches.

CHAPTER 123
Growth of the French Resistance

by Colonel Rémy

At noon on Monday, June 17, 1940, a young cadet at the Cavalry School at Saumur burst into the room where one of his officer-instructors was taking a hasty meal. The cadet seemed to be in a state of shock, and the breathless words with which he addressed the officer made no sense to the woman servant in the room. She looked on while the officer pushed back his chair, jumped to his feet, and strode to the door, wiping his eyes with the back of his hand as he went out.

Minutes before, the radio had broadcast a proclamation by Marshal Pétain which was to be repeated every hour until that evening:

"Frenchmen!"

"Called by the President of the Republic, I am taking over the direction of the government of France as from today.

"Certain of the devotion of our superb army, which is fighting with a heroism worthy of its long military tradition against an enemy superior both in numbers and in arms; certain that by its magnificent resistance it has fulfilled our duties to our allies; certain of the support of our old soldiers, whom I have been proud to command; certain of the confidence of the entire nation, I offer myself to France in order to lessen her suffering.

"It is with a heavy heart that I tell you today that the fighting must cease. Tonight I will contact the enemy and ask him if he is prepared to discuss with me, as between soldiers, after fighting the battle and defending our honour, the steps to be taken to end hostilities."

Twenty-four years before, the famous old soldier who made this announcement had galvanised the Verdun garrison with his immortal battle-cry *"Courage, on les aura!"*; and there can be no doubt that his heart was indeed torn by the need for France to lay down her arms in 1940. Those who heard him broadcast at the time still remember how his voice trembled as he concluded his speech. But as his words went out to the French people the roads of France were choked with countless refugees, haggard, desperate, swamping the fighting troops with their numbers and thus preventing any chance of a counter-attack, converting the retreat to a stampede on all sides. To take just one example, terrible scenes had occurred at the bridge at Gien, where nearly a million people had forced their way across the Loire in three days; and those scenes would be repeated as far afield as the Pyrenees and the Alps unless the fighting ended at once. Those who wanted to carry on the fight had to consider not only the chaotic state of the armies in the field. They could not ignore the sufferings of those hundreds of thousands of women, children, and old folk who had travelled (for the most part on foot) from Holland, Belgium, and north-eastern France, pushing their pitiful bundles of possessions on barrows.

It is a grim fact that Pétain's premature

▽ *De Gaulle in Britain, addressing the ship's company of the Fighting French sloop* Commandant Duboc.

announcement of his intention to request an armistice only added to the confusion and did nothing to alleviate the sufferings of the civilian population. The Luftwaffe's Stukas and the Italian bombers continued to terrorise the floods of refugees streaming south, while Pétain's proclamation only troubled and demoralised the majority of the troops. Very few of them came to the decision that nothing would be changed until an armistice was actually signed, and that their duty was to fight on where they stood. Among these few were the officers and men at Saumur, whose stand on the banks of the Loire was one of the most heartening episodes in the overall tragedy of the 1940 campaign.

De Gaulle's reply

If Pétain's speech had not included that last paragraph, the people of France would have been immeasurably encouraged to hear that the man who had saved the French Army in 1917 and led it to victory in the following year had become their leader. But as it stood, it was a mistake, and in the prevailing conditions it prompted an immediate reply, for the good of France, which only led to more rivalry in the future.

This reply came on the following evening. Over the British radio came the voice

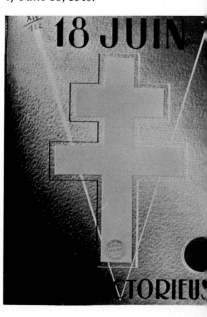

◁ *"Whatever happens, the flame of French resistance must not be quenched and will not be quenched"—in the darkest hour of France's defeat in 1940 de Gaulle stood out as the natural focus for the resistance, both in France and abroad.*
▽ *Poster commemorating de Gaulle's electrifying broadcast of June 18, 1940.*

of General de Gaulle, a generally unknown figure whose appointment three days before as Under-Secretary of State for National Defence had caused much surprise. Many a French officer regarded de Gaulle's initiative as a call to desertion. In fact it had the opposite effect: to proclaim to the world that France refused to accept that she had been decisively beaten. It was to de Gaulle's proclamation that France owed the right to join the victorious Allies at the conference table, to receive the surrender of Germany with an assurance which would have seemed insane in June 1940, with Germany victorious on all fronts. In his speech the day before, Pétain had paid tribute to the resistance of the French Army – too often discounted, despite the 100,000-odd deaths it had suffered since May 10. But de Gaulle gave the word "resistance" a new interpretation. "Whatever happens," he said,

▽ *Opposite number to "Colonel Passy", head of de Gaulle's secret service: Colonel Maurice Buckmaster (standing, centre), head of the French section of Special Operations Executive.*

"the flame of French resistance must not be quenched and will not be quenched."

France can always be proud that these words were spoken by a Frenchman at a time when it seemed that all was lost. The flame lit by de Gaulle, however, spread to all countries under German occupation, and France was not the only country which would see the scrawled "V for Victory" sign combined with the Lorraine Cross, symbol of "Free France". De Gaulle's speech of June 18 was for the benefit of the whole of occupied Europe, and "resistance" would become the key rallying-cry against the common enemy.

De Gaulle's appeal was little understood at the time, and is often confused with the famous leaflet, bearing the tricolour flag, which appeared in London a few weeks later with the announcement beginning "France has lost a battle, but France has not lost the war." What mattered was that the appeal existed. From its opening words Pétain – without being named – came under fire. "The commanders who have led the armies of France for many years have formed a government. This government has agreed with the enemy to end the struggle." On the following day de Gaulle's attack intensified: "Before French minds are confused, before the dissolution of a government under enemy control. . . ." And on June 22 the armistice was condemned in advance as "not a capitulation, but an enslavement".

A disastrous breach

Four days later de Gaulle, to his discredit, took up the word "enslavement" and flung it in Pétain's face. In so doing he created a breach which would have grave results for the destiny of France and was the source of unspeakable injustices and sufferings. The aggressive attitude he advocated was contrary to national opinion. The Parisians who would turn out to cheer de Gaulle on August 26, 1944, during his triumphal progress down the Champs Elysées, would nearly all be the same citizens who had greeted Pétain with equal fervour four months before on April 26, when he visited the occupied capital. Rouen, Dijon, Lyon, Nancy, and Epinal – the last being the closest Pétain got to Strasbourg, which the Germans forbade him to enter – and even Saint-Etienne, on D-Day itself, would welcome Pétain with the same infectious enthusiasm.

Nearly all Frenchmen believed that there was a secret agreement between de Gaulle, who "took up the broken sword" on June 18, 1940, and the old Marshal, who at the same time used his personal aura to try and save his country from the excesses of the enemy. These Frenchmen believed vaguely that the welfare of France demanded unity, and they were right. All the evidence shows that Pétain did indeed "resist" in every sense of the word, and that his sentence by a vengeful court in August 1945 for "dealings with the enemy" was a grave miscarriage of justice for Pétain and for France.

De Gaulle's resistance

The resistance inspired and led by de Gaulle was different. Several former members of the "Free French" have argued that active resistance to the Germans would have existed in France without de Gaulle. This is true: acts of sabotage and attacks on German officers and soldiers were carried out by men who had not followed de Gaulle's lead. But the fact remains that without de Gaulle, resistance would have taken another form – and France would have been lost.

Everyone knows of the achievements

AVIS

En vue d'inciter la population à entrer dans les groupes de résistance, les puissances ennemies tentent de répandre dans le Peuple Français la conviction que les membres des groupes de résistance, en raison de certaines mesures d'organisation et grâce au port d'insignes extérieurs, sont assimilés à des soldats réguliers et peuvent de ce fait se considérer comme protégés contre le traitement réservé aux francs-tireurs.

A l'encontre de cette propagande il est affirmé ce qui suit :

Le Droit International n'accorde pas, aux individus participant à des mouvements insurrectionnels sur les arrières de la Puissance Occupante, la protection à laquelle peuvent prétendre les soldats réguliers.

Aucune disposition, aucune déclaration des puissances ennemies ne peuvent rien changer à cette situation.

D'autre part, il est stipulé expressément, à l'article 10 de la Convention d'Armistice Franco-Allemande que les ressortissants français qui, après la conclusion de cette Convention, combattent contre le REICH ALLEMAND, seront traités par les troupes allemandes comme des francs-tireurs.

La puissance occupante, maintenant comme auparavant, considérera, de par la loi, les membres des groupes de résistance comme des francs-tireurs. Les rebelles tombant entre leurs mains ne seront donc pas traités comme prisonniers de guerre, et seront passibles de la peine capitale conformément aux lois de la guerre.

◁ *Grim warning from the Germans – a public announcement in Paris: "In order to persuade the population to join resistance groups, the enemy powers are trying to convince the people of France that members of resistance groups, by virtue of certain organisational measures and the wearing of insignia, have the status of regular soldiers and may therefore consider themselves protected from the treatment reserved for terrorists.*

"In view of this propaganda the following is announced:

"International Law does not grant to individuals taking part in subversive activity within the territory of the Occupying Power, the protection which regular soldiers may claim.

"No resolution or declaration made by the enemy powers can change this situation.

"Moreover, Article 10 of the Franco-German Armistice Convention expressly states that French nationals who take up arms against the German Reich after the conclusion of that Convention, will be treated by German troops as terrorists.

"The occupying power considers and will continue to consider members of resistance groups as terrorists. Rebels falling into their hands will not be treated as prisoners of war and will be liable to the capital penalty in accordance with the conventions of war."

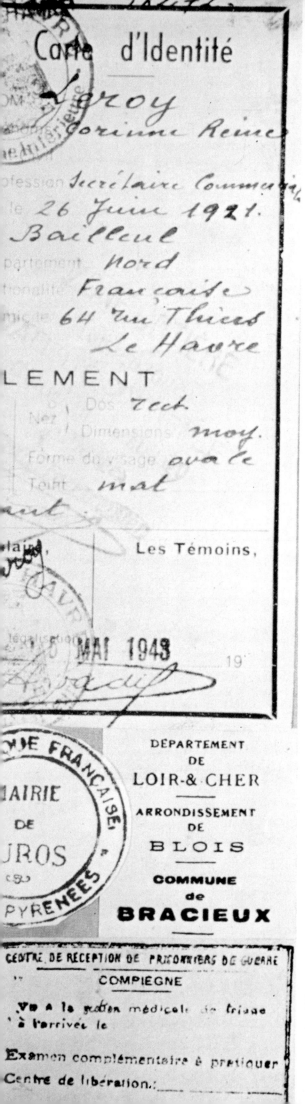

of the French Foreign Legion, but consider the case of the detachment in the Cameroons. Apart from its commander, Captain Danjou, and his two subordinate officers, very few of its number were Frenchmen. Its establishment was made up of Swiss, Belgians, Spaniards, Danes, Bavarians, Prussians, Württembergers, and Poles. Their achievement did not add to the battle honours of their original countries, but to the glory of France. And without de Gaulle's appeal of June 18, 1940, those men who crossed the Channel to carry on the fight in uniform would have been unable to do more than form a volunteer foreign legion which would have been part of the British Army. Without de Gaulle no Frenchman could have claimed, as de Gaulle himself persistently claimed, two years later: "The nation has thrilled with pride on hearing what its soldiers have achieved at Bir Hakeim—brave and true sons of France, who have written one of the most glorious pages in her history with their blood!"

The London organisation

As for myself, I had a better chance than others of crossing to England after the collapse in 1940. I was at my home in Brittany. Sheer instinct drove me to set out with my youngest brother on the morning of June 18. As I said to my wife: "If the Nazis win this war we will not only become their slaves, but the spirit of our children will be perverted, for they will be brought up under National Socialist principles." Not that I had a clear goal; the following evening found me at Verdon harbour, pleading in vain with the commander of a minesweeping sloop to take us to Morocco.

But a few days later, having been landed at Falmouth by a Norwegian ship, we gave in our names in a basement office near St. James's Palace, where "the man of June 18" had just set up his headquarters. Our particulars were recorded on a writing pad by a young second-lieutenant just returned from Narvik, and I heard that de Gaulle had had to pay for the pad out of his own pocket, his current finances being negligible. My spirits soared. I do not know of any great moral venture which has been launched with a full treasury, or with financial backing. We were there to defend the Christian idea of mankind as best we could, and as

◁ *A selection of forged forms and stamps used by agents. They include French and Dutch municipalities, birth certificates, police and forced labour offices, and Wehrmacht and Gestapo stamps. There are also forged signatures of S.S. and other officials. The identity card in the name of "Corinne Reine Leroy" was carried by the British agent Violette Szabo.*

long as we were poor all would be well. I felt already that we would win.

Shortly afterwards, however, I was being entertained with lavish hospitality by some British friends in a fine country house. I could not help wondering if I had been right to leave my family to the mercies of an enemy portrayed by the British press as acting with a total lack of pity towards occupied territory; and I looked around for a way of rejoining them without breaking my new undertaking. Finally I thought I found the answer in volunteering for a mission in France, although I knew nothing even of the most elementary facts of a secret agent's job. If I had had the least idea I would have realised that the plan would only have put those whom I wished to protect in greater danger.

My application was received by a young captain who went by the pseudonym of "Passy", which he had taken from a Parisian *métro* station in imitation of the first French volunteers, who came from the Narvik expeditionary corps. Lacking officers–as he then lacked everything else!–de Gaulle had put him in charge of the 2nd, 3rd, 4th, and 5th Bureaux of his skeletal staff; and although my military experience was very limited I thought that this was too much for one man to handle. Barely past his 30th birthday, André Dewavrin was a brilliant officer, although quite inexperienced in his new functions.

He asked me to leave him my passport, however; and an examination of its pages, with its Spanish stamps, suggested to his contacts in the Intelligence Service that I could be sent to France without much trouble. So it was that in early August I set out for Lisbon in a comfortable flying-boat. My secret agent's gear consisted only of a very simple code, which I carried in my head; a small bottle of invisible ink, which I never used at all; and 20,000 francs, which Passy had scraped together with some trouble. My mission was to report on German movements between the Spanish frontier and Mont Saint-Michel, through Brest. From my complete ignorance on how to collect such information, let alone pass it on, one would have thought that my zone extended to Scandinavia. To my tentative request for a radio transmitter, the British replied that their own army (still re-equipping after Dunkirk) had priority.

The growth of the network

Two years later, my network–which I had christened the *Confrérie Notre-Dame*–

continued on page 1719

▽ *Agents prepare for a mission to occupied France.*
▽ ▷ *Dropping supplies.*
▷ ▷ *A "body" arrives, photographed by one of the "welcoming committee".*

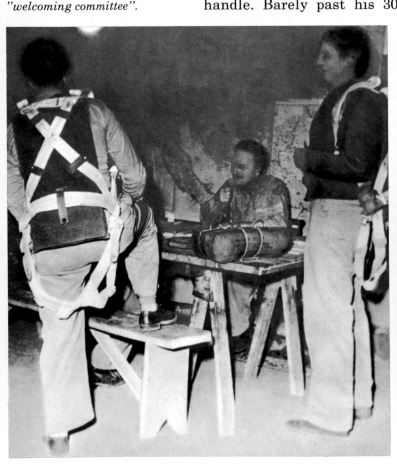

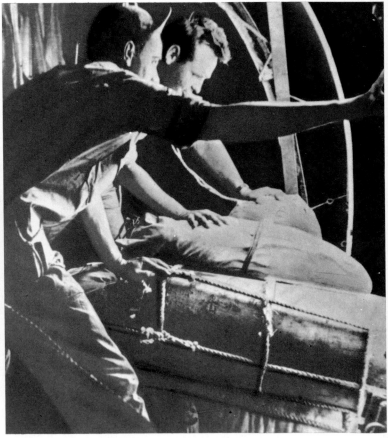

Ree, Captain Harry. *Known to the resistance as "Henri". Operated first in Jura region, setting up resistance networks. Organised sabotage of Peugeot motor works at Sochaux, oil tanks of the Usines Marti, and Leroy Machine Company factory at St. Suz. Network betrayed by French double agent. Constantly hunted and forced to take refuge in Switzerland. November 27, 1944, badly wounded in fight with Gestapo man. Sheltered and nursed by resistance; returned to London in July 1944 via Switzerland and Spain.*

Sansom, Odette. *Known to the resistance as "Lise". Operated in south of France as courier for Peter Churchill's network. Moved to St. Jorioz in the Savoy mountains with Churchill, posing as his wife. Arrested with Churchill after their network was penetrated by the brilliant Abwehr counterspy agent, Hugo Bleicher. Tortured to supply information on other members of the Churchill network, but survived. Deported to Ravensbrück, but lived.*

Churchill, Captain Peter. *Known to the resistance as "Michel". First mission February 1942, delivering money to networks in south. Second mission delivering radio operators. August 1942, back to south of France to organise networks; forced to move from Cannes to Toulouse after German occupation. Shifted headquarters to St. Jorioz in Savoy mountains; arrested with Odette Sansom, April 1943. Survived Flossenbürg and Dachau.*

Inayat Khan, Noon. *Known to the resistance as "Madeleine". Radio operator for "Prosper" network in Paris. Left virtually on her own after mass Gestapo round-up in June-July 1943. Betrayed by woman informer and arrested. Shot at Dachau, September 1944.*

Dufour, Jacques. *Known to the Resistance as "Anastasie". maquis leader. Called "the biggest bandit in the Limoges region" by Germans. String of daring and successful sabotage actions. June 1944, set out to prevent S.S. "Das Reich" Panzer Division from moving north to Normandy. Operating with Violette Szabo, narrowly escaped capture when ambushed by S.S. at Salon-le-Tour. Continued operations against "Das Reich"; linked up with advancing Allies.*

Szabo, Violette. *Known to the resistance as "Corinne". Penetrated prohibited coastal zone and reconnoitred Rouen area, April 1944. Second mission in June (D+1), to work with maquis in the Limoges area. Captured after two-hour gun battle with "Das Reich" troops, allowing "Anastasie" to escape. Shot at Ravensbrück, January 1945.*

◁ *The Belgian resistance worker Françoise Labouverie, seen at far left disguised as "Nicole Desmanets" in February 1944. The two pictures were taken at about the same time.*

One agent's story

Françoise Labouverie was 20 when Belgium was invaded in May 1940. She and her family were swept up in the flood of refugees which fled from the German advance. They first headed for the coast at Dunkirk, and finally made for St. André in southern France, via Rouen and Bordeaux, where they stayed with a friend of Madame Labouverie for the next three months.

Then came the return to occupied Belgium. Françoise spent the winter of 1940-41 in an office job in Brussels until ill health forced her to go home to Céroux. Her mother decided to convert their home to a guest house, and there Françoise made her first contact with resistance: the black market, maintained by the farming community.

In March 1941 Françoise became engaged, having heard that her fiancé was planning to escape to England. As the summer of 1941 wore on her determination to escape as well hardened. She planned two training journeys: a bicycle trek through the Ardennes and a skiing holiday in the Jura. But eight tedious months of waiting passed before the first chance of escape materialised.

Via an old friend from her days as a Wolf Cub leader, Françoise met "Etienne", who gave her a message to deliver in the south of France. "You will go to Carcassonne and on the third floor of the fifth house on your left in the Market Street, as you come from the market, you will find Madame Ladinde. Tell her Etienne and Paulette send their love – they remember the fireside chats. Tell her Hibou is holding on."

Françoise chose St. André as the point from which to attempt the tricky crossing of the demarcation-line. Escorted across into Vichy France by a seasoned *passeur,* she headed for Lyon, where her cousin Jacques was attaché to the U.S. Embassy. She delivered her message to Madame Ladinde in Carcassonne, and, back in Lyon, met "Oncle Roger", who was to escort her across the frontier into Spain. But it was not to be. She was turned back at the frontier, and began to work as secretary to "Oncle Roger".

Her work consisted mainly of copying maps and reports, "mainly concerning airports and landing fields in Belgium". But this phase ended abruptly when the Germans marched into Vichy France on November 11, 1942. "Oncle Roger" flew to Algiers – taking Françoise's passport with him. She spent a month caring for the five children of a Belgian family, then made two more attempts to cross into Spain. But these, too, failed; Françoise knew that the longer she stayed in southern France she was risking herself and her contacts there – and so she set off for Belgium again, arriving home at the end of December 1942.

As soon as possible she went to Brussels, looking for "Etienne", and agreed to work for him. "Etienne" – his real name was Pierre Hauman, a former captain of Belgian cavalry – had been running a small Intelligence *réseau* (network) for a year. It was called "Tégal"; the story went that when "Etienne" was asked to coin a cover-name for his group he had answered *"Ca m'est égal!"* ("It's all the same to me!") and the name stuck.

"Tégal" was a small and compact group: "Etienne" and his assistant Franz, the radio operator, Bob, and Françoise as secretary formed the hard core. They passed on the reports of innumerable agents; "you found them all over Belgium, eager, courageous, selfless, they knew no one and asked no questions."

Known as "Nicole" in the "Tégal" *réseau,* Françoise was called upon to make many hazardous trips through occupied Belgium to contact agents. In the rented Brussels flat which served as the "Tégal" office, she typed lists of information, copied sketches, and helped while the information was put on microfilm before being conveyed to England. Then, on September 23, 1943, "Etienne" was betrayed and arrested. The "Tégal" members dispersed and went underground.

Françoise spent nine months on the wanted list, moving from address to address and existing with the help of relatives and friends, before her turn came. On June 13, 1944 she was arrested by the Rexists, Belgian quislings collaborating with the Germans. Held in St. Giles prison, she was interrogated by the Rexists and the Germans and was swept up with the other inmates of St. Giles on the approach of the Allied armies. They were entrained for Germany – but sabotage by railway workers kept the train in Belgium; the prisoners were liberated on September 2.

◁ An English radio receiver-transmitter specially designed for the Resistance. Radio operators in the field ran the constant risk of capture; the Germans operated radio-detection vans to track down intercepted transmissions to their source.

▷ Two years later (1943) than the model above, and much more compact: a pocket receiver used by resistance workers in the south of France.

continued from page 1714

covered the whole of occupied France and Belgium, proving that Passy had been right and the experts of the British Intelligence Service wrong. The latter had put their faith in a long-term training programme for candidates like myself, using special schools, before putting the fully-trained agents "in the field". Passy replied to this by arguing that the war moved fast, and the conditions awaiting us in France did not match up with classic theories of espionage. Working in our own country, we would be able to count on the help of innumerable Frenchmen whom the Germans had been obliged to leave at their posts: in government departments, the railways, the ports, and the factories. Our agents, claimed Passy, would be able to use these Frenchmen to amass quantities of information which no agent working in a foreign country would otherwise be able to obtain – and, what was vital, to do it without delay and relay it back to headquarters at top speed.

Passy's views were correct. Between December 1940, when I sent him my first despatch (a very slim package, containing the vaguest of information), and the beginning of November 1943, when a betrayal virtually annihilated my network, we sent nearly 80 agents back to London. They were crammed with information – military, political, and economic – which often proved to be of the highest value, and carried bundles of scale drawings and maps and a good thousand radio messages. By this time, the end of 1943, Passy was a colonel, the head of the B.C.R.A. or *Bureau de contre-espionnage, de renseignements et d'action*. He gave me the job of setting up the *Section du Courrier Militaire*. I had daily to circulate between the various French and Allied services based in London some 10,000 roneoed reports, 3,000 photocopy sketches, and 500 photographs, some of which were often collages. To read, classify, collate, compile, reproduce, and distribute the incoming material from occupied France, I had the services of 120 skilled and keen volunteers who worked with me in the vast offices allocated to me in Palace Street. This was quite an advance from July 1940, when I had first entered Passy's modest office in St. Stephen's House, furnished as it was with nothing more than a plain wooden table and a couple of benches! Here, surely, was proof that above everything else the resistance was a matter of faith as well as of material resources.

Areas of operation for the resistance units

At the time of the armistice France had been divided into two zones, separated by an official "demarcation line". An appendix to the armistice convention defined this line with considerable precision; but in fact it was only settled after discussion between the districts directly involved, with the delimitations being settled on the spot. It is doubtful that the Germans had the last word. They did make some subsequent adjustments to the demarcation line in agreement with the local French authorities, but never got themselves involved in territorial squabbles. Nor was "The Line" the only frontier arbitrarily imposed on French territory. On August 7, 1940, a decree from Hitler annexed Alsace to the *Gau* of Baden in the Reich; and on November 30 of the same year Lorraine was proclaimed the *Gau Westmark* and annexed to the Third Reich in its turn.

The Germans imposed yet another zone. Its western limit ran from the Somme estuary through Abbeville, Amiens, Soissons, and Laon, meeting the "demarcation line" south of Dôle. This area came under the authority of General von Falkenhausen, Military Commander of Holland, Belgium, and northern France, who had his headquarters at Brussels. Stretching south to the Rhône at its exit from Lake Geneva, this zone was curiously similar to the western province of the original Holy Roman Empire; one German officer of the garrison at Salins-les-Bains in the Jura had declared: "We will reconstruct Lotharingia." This immense area of French territory the Germans called the "Green Zone"; it would be detached from France when final victory was won by the Reich. The French called it the "forbidden zone", for German control was stricter there than elsewhere; and especially along the Channel coast, which was known as the "Red Zone" in London. These refinements did not affect resistance workers in the Unoccupied Zone, whose preoccupations were very different. Their resistance took a political form, with the Vichy régime as its prime target. As for the Germans, they were only a secondary problem in the south – until the occupation of November 1942, which changed the situation completely.

△ *One of the many women who played a vital part in the Resistance.*
Overleaf: *Hero of the hour – a* maquis *fighter in confident pose, cradling his Bren gun.*

Developments in Vichy

Attitudes towards the Germans varied between the occupied zone and Vichy France. In occupied France it became possible to sense an attitude of condescension towards compatriots in the *"zone nono"*. This was unjust, but certainly resistance in southern France did not become effective before the Germans took over in November 1942. But there were compensatory factors. As from February 27, 1942, when one of the very first successful air supply missions was accomplished, the Unoccupied Zone was an invaluable help in getting our information back to London. Contained in a parcel whose contents would be unknown to the bearer, our message would be entrusted to the guard of the Pau-Canfranc train. At Canfranc it would be taken over by our friend Le Lay, controller of customs, who would send it on to Jacques Pigeonneau, French Ambassador in Madrid. Pigeonneau would then deposit it in our "letter-box", repre-

sented by a British commercial traveller in Madrid. By diplomatic pouch it would then be passed on to Lisbon and flown back to London. We had no mishaps, although the system had its risks, but it

△ A maquis *camp: weapon-cleaning time.*
◁ *The inner man. A maquis group toasts the coming of liberation.*

△ *Sten gun instruction in the field. The Sten was an ideal weapon for resistance work: tough, easy to operate, and simple to dismantle for concealment purposes.*

was very slow; and the same went for messages sent out by Passy from London. This was the route by which, at the beginning of 1941, I finally received my long-awaited radio transmitter, which arrived in a heavy and bulky suitcase. Our first radio contact with London was made from the house of Louis de La Bardonnie at Saint Antoine-de-Breuilh in the Unoccupied Zone, not far from the demarcation line cutting the road from Libourne to Sainte Foy-la-Grande. Shortly afterwards the transmitter was moved to Saumur, where it fell into the hands of the Germans at the end of July 1941. But

in its brief career it had been instrumental in keeping the battle-cruisers *Scharnhorst* and *Gneisenau* immobilised in Brest, and thus, more remotely, in the destruction of the *Bismarck*.

German counter-measures

Until the end of 1941 the main contribution of the French resistance was not acts of sabotage but the steady flow of sketched Intelligence matter. The German reaction was swift and severe. I can remember a

to the resistance as "Saint-Jacques", whose mission had preceded mine by a few days. Five names; five typical examples of sacrifice. At least they died under the bullets of a firing-squad and were spared the long agony of the camps.

After the outbreak of the Russo-German war on June 22, 1941, the effective strength of the Resistance in occupied France grew at such a speed that it caused us much suspicion at first. We had no way of knowing that the Communist Party would throw in its lot with the common cause. It did, at least in theory, put its French *Francs-Tireurs et Partisans* (F.T.P.) under de Gaulle's authority, in a letter written at the end of 1942 which I took to London together with Fernand Grenier, a member of the Party Central Committee. The superb courage of the men and women of the F.T.P. overcame many initial suspicions, although many of them could never reconcile their own beliefs with the Communist ideal. Yet the F.T.P. was not prevented by Communism from fighting and dying for France, and they should not be confused with the thugs and bandits who called themselves F.T.P. after their territory was liberated. In 1941 the F.T.P. concentrated on "action" planning – sabotage and attacks against the Germans – rather than on pure Intelligence work. The tight control of the Party slowed down the flow of information so much that it frequently lost its highest value.

In 1941 liberation seemed a very long way off, and hopes of insurrection against the still formidable German occupation forces seemed impossible. The *maquis* was still a thing of the future (it was born of the refusal to obey the *Service de Travail Obligatoire,* the S.T.O. or "compulsory labour service", at the end of 1942). Yet optimistic and far-sighted leaders were already at work recruiting for the future, concentrating on men who would stick by their combat groups when the time came to come out into the open and fight weapon in hand, against the German forces of occupation.

Operational groups

Foremost among these groups was the *Organisation Civil et Militaire* (O.C.M.). In April 1942 its leader was Colonel Alfred Touny, who was shot with 12 of his comrades at Arras two years later. Then there were the *Chantiers de la Jeunesse,*

continued on page 1730

△ *French postage stamps commemorate resistance workers who died in the war.*

poster, dated August 29, 1941, displayed in the *métro*. It announced the execution of Commander d'Estienne d'Orves, Maurice Barlier, and Jan Doornik, all three of them shot "for acts of espionage". Until I saw this poster I had not known their names. On October 24 it was the turn of my first radio operator, Bernard Anquetil, arrested at Saumur three months before, who had refused to save himself by betraying me. Like the other three he was shot at Mont-Valérien. The same fate was suffered by Charles Deguy on July 29, 1942. Deguy was the "number two" of my friend Maurice Duclos, known

Gestapo terror...Firing-squad...

More than any other organ of the Nazi state, the Gestapo won international notoriety as the most feared and efficient instrument of Hitler's "New Order". Like the S.S., however, the Gestapo could never have earned this reputation if it had merely consisted of brutal thugs. In fact it was staffed with brilliant and ruthless detectives whose brainwork was devoted to tracking down the enemies of the state.

Its full style and title was *Geheime Staatspolizei* – Secret State Police – and it was as old as the Nazi state itself. Göring established the Gestapo in Prussia on April 26, 1933, months before the death of Hindenburg and Hitler's accession to total power over the Reich. From the start its task was a witch-hunt against all opponents of the Party and the régime. It was deeply involved in the Reichstag fire and the crushing of Röhm's S.A. Fear of the Gestapo was instrumental in securing the massive *"Ja"* plebiscite votes which strengthened Hitler's hold on Germany and Austria. But as the 1930s drew on it became apparent that the Gestapo's rôle as a direct instrument of state power had hardly begun.

Typical of this was the Nazi attempt to charge General von Fritsch, commander-in-chief of the Army, with homosexual offences. It was the Gestapo who found the unsavoury figure of Hans Schmidt, who trailed a long record of blackmailing homosexuals, to swear that he had caught Fritsch *flagrante delicto* in a Berlin back alley with an underworld character who rejoiced in the title of "Bavarian Joe". The Army won one of its last victories over the régime when Fritsch was cleared in a court of honour – but the Gestapo escaped from the whole depressing affair without being indicted in turn, although it had been caught out in an attempted perversion of justice of almost farcical dimensions.

When the time came for Hitler's invasion of Poland, the Gestapo was in the forefront. Heinrich Müller, its chief, was ordered to provide convicted criminals for an operation known as "Canned Goods". A party of Germans,

dressed in Polish uniforms, were to raid the German radio station at Gleiwitz, make a rapid broadcast, fire a few shots, and vanish, leaving the body of a uniformed "Pole" for discovery by the outraged Germans. This was duly done and the whole affair trumpeted to the world as the last Polish act of aggression which Germany would ever have to tolerate.

With the coming of the war the Gestapo's activities radiated out into the occupied territories, hunting down Jews and resistance leaders. No less than the Stuka and the Panzer division, it was an instrument of war, to root out resistance at source and

keep enemy populations cowed by the terror of its name.

As the French Resistance grew in confidence and stature, so the Gestapo was forced to refine its tactics. One of the most successful counter-espionage *coups* in the story of the French resistance was achieved not by the Gestapo itself but by Sergeant Hugo Bleicher of the *Abwehr*, who used the terror of the Gestapo's name to induce captured agents and resistance workers to co-operate with the Germans. By passing himself off as a Luftwaffe officer who had decided that Germany had lost the war, and that he wanted to go over to the Allies, Bleicher later managed to pene-

trate Peter Churchill's resistance network based on St. Jorioz in the Savoy Alps and destroy it, adding to his laurels with the arrest of Churchill and Odette Sansom.

It was the work of expert counterspies such as Bleicher which made the task of the Gestapo much easier than it would otherwise have been in France. The Gestapo was more than willing to work with its military counterparts – the *Feldpolizei* and the *Abwehr*. The subtlety used to track down the key men in the resistance was taken to considerable extremes. But once an arrest had been made the subtlety ended.

Brute force was the basic

1

2

1. *Awaiting their next victims: splintered firing-posts in a bullet-pocked cellar in Paris.* 2–5. *Grim sequences of German photographs record the last seconds of resistance workers in Paris. The numbers on the back wall make the yard a horrible parody of a shooting-range.*

3

4

5

... and torture chamber

6 method employed on Gestapo prisoners. For a start, the Gestapo knew very well that if an arrested agent could hold out for 48 hours his contacts would have time to disperse and a general alert sounded in the local resistance network. Speed was therefore of the essence.

A Gestapo interrogation had a standard, no-nonsense opening to show the victim that he was utterly in the power of his tormentors: two or more men at work on him at once, slaps, punches, kicks, and abuse, until the victim slumped on the edge of his chair on the verge of unconsciousness. He would then be revived and as likely as not subjected to a period of "soft" treatment – his handcuffs loosened, a cigarette offered and

lit, coffee and food provided. But this phase could not be unduly protracted because it gave the victim time to recover and build up his strength to face the next onslaught.

The next phase would redouble the ferocity of the first. In the case of Yeo-Thomas, the "White Rabbit", it consisted of being stripped naked and hustled into a bathroom where a chain was wrapped round his ankles. He was then thrown into the bath which was full of icy water and his feet were hoisted out of the water, plunging his head beneath the surface. Despite his struggles he was held in that position until he passed out; he was then hauled out, given artificial respiration to bring him round, and the process repeated

again and again.

In the case of Yeo-Thomas this was then followed by being hoisted from the ground by his hands, which were manacled behind his back, until his shoulders were dislocated and he passed out again. This in turn was followed by a terrifying beating with rubber coshes, including his genitals. Holding out against all these appalling tortures, Yeo-Thomas finally convinced the Gestapo that he was a hopeless case. He was sent to Germany for extermination, but escaped from Buchenwald.

Only against men and women of the calibre of Yeo-Thomas did the terror brutality of the Gestapo fail. But when it did it was found that the failure was total.

7

6-7. There was nothing subtle about the way the Gestapo went to work. They were out to get confessions and information in the shortest possible time and they brought the art of physical torture to a pitch unheard-of since the days of the Inquisition. And with the benefits of 20th Century civilisation they were able to use a particularly horrible form of persuasion: electrocution.
6. Suspended on these contacts the victim would jerk in helpless agony while the current flowed.
7. Testament of anguish: human hand-marks scoured in the wet concrete of a cellar wall. The victims would be shoved into the cellar, the concrete would be soaked to improve the electrical contact – and the current would then be turned on ...

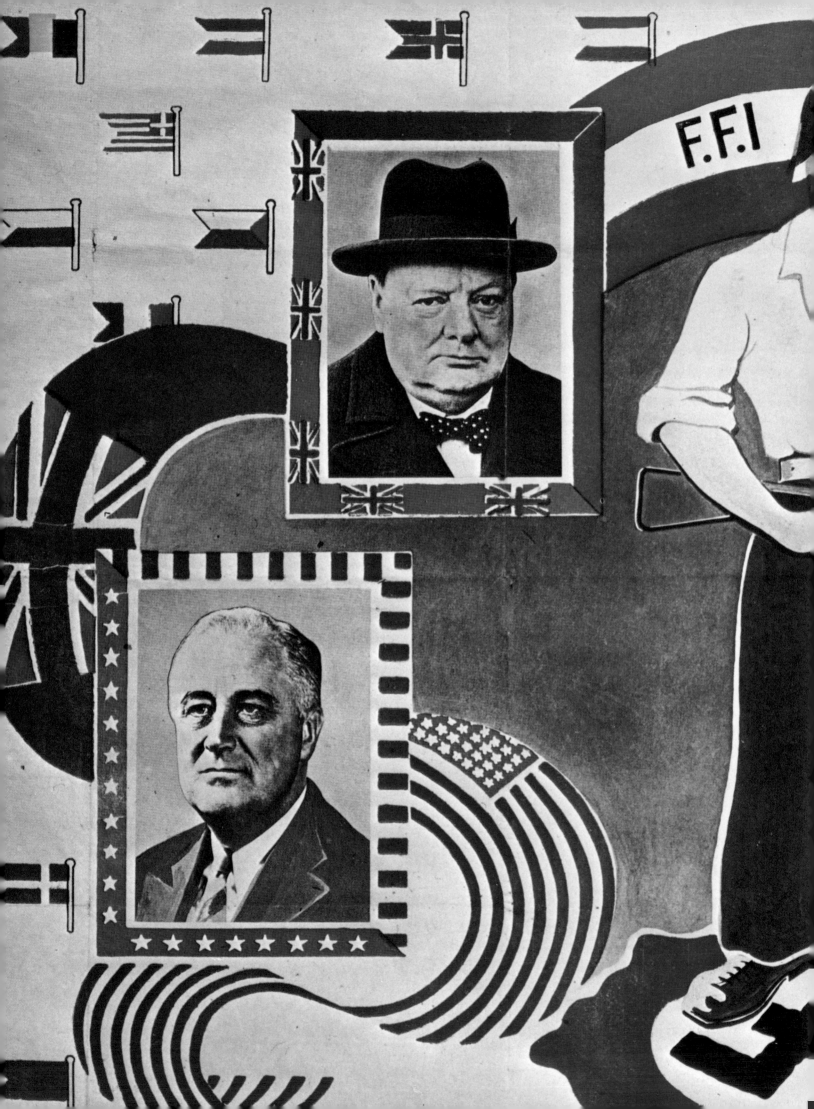

△ *Interrogation in the field: grilling a suspected collaborator.*

Previous page: *A poster honouring the F.F.I.–*Forces Françaises de l'Intérieur. *It reflects the pride felt towards the resistance fighters as the "home army" of France.*

continued from page 1723

or "youth camps", which traced their origins back to June 2, 1940. On that day General de La Porte du Theil resigned the command of VII Corps and the War Ministry gave him the difficult and unenviable job of regrouping the young men called up in 1940, who were out on the roads in tens of thousands, living by looting. Given this unpleasant job, de La Porte du Theil saw in it a way of preserving the system of compulsory service and military instruction despite the very strict terms of the armistice, and Marshal Pétain backed him to the hilt. The title *Chantiers de la Jeunesse* was a blanket term to deceive the Germans. It took them a long time to find out what de La Porte du Theil was really doing; the Gestapo did not arrest him until January 4, 1944. Such was the confusion which accompanied the liberation that this veteran resistance worker was charged with collaboration with the Germans after his own liberation in Germany; but orders from the top saw the charge dismissed before any injustice could be done. Many of those who had been formed into *Chantiers de la Jeunesse* made up the framework of the *maquis*, and a large part of de Lattre de Tassigny's 1st

Army consisted of recruits from the *Chantiers* along the road from the south of France to Alsace–apart, that is, from those troops mobilised in North Africa. Only a short time was needed to train these young recruits–a matter of hours–and their conduct in action was superb. Finally, in the Vichy zone, there were the *Compagnons de la France* ("companions of France"). They played an important part in the liberation, and one of the most famous names in our network, *Georges Lamarque*, came from their ranks.

A brave gesture

On November 11, 1940, there was a brave demonstration in Paris which completely flouted the German occupation decrees. From morning to evening, despite brutal German counter-measures, thousands of students and schoolchildren (some of whom were not yet 15 years old) turned out to lay wreaths on the tomb of the Unknown Soldier at the Arc de Triomphe. Similar demonstrations took place in Brussels and Luxembourg.

Resistance outside France

Like Belgium, Luxembourg had endured four years of German occupation in World War I while Holland preserved her neutrality. This time, while King Léopold III declared himself a prisoner of the invaders of his country, Grand Duchess Charlotte and Queen Wilhelmina left their countries for London, from where they inspired their subjects to resist. Holland now had to begin learning the art of resistance which Belgium and Luxembourg had learnt 22 years before. As early as June 15, 1940, the citizens of Brussels and Liège – to the fury and consternation of the German occupation authorities – were circulating two subversive leaflets: *Ssh!* and *The World of Labour*. The Belgians were not content with this. When the Belgian Army surrendered, Major William Grisard had ended his last order of the day with words that heralded de Gaulle's later appeal to the French: "This is not the end. This is only a phase, and we will meet again." In the second fortnight of June, Brevet-Colonel Lentz, chief-of-staff of

△ and ◁▽ *Mustering for a strike against the Germans – with a motley collection of Allied and captured German weapons.*

△ and ▽ *The confidence of coming victory: formal parades.* ▷ *German counterblast to the resistance: a poster deploring the "terrorist" activities of captured and executed resistance workers in other occupied territories.*

the 17th Infantry Division, began to re-group the most reliable and determined men from the regiments of that division who had evaded captivity. At about this time Captain-Commandant Claser began to organise the "L.B." or *Légion Belge*. While Lentz concentrated on garrison towns for his recruiting, keeping his net-work essentially military, Claser took in civilians, with reservists and professional soldiers recruited on a regional basis.

By October 1940 the whole of Belgium had been organised into three zones and nine provinces, grouped in regions and sub-regions. Claser and Lentz worked to-gether, with Lentz retaining the military command. Claser, aided by Lieutenant van de Putte as head of information and by reserve Captain Boerenboom, acted as chief-of-staff to what eventually became

first the "Army of Belgium" and later the "Secret Army". The reserve units, organ-ised on a regimental basis, were com-manded by Brevet-Colonel Bastin, a World War I hero, and director of the Red Cross P.O.W. parcel service. In accordance with previous plans, Bastin took over the L.B. from Lentz when the latter was arrested on May 8, 1942. Claser was arrested and died in captivity. Lieutenant van der Putte and Captain Boerenboom were also rounded up. However, before his capture, Lentz had succeeded in unifying the various elements of the Belgian resistance, forming a central committee under the presidency of Colonel Heenen, whose general secretary was Frans Bodaert, Lentz's liaison officer.

The geographical position of Holland, Belgium, and Luxembourg led to the early

DES LIBÉRATEURS?

GRZYWACZ
JUIF POLONAIS
2 ATTENTATS

ELEK
JUIF HONGROIS
8 DÉRAILLEMENTS

WASJBROT
JUIF POLONAIS
1 ATTENTAT - 3 DÉRAILLEMENTS

WITCHITZ
JUIF POLONAIS
15 ATTENTATS

FINGERWEIG
JUIF POLONAIS
3 ATTENTATS - 5 DÉRAILLEMENTS

BOCZOV
JUIF HONGROIS
CHEF DÉRAILLEUR
20 ATTENTATS

FONTANOT
COMMUNISTE ITALIEN
12 ATTENTATS

MANOUCHIAN
ARMÉNIEN
CHEF DE BANDE
56
ATTENTATS
150 MORTS
600 BLESSÉS

RAYMAN
JUIF POLONAIS
13 ATTENTATS

ALFONSO
ESPAGNOL ROUGE
7 ATTENTATS

LA LIBÉRATION!
PAR L'ARMÉE DU CRIME

appearance of a form of resistance which was only found in France along the approaches to the "forbidden zone" and the demarcation line. The first task was to conceal from the Germans those British servicemen who had failed to embark from Dunkirk. The close German watch on the North Sea coast made it too difficult to get the fugitives home by sea. It was therefore a matter of establishing, with the co-operation of the people of the French frontier zones, escape routes or "chains" whose links were gradually extended as far as the Pyrenees. These British escapers were immediately joined by Belgians who wished to carry on the fight in uniform. Soon there appeared, in their thousands, French escapers from German prison camps, who followed R.A.F. bomber crews shot down during missions over the Ruhr.

So many men and women devoted them-

selves to helping the escapers that an accurate estimate count of their numbers is impossible. Two escape networks in Belgium deserve special mention: "Comet" and "Pat O'Leary". The latter was set up by Dr. Albert-Marie Guérisse. He was a Belgian Army surgeon who escaped at Dunkirk, returned to France to continue the struggle, was captured, and escaped shortly after the armistice. Returning to France on a secret mission he was captured but escaped again, and set up one of the most important escape networks before being captured a third time and deported to Germany. "Comet" was formed by a girl, Andrée de Jongh, who had often heard the story of Edith Cavell's heroism in World War I from her father, a headmaster at Schaerbeek in the suburbs of Brussels. From strenuous personal efforts she built up an escape route from Belgium to Bilbao. She took

personal charge of her "children", crossing the Somme (often swimming, if necessary), taking them by train to Bayonne and into Spain by a hazardous mountain crossing. Andrée de Jongh was also arrested and deported. "Comet" paid a heavy price, but its efforts enabled almost a thousand airmen of the R.A.F. and U.S.A.A.F. to escape and fight again.

In Holland, Belgium, and Luxembourg, many ordinary houses concealed hundreds of French ex-P.O.W.s who had escaped from Germany. These men had to be hidden, fed, and provided with clothing and shoes – duties which were made almost impossible by the hard conditions of the occupation, and which raised the most difficult problems. Women resistance workers learned to bake bread in their own ovens; their menfolk learned how to butcher pigs and cattle. Fed and cared for – often provided with money saved by household economy – the prisoners would then be taken to another hiding place on the next stage of their journey to freedom,

▽ Out in the open at last, to join forces with the Allies. Resistance fighters drive through Rheims beneath the tricolour.

gradually approaching the last barrier: the demarcation line. In this dangerous underground game, the Dutch, Belgian, Luxembourg, and French resistance workers, helped by priests, played a rôle of vital importance. With incredible self-sacrifice, ingenuity, and courage, they threw themselves into the task of conveying the fugitives into the Unoccupied Zone, despite the formidable advantages held by the Germans. The number of successful escapes ran into tens of thousands.

German vigilance and oppression bore down particularly hard on Luxembourg, considered by the invaders as part of the Fatherland which had been arbitrarily detached, and now to be thoroughly "Germanised". On the orders of Gauleiter Gustave Simon the slogan *"Heim ins Reich!"* (Home to the Reich!) was everywhere displayed. On August 30, 1942, Simon announced the compulsory call-up for the Wehrmacht of all Luxembourgers between the ages of 20 and 24. The reply of the people of Luxembourg was immediate and remarkable: a spontaneous general strike, which even saw teachers and pupils staying away from their schools. The key centres were Wiltz in the north, and Esch in the south. It was a superb demonstration of how the Luxembourgers felt about the German intention to annex the Grand Duchy.

The grim year of 1941 ended with a dark and hard winter. Its gloom affected heart and soul, for it was clear that the war was still only in its opening phase. It would be many weeks and months before the first definite hope of liberation showed over the horizon, and then only at the price of untold sacrifice. The wife of one of my friends—one of the first recruits in my network—recently reminded me of how I replied to her fears of the risks her husband was running. I had told her, "But we are already all dead men!" In view of the losses already suffered and the dangers still to be run, it seemed impossible to me that any of us would escape with our lives. Why is it that many of us who did survive still feel nostalgia for those times when grief was second nature to us? The simple reason was that in the resistance there was no place for double-dealing, and we learned what confidence means when it has to be absolute. We depended totally upon each other and extended this sense of mutual loyalty to all our colleagues, even if they were not personally involved in what we happened to be doing.

This confidence gave us tremendous strength, for it allowed no compromise. When I heard that my radio operator Bernard Anquetil had been arrested, I had a moment's doubt. He knew the small flat where I lived; he had been there several times. And I knew what methods the Germans use to extract information from even the bravest men. But I could not help thinking that if my friend were to hear that I had quit my address, he would think that I had doubted his trustworthiness. I stayed where I was. And indeed Bernard Anquetil went before the firing-squad without having told his interrogators of my whereabouts.

That, basically, was what made the opening phase of the Resistance so inspiring: the discovery of what life really meant, in the company of men and women inspired by the same ideal. We shared a common faith in the destiny of our country, and the much more intangible (but no less real) respect for the freedom and dignity of mankind. And those who lost their lives during the most hopeless phase of the struggle surely played the finest part.

Revenge on the collaborators

The story of the French resistance included a running fight between the agents and workers in the field and the German skill at using counterspies and double agents. These traitors had different motives. There was "Horace", a liaison agent dismissed by Yeo-Thomas, the "White Rabbit", for unpunctuality and mendacity. A weak and greedy young man, "Horace" became a double agent for the Gestapo and Yeo-Thomas had the grim satisfaction of unmasking him to the Germans at a confrontation after his arrest.

Then there was the case of "The Cat", radio operator for the *Interallié* network. This was another coup for the *Abwehr* ace, Hugo Bleicher. It began with the arrest of a section leader, Raoul Kiffer. Bleicher broke him down by telling him that his comrades had betrayed him, and Kiffer

agreed to work for the Germans. On his information Mathilde Carré, "The Cat", was arrested in her turn. Bleicher gave her the full V.I.P. luxury treatment transferring her from jail to a hotel suite. He told her that he had all the information he needed to send all her comrades before a firing squad, and followed this up by telling her that if she helped him he could keep them out of the Gestapo's clutches and see that they were treated as prisoners-of-war. "The Cat" agreed. All the key members of *Interallié* were rounded up–and Bleicher prepared for the second phase of his plan, using "The Cat" to send bogus radio messages back to London as if the network were still intact, and so trap other agents. To begin with this was successful; but soon doubts began to creep in across the Channel. By the time that Bleicher took the

bold step of sending "The Cat" back to England, suspicions were thoroughly aroused at S.O.E. and "The Cat" broke down and confessed on being taxed with being a double agent. But the damage she had done lived after her, and several agents were arrested by the Germans after her capture.

The Jura resistance had the problem of "the man who drove for the Gestapo", Pierre Martin, who gave the resistance much valuable help before being unmasked as a double agent. Harry Rée, chief S.O.E. agent in the Jura, made repeated attempts to settle accounts with Martin. The traitor was eventually gunned down by a vengeance *équipe* headed by Paul Simon, who caught Martin alone in a hotel restaurant in Besançon. Fate was not kind to Simon; he was trapped by an S.S. squad at the Café

Grangier at Sochaux early in 1944 and died trying to shoot it out with the Germans.

Strangely, many of the "V-men"–as these double agents were known–often retained much of their loyalty towards their former employers and tried to shield them. Conversely, German counterspy aces such as Bleicher were as often as not fully aware that their tools were not giving them full information, but kept them on to add to their own knowledge. Thus, via Roger Bardet–who had been instrumental in the destruction of the St. Jorioz circuit – Bleicher made contact with network leader Henri Frager, and began to drop heavy hints that he "knew all". He nevertheless allowed Frager to return to England by Lysander, an act for which Bleicher was severely reprimanded by his superiors in *Abwehr*. Finally,

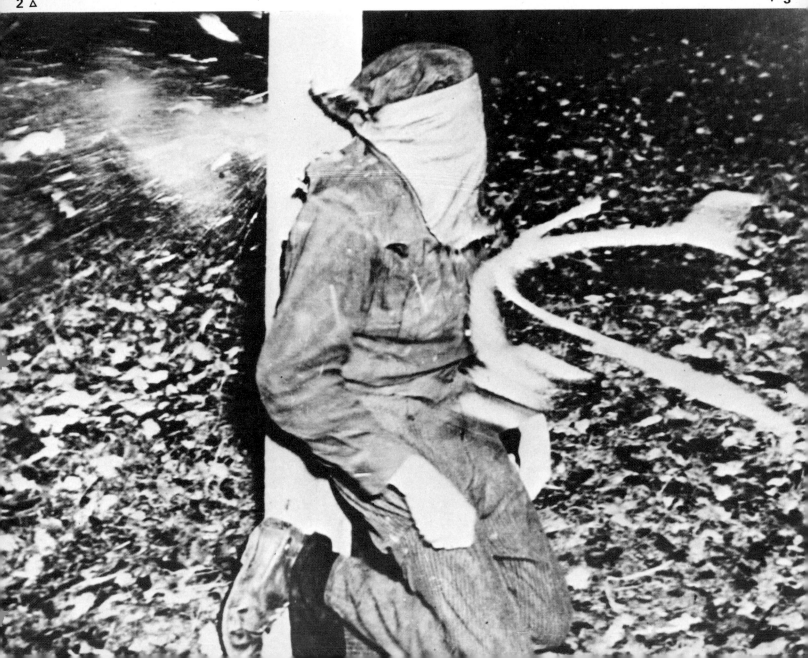

given a blunt ultimatum by the S.D. – the prompt arrest of Frager, or the ignominy of a People's Court trial – Bleicher found himself with no alternative but to put an end to Frager's activities. The Frenchman had genuinely believed in Bleicher's *bona fides;* Bleicher, in turn, had developed genuine respect for Frager's courage and patriotism. Bleicher's attempts to arrange fair treatment for Frager came to nothing; he died in Buchenwald concentration camp.

These are only a few of the many strange cases in the story of the resistance when personal concepts of treachery and loyalty became so enmeshed as to become almost indecipherable. It was a weird and paradoxical mixture; the heights of devotion to duty and the depths of personal self-seeking, a game played for mortal stakes in which the contestants made use of everything they could get their hands on to achieve their aim.

At the other end of the scale the people of the occupied territories had to live with collaboration of a more basic nature. This sprang from the basic human instinct to "beat the system", sharpened by the more immediate hardships of the occupation – shortage of food and comforts, the curfew, travel restrictions. Those Frenchmen who turned informer were very soon in need of German protection; there were many cases of stool-pigeons and toadies being murdered. And it

was inevitable that there was little or no tolerance for women who slept with *"les Boches"*, despite the traditional French respect for *affaires du coeur.*

With the coming of liberation the revenge taken on collaborators was savage. Men were beaten up by mobs and given scant attention by the authorities; women marked down as "Boche lovers" went through the humiliation of having their heads shaved and being paraded through the streets. This caused much concern to the British and American troops who witnessed these scenes; the standing order was on no account to get involved in how the French chose to settle their own accounts. But there were several cases of Allied officers intervening and stopping the shaving of old women whose daughters and relatives had been judged guilty, or even those who were considered to have shown insufficient distaste at having troops billeted in their homes.

The two most prominent Frenchmen to be accused when their country was liberated were, of course, the Vichy leaders, Pétain and Laval. Few tears were shed over Laval, who had always been the most outspoken collaborator of them all. But Pétain's case was a tragic one, proving the shortness of men's memories and the fragility of their gratitude.

In 1916 Pétain had saved Verdun and become a national hero; in the following year, when General Nivelle's offensive on the

Chemin des Dames completely broke the French Army's morale, it was Pétain who picked up the pieces and restored morale. By 1940 he stood out as the Grand Old Man of French military tradition and glory. But what he had seen in World War I had had a fatal effect on his outlook. During the bloody struggle for Verdun his watchword had been "one does not fight with men against *matériel";* by 1940 he was determined that at all cost France must be spared from needless suffering, and that it was his duty to see that this was done. Widely respected in France during the war – he was given enthusiastic welcome in many major French cities – he suddenly appeared in 1945 as the *capitulard* of 1940.

He faced his trial with dignity, wearing a plain uniform with no decorations apart from the *Médaille Militaire* and refusing to take his baton into court – "that would be theatrical." Condemned to death (the sentence was later commuted to life imprisonment), Pétain accepted the verdict stoically. His humiliation extended to having his name chopped out from the head of the Roll of Honour at Verdun. He died in 1951.

Pétain's sentence was typical of the cruel and vengeful mood at work in France after the war. And his tragedy was summed up by one of his *aides-de-camp*: "You think too much about the French and not enough about France."

1. (Previous page): *The ugly side of liberation. A policeman drags a beaten-up collaborator to captivity by his hair.*
2. *A mass execution.*
3. *Death of a traitor. His bonds are flying loose, sliced by the bullets.*

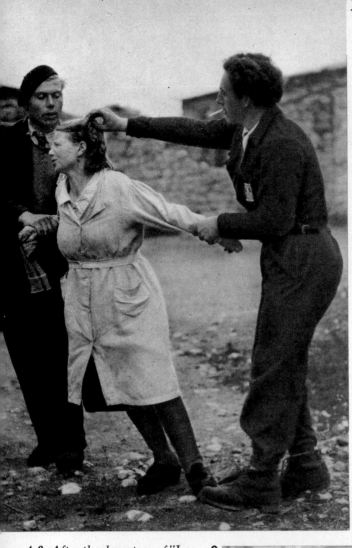

4-6. *After the departure of "Les* **6** *Boches" – humiliation for women accused of having collaborated with the invaders. Although this collaboration had often taken the form of betrayal of friends and relatives, most of the women and girls concerned had done nothing more treacherous than succumb to the temptation of extra food and more favourable treatment for services rendered. Others were victims of genuine love affairs – but not even the French toleration for "affaires du coeur" saved them from the bitterness of their compatriots when liberation came. The mood of the hour was vicious, and women collaborators nearly all suffered the fate of being seized, shorn, and exposed to public execration.*

4, 5. *Women are prepared for the scissors.*

6. *Headscarves mitigate the shame of shaven skulls.*

CHAPTER 124

DRAGOON:
The drive through southern France

Operation "Dragoon", supervised by General Maitland Wilson, C.-in-C. Mediterranean, was to be the landing between Saint Raphael and le Lavandou of the American 7th Army under Lieutenant-General A. M. Patch, who the previous year had been so successful in cleaning up Guadalcanal. The landing operation was to be carried out by the American VI Corps with its 3rd, 36th, and 45th Divisions, well experienced in amphibious operations. It was to be supported by an Anglo-American parachute division under Major-General Robert T. Frederick landing in the area of le Muy with the object of opening up the Argens valley. A position nearer Toulon was not chosen because of the danger of the two twin turrets at Cap Cépet whose guns could hurl a 119-pound shell a distance of nearly 22 miles.

A thousand ships were required: warships, troop transports, and supply vessels. These included five battleships, nine escort carriers (216 aircraft), 24 cruisers, 122 destroyers and escort vessels, and 466 landing craft, all from five navies: American, British, Australian, French, and Greek. The fleet, named the Western Task Force, was commanded by Vice-Admiral H. Kent Hewitt. On board his flagship was James Forrestal, the new U.S. Navy Secretary.

Air support came from the U.S. 12th Air Force, under Brigadier-General Gordon P. Saville, with 2,100 aircraft. Its heavy bombers operated from the area of Rome, its medium bombers, fighter-bombers, and fighters from 14 airstrips which had been built in the Bastia area. Any objectives out of range of the latter would be dealt with by carrier-based aircraft under Rear-Admiral T. H. Troubridge, R.N. On August 13 and 14, the four-engined bombers prepared the way for the landings by attacking gun-emplacements, communication centres, bridges, and viaducts. These attacks were spread over an area from Port-Vendres to Genoa to deceive the enemy.

The German defences

The defence of the 400 miles of coastline between Menton and Cerbère was the responsibility of the German 19th Army.

▽ *American transport speeds the advance to the north.*

△ *Build-up. Massed vehicles in Italy, earmarked for "Dragoon".*
▷ ▷ △ *On the way. Part of the impressive task force which screened the armada.*
▷ ▷ *Closing the beaches.*

On D-day it had six divisions, deployed with three on each side of the Rhône. Between June 6 and August 4 it had had to give up its 217th, 272nd, and 277th Divisions, receiving in exchange only the 198th and the remnants of the 716th, which had been thrashed at Caen. Colonel-General Blaskowitz, C.-in-C. Army Group "G", wrote to C.-in-C. West on that day:

"The Army Group does not in the least deny the necessity of weakening the 19th Army to this extent, having regard to the situation of Army Group "B". It nevertheless feels obliged to point out that the consequences of these losses of men and *matériel* will be such that the Army's defences will be so diminished that it cannot guarantee to hold the coastline."

On August 10, however, the 19th Army had to lose its 338th Division. 11th Panzer Division was ordered to Avignon from Montauban by Hitler, but not until August 13, so that by the following day the whole of this division was still over on the right bank of the Rhône. This was the situation facing General Wiese, C.-in-C. 19th Army.

The German naval forces in the south of France consisted of only a limited number of small units and a few U-boats. The American air forces increased their attacks on Toulon, however, and four U-boats were sunk on August 6. The Luftwaffe had only 70 fighters and 130 bombers, a total of only one-tenth of the Allied aircraft used in Operation "Dragoon".

The first landings

On the single day of August 15, Allied aircraft flew 4,250 sorties and only 60 German planes managed to get off the ground. Admiral Hewitt's fleet fired 50,000 shells, including 3,000 12-inch or heavier, either during the preparations or at the request of the troops landing. The American VI Corps' attack, supported by the "Sudre" Combat Command of the French 1st Armoured Division, was against the German 148th Division (Lieutenant-General Otto Fretter-Pico) on the right and the 242nd Division (Lieutenant-

continued on page 1749

△ *The first paratroops are dropped. The main paratroop force was carried by 396 aircraft in nine relays, and was preceded by pathfinders.*
▷ *One of the glider landing zones. Much had been learned from earlier fiascos, and the German anti-glider defences gave little trouble.*

△ *A spectacular sight – the sky of southern France fills with parachutes. The "Dragoon" operations saw the most successful mass drop to date, with 60 per cent of the paratroops landing on their dropping zones or nearby.*

△ *Familiar scenes on the beaches – order emerges from apparent chaos.*

▷ *Homage to a colossus – a G.I. surveys the deck of one of the two French battle-cruisers in Toulon. (Strasbourg and Dunkerque had both been scuttled at Toulon when the Germans occupied southern France in November 1942.)*

▷▷ *A party of Germans surrenders in Marseilles under a hastily-improvised flag of truce.*

△ *Out in the open at last—the F.F.I. joins up with the liberators.*
▷ *F.F.I. round-up of suspected collaborators in Marseilles.*

continued from page 1742

General Bässler) on the left, the latter being responsible for the defence of Toulon. Both German units were part of LXII Corps (General Neuling) but corps H.Q. at Draguignan was cut off from its troops by the landing of the "Frederick" Division, supported by the Var *maquis*. The only Allied unit to run into difficulties was the U.S. 36th Division (Major-General John E. Dahlquist) in the area of Agay. Everywhere else the operation went like clockwork. By evening the Allies had landed 60,000 men, 6,000 vehicles, and 50,000 tons of *matériel,* all at the cost of 320 killed who, for the most part, had stumbled onto mines.

Amongst the day's exploits those of Colonel Bouvet's commando are worth recording. It landed in the middle of the night between Cavalaire and Cavalière and captured the fortifications on Cap Nègre. By the evening of the 15th it had advanced over nine miles and taken 1,000 prisoners.

Twenty-four hours later the 7th Army beach-head extended from Anthéor on the right through Draguignan, where General Neuling and his staff were taken prisoner, to le Luc on the road to Aix and over 24 miles from Fréjus, then back to the Mediterranean between Cavalière and le Lavandou. On the beaches Patch's second echelon arrived ahead of time and landed with the 1st Moroccan (General Brosset), the 3rd Algerian (General de Monsabert), and the 9th Colonial (General Magnan) Divisions, the remainder of the French 1st Armoured Division (General Touzet du Vigier) and General Guillaume's Moroccan *goumiers,* North African mountain troops.

De Lattre

On the following day this vanguard of the French 1st Army went into battle under General de Lattre de Tassigny. In the exercise of his command de Lattre seemed to be everywhere and to appear as if by miracle in places where his decision was needed. He cared deeply for the fate of his men and was often rude to staff and services on their behalf if the occasion warranted it.

Two men from very different backgrounds have borne witness to his character. On September 30, 1935, as he left manoeuvres at Mailly, Captain Hans Speidel, assistant military attaché at

the German Embassy in Paris, made the following comment on the officer commanding the 151st Regiment: "De Lattre makes an exceptional impression: he is a man of great vitality and fine intelligence and his bearing and discernment are quite out of the ordinary. His fellow-officers predict a great future for him in the French Army." This judgement by Rommel's future chief-of-staff is echoed by General de Gaulle in his memoirs:

"De Lattre was emotional, flexible, far-sighted and a man of wide interests, influencing the minds around him by the ardour of his personality, heading towards his goal by sudden and unexpected leaps, although often well thought out ones.

"De Lattre, on each occasion, courted opportunity above all. Until he found it he endured the ordeal of his tentative efforts, devoured by an impatience that often provoked scenes among his contacts. Suddenly seeing where, when and

▽ *From the beaches of Provence to the Vosges. When the "Dragoon" force joined hands with the right-wing armies advancing from Normandy, the Allied front was extended from the Channel to the Swiss frontier.*
Overleaf: *Another testament to Allied air power—bombed bridges across the Rhône.*

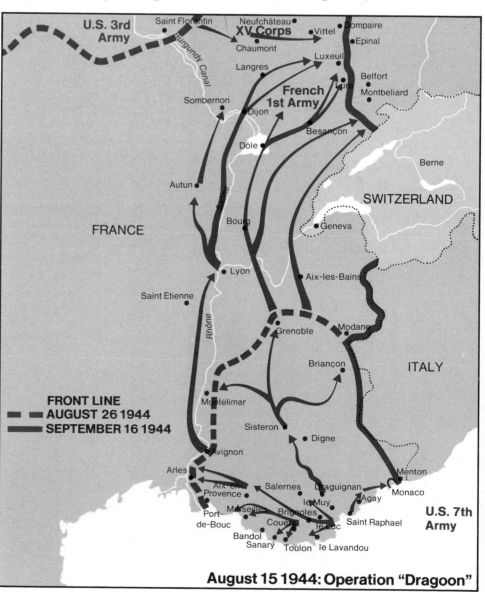

August 15 1944: Operation "Dragoon"

▷ A group pose by exultant F.F.I. fighters.
▽ New weapons for the F.F.I., courtesy of the Allies.

△ F.F.I. men shift a wrecked vehicle while the Shermans roll past in the background.
◁ A wealth of new equipment.

△ *Keeping up the pressure: a tank pushes north. Despite the pace of their advance the French and Americans failed to cut off and annihilate the Germans in the south.*

how the issue could be determined, he then set about the task of building it up and exploiting it. All the resources of a rich personality and extraordinary energy were put to work, demanding a limitless effort of those he engaged in it, but certain that he was preparing them for success."

It is no disrespect to this strategist and leader of men to say that the weapon Weygand and Giraud had forged for him, and which General Juin had tempered in the recent Italian campaign, had a keen edge. The Frenchmen from North Africa were enthusiastic at the idea that they were going to liberate their brothers in the home country, and were encouraged by the presence amongst them of 18,000 escapees from the unhappy armistice army. Considering the 9th Colonial Division's attack on the German positions in the area of Villars-les-Blamont on November 14 and 22, when the division's artillery crushed the 198th Division in the area of le Puix-Suarce, we can say with some justice that the 1st Army, by its bravery and its accomplishments, was the equal of any other Allied force.

A better judge was Major-General von Mellenthin, then chief-of-staff of Army Group "G". In *Panzer Battles* he writes: "The French tanks, reflecting the tempera-

ment of their army commander, General de Lattre de Tassigny, attacked with extraordinary spirit and *élan.*" A worthy tribute from an enemy who knew what he was talking about, to General du Vigier and his colleague Vernejoul, commander of the French 5th Armoured Division. The French opened their score with the capture of Salernes, Brignoles, and Cuers, the latter some nine miles north-east cf Toulon.

The American VI Corps, acting on local information, sent a motorised column along the axis Digne–Sisteron with orders to intercept the German 19th Army at Montélimar. Close on its heels was the 36th Division. The 45th Division (Major-General William W. Eagles) had taken the road to Aix-en-Provence.

Hitler orders retreat

In view of the reports he had received, and réalising that there was no longer any hope of throwing the enemy back into the sea, on August 16 Hitler ordered Colonel-General Blaskowitz to begin at once the evacuation of south and south-west France. Army Group "G" would

▷ *Abandoned transport in the wake of the German retreat. Unlike the advancing Allies, Blaskowitz had the advantage of being able to fall back on well-stocked depots as he pulled back up the Rhône valley.*

link up in the region of Sens with Model's left as the latter fell back to the Seine, whilst the 19th Army would proceed up the Rhône valley and hold as long as possible the line Côte d'Or–Lyon–Aix-les-Bains so as to keep Switzerland encircled. The 242nd Division at Toulon and the 244th at Marseilles (Major-General Schaeffer) would defend the ports to the last and raze their installations to the ground. The 148th Division, fighting in the Estérel massif, and the 157th in the Dauphiné, would come under Field-Marshal Kesselring's command and hold the French side of the Alps.

General von der Chevallerie, C.-in-C. of the German 1st Army, had transferred his H.Q. from Bordeaux to Fontaine-bleau on August 10 and so the conduct of the German retreat in the south-west fell to General Sachs, commander of LXIV Corps (158th and 159th Divisions). He left strong garrisons in the "fortresses" of la Pointe-de-Grave, Royan, and la Rochelle. General Wiese's task was to co-ordinate the movements of the Luft-waffe IV Corps (General Petersen: 189th, 198th, and 716th Divisions) and LXXXV Corps (338th Division). The 11th Panzer Division, under a particularly distin-guished commander, Lieutenant-General Gustav von Wietersheim, was ordered to cover the retreat.

Hitler's new directive

On August 20, as a consequence of this order to Army Group "G" and the in-creasingly serious situation of Army Group "B", whose left flank was being rolled up by Patton and the American 3rd Army, the Führer issued a new direc-tive. This has been summarised by Pro-fessor Percy Ernst Schramm, then editor and now publisher of the O.K.W. war diaries for 1944 and 1945:

"C.-in-C. West was ordered to hold the bridgehead west of Paris and prevent the enemy drive towards Dijon. First of all what remained of the 5th *Panzerarmee* and the 7th Army had to be withdrawn behind the River Touques and reorganised so that their armoured formations could be brought back into the left flank. If it turned out to be impossible to hold out in front of the Seine, the Paris bridgehead had to be held and also the line Seine–Yonne – Burgundy Canal – Dijon – Dôle –

Swiss frontier. The withdrawal of the 7th Army behind the Seine was to be prepared at once. The 5th *Panzerarmee* would protect its crossing over to the right bank so as to prevent the enemy engaged in the Seine valley from driving north and then eastwards after crossing the river."

Downstream from Paris the 1st Army, now under Army Group "B", would block off the narrow valleys on either side of Montargis to allow the occupation of the Burgundy Canal and the area north-west of Dijon.

300,000 Germans cut off

This directive calls for two remarks. Firstly, it took no account of the 230,000 men from the army (86,337), navy and air force trapped in the "fortresses" in the West.

Amongst these, Saint Malo had fallen on August 17 after epic resistance. It

◁ ◁ △ *Battle-stained G.I.s throng a field kitchen.*
◁ ◁ *The new occupants take over—Americans in a former German headquarters.*
△ *An American M3 half-track is utilised in an anti-aircraft role.*

took the 8-inch and 240-mm howitzers of the U.S. artillery, the 15-inch guns of the battleship *Warspite,* and the use of napalm to force Colonel von Aulock to hoist the white flag on the little island of Cézembre, the last centre of resistance, on September 2. The Brest garrison was attacked by the U.S. 2nd, 8th, and 29th Divisions and defended with equal tenacity by Lieutenant-General Ramcke and the 2nd Parachute Division. On September 17 fighting ceased in this unhappy town, which had been very heavily shelled. A further 48 hours were to elapse before Ramcke gave up the struggle in the Crozon peninsula.

Neither of the "fortresses" of Lorient or Saint Nazaire on opposite banks of the Loire was attacked; nor were the Channel Islands, where the 319th Division (Lieutenant-General von Schmettow) had some 30,000 men. The latter were sufficiently aware of the futility of their mission to call themselves the "Guernsey P.O.W.s" or the "non-stop card-players". But on the other hand, the shortage of usable ports was to prove a considerable handicap to the Allied supply network, and hence to the whole advance to Germany.

German divisions bled white

Our second remark is that this directive certainly came too late. It might have been possible to carry it out on August 1, when the vanguard of the 4th Panzer Division was forcing a crossing of the Sélune at Pontaubault. But it was no longer possible on the 20th, when Patton was driving his XII and XX Corps towards Sens and Montereau and ordering XV Corps to cross the Seine at Mantes without a moment's delay.

Hitler's directive, overtaken by events, was also at fault because it was issued without regard to the means left at Field-Marshal Model's disposal. In effect,

△ *By the end of 1944 the southernmost extremity of the Maginot Line had been reached.*

according to H. M. Cole of the historical service of the U.S. Army, who bases his figures on minute research of German military archives, on August 31 the 60-odd divisions of the Wehrmacht and the *Waffen*-S.S. then engaged on the Western Front had lost 293,802 officers, N.C.O.s, and men killed, wounded, and missing since June 6. This was an average of about 5,000 men per division, a loss which must have sapped the strength of every formation.

Losses in *matériel*

In July Guderian, the Inspector General of the *Panzerwaffe*, recorded the destruction of 282 Pzkw IV, 375 Panther, and 140 Tiger tanks; in August these figures were respectively 279, 358, and 97, giving an overall total of 1,529 in 62 days of fighting. It was the same for the rest of the equipment: by August 25, 1,500 guns, (field, A.A., and anti-tank) and 500 assault guns had been destroyed. The Führer's order to the C.-in-C. West might have been impossible to carry out, but there was also little chance of the latter's beaten armies establishing themselves in the position just reconnoitred by General Kitzinger of the Luftwaffe behind the Seine and the Burgundy Canal.

This line ran along the Somme, the Crozat Canal, the Aisne at Soissons, the Marne from Epernay to Chaumont, the Langres plateau, and ended up at the Swiss frontier in the region of Pontarlier.

A new defence line

On August 24 Hitler dictated to Seyss-Inquart, the Nazi High Commissioner in Holland, *Gauleiters* Simon, Bürkel, and Wagner (his representatives in Luxembourg, Lorraine, and Alsace), and the military authorities concerned an order to develop a "German position in the West" for which they would have recourse to a mass levy.

There would be a continuous anti-tank obstacle, behind which the land would be laid waste and positions in depth organised. It would straddle the Scheldt estuary, use the line of the Albert Canal, cover Aix-la-Chapelle and Trier, the fortified complex of Thionville–Metz, turn up the Moselle as far as Saint Maurice and finally block the gap at Belfort.

Did Hitler realise that, from Model's reports, his directive of August 20 was out of date by the 24th? The fact remains that twice in four days he had recognised that he was beaten in the West.

CHAPTER 125
"Paris Liberée!"

On August 16, the very day when the American XX Corps reached Chartres, the Paris police went on strike. This was the start of the uprising in the city. S.H.A.E.F.'s plan was not to mount a frontal attack on an urban area of this importance, but to outflank it on both sides so that it would fall of its own accord, thus sparing the city the fighting and all the destruction this would entail. According to calculations made in London, this operation was to take place between 120 and 150 days after D-Day. On August 16 at Chartres General Patton was about 20 days ahead of schedule.

"What to do about Paris?" Eisenhower asked himself. A critical problem indeed, as he has pointed out in his memoirs, since the liberation of Paris would bring the need for supplying food to the capital at a rate calculated by S.H.A.E.F. experts

at 4,000 tons a day. This figure caused the C.-in-C. 12th Army Group to refuse.

"However, in spite of this danger of famine in Paris, I was determined that we would not be dissuaded from our plan to by-pass the city. If we could rush on to the Siegfried Line with tonnage that might otherwise be diverted to Paris, the city would be compensated for its additional week of occupation with an earlier end to the war. But we had not reckoned with the impatience of those Parisians who had waited four years for the armies that now approached their gates. My plan to pinch out Paris was exploded on an airstrip near Laval the morning of August 23."

General de Gaulle, in his rôle of head of the provisional government, had also addressed himself to the Allied C.-in-C. On August 21, newly arrived at Rennes

▽ The ecstasy of liberation. A convoy of civilian cars follows Allied vehicles in a spontaneous demonstration during the liberation of Paris. It was some days before the city was completely free of snipers, though the bulk of German forces had surrendered by August 25.

△ *Shooting continued after the surrender. Here members of the "F.F.I." return fire during General de Gaulle's visit to Notre-Dame.*

from Algiers, he had said:

"Information reaching me from Paris leads me to believe that as the police and the German armed forces have almost disappeared from the city, and as there is an extreme shortage of food, serious trouble may be expected within a very short time. I think it is vital to occupy Paris as soon as possible with French and Allied troops, even if some fighting results and there is some damage in the city.

"If a disorderly situation arises now in Paris, it will be difficult later on to get control of the city without serious incidents and this could even affect later operations.

"I am sending you General Koenig, who has been nominated Military Governor of Paris and C.-in-C. of the Paris Region, to study the occupation question with you in case, as I request of you, you decide to proceed without delay."

In his war memoirs de Gaulle tells us

why he intervened. It was a matter of preventing the formation, under cover of an uprising, of a predominantly Communist government. If this were to happen, he said, "on my arrival I should find this 'popular' government functioning: it would crown me with a laurel wreath, invite me to take my place within its organisation, and then pull all the strings. For those in control the rest would then be alternate boldness and prudence, the spread of state interference everywhere under cover of purges, suppression of public opinion by control of information and a militia, the progressive elimination of their earlier associates until the dictatorship of the proletariat was established."

Eisenhower agreed to the request, and Leclerc's division was sent off to Paris. This was what they had been waiting for, stamping with impatience until they were given free rein, ever since they had been transferred from North Africa to Great

the Soviet advance would sooner or later burst over the dykes the Germans were erecting to hold it, and flood out all over Germany. Events since 1943 had only served to confirm his pessimism. When he left the O.K.W. meeting on August 7 after being invested by Hitler with the command of *Gross Paris* he had the impression that he had been dealing with a madman:

"Finally Hitler came to July 20 and I witnessed the explosion of a man filled to bursting with hatred. He yelled at me that he was glad to have bagged the whole opposition at one go and that he would crush it. He was in a state of feverish excitement. Saliva was literally running from his mouth. He was trembling all over and the desk on which he was leaning shook with him. He was bathed in perspiration and became more agitated still as he shouted that his generals would be 'strung up'. I was convinced there and then: the man opposite me was mad!"

If the means at Choltitz's disposal were enough to contain an uprising within the capital, the situation became completely different on August 21 as soon as O.K.W. ordered that the "Paris bridgehead" was to be held against the Americans. Hitler himself wrote to him, in order to underline the "supreme importance of the defence of Paris from the military and political points of view" and declared that "its fall would cause the breakdown of the whole coastal front north of the Seine and compel us to abandon bases used by

△ *A German officer, pistol in hand, races past a Parisian café. He was photographed from one of the commanding positions held by the F.F.I. just before he was shot. The Germans fought at a disadvantage in Paris since they did not dominate the rooftops, which in turn meant that they could not control the streets. As in Warsaw they retreated to the major buildings, which they held as strongpoints.*

▽ *Two soldiers of the U.S. 4th Infantry Division shelter behind a truck as they watch for snipers.*

Britain. Meanwhile this French 2nd Armoured Division had been moved from the U.S. 3rd to the U.S. 1st Army and put under V Corps. The least that can be said about this new arrangement is that Generals Gerow and Leclerc just were not on the same wavelength.

Choltitz and Hitler

On the German side the principal actors in the drama were General Dietrich von Choltitz, the Swedish Consul-General Raoul Nordling, and the leaders of the Paris insurrection.

Choltitz's behaviour is to be explained thus: since the previous autumn, when he had commanded XLVIII Panzer Corps on the Dniepr, he had maintained, in the presence of his chief-of-staff, Major-General von Mellenthin, that the tide of

18 au 25 Août 1944

Colonel Roll-Tanguy

Colonel Fabien

PARIS *SE LIBÈRE*

our V-weapons against England". And Choltitz could also be reminded that "in the course of history the loss of Paris has also meant the loss of France". This did not, however, alter in any way the situation of the 22,000 men from two or three different divisions with whom he was being asked to hold a bridgehead from the Seine at Poissy to the Marne at Creteil (about 32 miles). The end of the order: "The Seine bridges will be prepared for destruction. Paris must only fall into enemy hands as a heap of rubble", revealed more a state of terrorism than sound strategic thinking. As an experienced soldier Choltitz was well aware that neither the heap of rubble nor the destruction of the bridges (if they were all blown) would slow down the Allied advance. There would have to be more than 60 demolition charges laid, two or three at least would fail to go off and all the experience of the Blitzkrieg had shown that destroyed bridges are no good unless protected by covering fire. For all these reasons the C.-in-C. *Gross Paris* lent a willing ear to Raoul Nordling, not however forgetting that in Germany the freedom and perhaps the lives of his wife and children might depend on the way his behaviour was judged by the Führer. In this double life he was compelled to live he was ably seconded by Lieutenant-General Speidel, chief-of-staff of Army Group "B", though they both had to converse in guarded terms because their telephones were liable to be tapped.

Paris liberated

On August 23 the French 2nd Armoured Division bore down on Paris, the "Langlade" and "Dio" Combat Commands along the axis Sées–Rambouillet–Pont de Sèvres, and the "Billotte" Combat Command via Alençon–Chartres–Arpajon–Porte d'Italie, causing an overlap along the sector given by U.S. V Corps to its 4th Division and a new disagreement between Generals Gerow and Leclerc. During the advance German 8.8-cm guns in ambush along the roads caused the loss of 317 men and 41 tanks and self-propelled guns. In the night of August 24-25 Captain Dronne and the tanks *Romilly, Champaubert,* and *Montmirail* passed through the Porte de Gentilly and reached the square in front of the Hôtel de Ville.

△ *A group of German soldiers emerges from a building to surrender to the F.F.I.*
◁ *A German officer stands perilously outside the Chamber of Deputies, during the negotiations for the surrender of the 400 Germans who had held out inside.*
◁◁ *A children's magazine with a rather imaginative picture of the liberation.*
▽ ◁ *General Koenig and staff. Cdt. Duperior, Col. de Chevigné, Capt. Lucas, Koenig, Col. de Wavrin, Comm. Raulin.*

▽ *A Renault R40 returned to its original owners: members of the "F.F.I." refuel a tank captured from the Germans.*

Summer in Paris. Crowds near the Opera ignore a burning vehicle as they surge into the square to celebrate the liberation. The battle for Paris was a curious blend of street fighting and the continued life of a city. Hitler had hoped to reduce the city to ruins with air and artillery attacks complementing the planned demolitions.

On the following day, with the aid of the *Forces Françaises de l'Intérieur* under Colonel Rol-Tanguy, the 2nd Armoured Division liberated Paris, and Choltitz, who had not left his headquarters in the Hôtel Meurice, surrendered.

"Destroy Paris!"

As soon as he heard that Paris had fallen, Hitler flew into a rage and ordered it to be wiped out. With this end in view he had the great siege mortar *Karl* readied. This huge gun had a calibre of 60 cms (23.6 inches), fired 2.2-ton shells, and had not been in action since Sevastopol'. The V-weapons and all available aircraft were now also to be brought into action.

Speidel forbade the transmission of this order. It had not the least strategic value and it would have caused thousands of civilian victims, and the destruction of buildings of inestimable artistic value. Speidel was later arrested on suspicion of being implicated in the July Plot and was lucky to escape the horrible

torture which befell Witzleben and Hoeppner. If any conclusion is to be drawn from this episode it must come in the form of a question: what stage would the intellectual and moral reconstruction of Western Europe have reached today if Generals von Choltitz and Speidel had not, at the risk of their lives, thwarted the bloodthirsty plans of Adolf Hitler?

De Lattre presses on . . .

In Provence, General de Lattre de Tassigny had meanwhile managed to wriggle out of the plan by which he was intended to concentrate all his efforts on Toulon, and only move on to Marseilles when the large military port had been mopped up. This plan was calculated to lead to the hoisting of the tricolour on Notre Dame de la Garde on D-day plus 45, that is on September 28, if all went well.

On August 18 two solutions seemed possible to this ardent, yet calculating leader, as he says in his memoirs: "Given our recent successes, ought I to stick to the original plan? Or should I try to extend its scope? These were the alternatives that faced me on that day. It was very difficult, for the consequences of an error of judgement could only be very serious. If I opted for prudence, I could attack in strength, but all the benefits of surprise, and the chaos this would have caused in the enemy's ranks, would be lost. The Germans would have time to redeploy, move up reserves, and make full use of the enormous capabilities of the Toulon defence system. Thus caution would mean a siege, with all its consequent delays and suffering.

"If, on the other hand, I opted for boldness, I could expect to profit from the confusion caused by the strength of Truscott's attack, but my men would have to attack with one man against two, in the open and against reinforced concrete and protected gun emplacements. Boldness could break the French Army before it was even brought together.

"These were dramatic moments for the soul of a commander, but they could not be prolonged. After all, if the surprise attack failed, I could halt it and allow another commander to try again with more reinforcements. The risk was small compared with the enormous gains that might result from a swift success."

De Lattre went for boldness and got the

Two scenes typical of the liberation.
△ *A Parisienne gives a G.I. a victor's greeting, watched by a smiling gendarme.*

▽ *Police and members of the "F.F.I." escort away a suspected collaborator. The round-up of suspects after the liberation was haphazard and at times unjust.*

approval of General Patch, who overcame the misgivings of his staff. The French commander was, we would suggest, bolstering up a right decision with wrong premises, because on the same day, far from thinking of reinforcing the defence of Marseilles and Toulon, his adversary, acting under a directive from O.K.W., was actually putting into effect an order for withdrawal which was to take his 19th Army back to the area Lyons–Aix-les-Bains. De Lattre did not know, and could not have known, that Wiese was getting ready to retreat. The risk he mentioned was a real one to him and had to be faced.

This points to the difference between the military historian and the war-time commander: the one draws upon documents calmly collated in the peace of a library; the other makes his decisions from information which is never complete and "works on human skin", as Catherine the Great remarked forcibly to the intellectual Diderot, who carried no responsibility.

Now left to its fate, 242nd Division defended Toulon to the last ounce of its

△ *Sheltering behind an American tank, civilians shoot at a building still held by German troops.*
◁ *Parisians take cover behind parked M7 "Priest" self-propelled guns, during a battle with a sniper. These fire fights were often one-sided, for no snipers were ever captured, and Frenchmen found on the roof tops claimed that they too were hunting Milice gunmen or German stragglers. (The Milice was the hated Vichy militia).*

strength. On August 21 the 1st Free French Division had got as far as Hyères, in spite of stiff resistance, and Colonel Bouvet's commandos, working under the 9th Colonial Division, had scaled the walls of Fort Coudon on ropes and hunted down the 120 men of the garrison in the galleries: "At 1530 hours," General de Lattre reported, "when the Kriegsmarine decided to give in, it had only six unwounded men. But at the moment of surrender, their commander signalled: 'Fire on us.' Violent shelling then began on the fort and lasted for several minutes. Germans and Frenchmen alike were hit, and amongst the latter was Lieutenant Girardon, one of the heroes of the assault."

Defended to the last man

The same thing happened the next day in the ammunition magazine at Toulon, where the galleries had to be taken one by one by Lieutenant-Colonel Gambiez's battalion of shock troops, supported by two tank-destroyers firing point-blank and a battalion of artillery, which reduced the works above the ground.

"Only the dead stopped fighting," de Lattre wrote when describing this action. At nightfall, when the flame-throwers had overcome the last of the resistance, he went on, "the inside of the fortress was no more than a huge open charnel-

house over which hung a frightful stench of death. It was being devoured by flames which caused boxes of ammunition to explode at every moment. There were 250 corpses strewn on the ground and only 180 men had been taken prisoner. Of these 60 were seriously wounded. This macabre spectacle suddenly reminded me of the most tragic sights at Douaumont and Thiaumont in 1916. It is a fine thing that our lads, many of whom are in battle for the first time, have equalled the exploits of the hardened *poilus* of Verdun. Their enemy was in no way inferior to the one their fathers faced. One of the defenders was asked to give the reason for this heroic and desperate resistance. 'We defended ourselves, that's all. I am an officer, a lieutenant. It's war for me as well as for you, gentlemen,' he replied.''

The victorious advance of the 9th Colonial Division through the defences of Toulon relieved the 3rd Algerian Division of its first mission, during which

◁ *Behind his own barricade, a French soldier covers a road with a .50 calibre machine gun.*
▽ ◁ *An M8 light armoured car of the 4th U.S. Infantry Division drives down the Champs Elysées. Four years earlier the soldiers and horses of the Wehrmacht had clattered down the same wide avenues.*
▽ *Two German officers and a medical orderly are escorted away by a mixed group of "F.F.I." and regular French soldiers. With the large numbers of small arms in circulation in August 1944, these Germans were still targets for revenge by individual Frenchmen even when they had become prisoners.*

▷ *Police and Allied servicemen link arms to keep back the crowds during the parade to celebrate the liberation.*
▽ *Another parade of trucks and soldiers, a painting by Floyd Davis "German prisoners in Paris". A 2½-ton truck with its human cargo drives past Notre-Dame in the bleak autumn months following the liberation.*

it had reached Sanary and Bandol, thus ensuring the investment of the western side of the fortress.

Reinforced in due time by General Guillaume's *goums,* General de Monsabert rapidly turned towards Marseilles, where the firemen, the sailors, and the F.F.I. had taken up arms on August 21. The French forces took the mountain route and outflanked 244th Division's defence points along the main axes. On the 23rd General de Monsabert presented himself at 15th Military District H.Q. He sent for Lieutenant-General Schäffer, who then refused to surrender.

Toulon liberated

The liberation of Toulon was completed on August 27 by the capitulation of Rear-Admiral Ruhfus, who had found a last refuge from the shells of the navy and the bombs of the air force in the Saint Mandrier peninsula. The assault on Toulon had cost the French 2,700 men killed and wounded, but they had taken over 17,000 prisoners and several hundred guns. The Cape Cépet battery, which had been such a thorn in the flesh of the attackers, was pounded by 1,400 shells of 12-inch calibre or higher and 809 1,000- and 2,000-lb bombs. There were four direct hits on its turrets. One jammed, the other had one gun put out of action. The only gun undamaged fired 250 shells, but without appreciable effect.

Marseilles falls

On August 23 de Lattre sent the 1st Armoured Division into Marseilles, and together with the 3rd Algerian Division and the Moroccan *goums* it overcame the resistance within the city. As in Toulon, the Germans defended themselves bitterly, using rocket launchers, mines, and flamethrowers. The loss successively of Notre Dame de la Garde and Fort Saint Nicolas, however, ended Schäffer's resistance and in the evening of the 27th he wrote to Monsabert:

"Prolonged resistance seems pointless in view of your superior strength. I ask you to cease firing from 2100 to 0800 hours so that surrender terms may be finalised for mid-day on the 28th and that I may have a decision from you which will

allow me either to surrender with honour or to fight to the finish."

Neither General de Monsabert nor his commander were men to overlook the valour of the 244th Division. And so the armistice was signed on August 28 shortly before 0800 hours.

Allied victory in Provence

The Allies were now a month ahead of schedule. The fury of their attacks had cost them 4,000 killed and wounded, but they had wiped out two enemy divisions and captured 37,000 prisoners.

Before ceasing all resistance the Germans blew up the port installations in Marseilles and Toulon. Until these were restored, the Provence beaches had landed 380,000 men, 69,312 vehicles, 306,000 tons of supplies and *matériel,* and 17,848 tons of fuel. By May 8, 1945, 905,512 men and 4,123,794 tons of *matériel* had passed through the hastily-reconstructed ports of Marseilles, Toulon, and Port de Bouc. These figures are taken from Morison, who claims, and we would agree with him, that for this alone Operation "Dragoon" was justified.

△ *General Dwight D. Eisenhower, Supreme Commander Allied Expeditionary Forces, at the Arc de Triomphe, when he visited Paris on September 1, 1944. With him are (left) Lieutenant-General Omar N. Bradley and (right) General Joseph Koenig, military commander of Paris, and Air Chief-Marshal Arthur Tedder (extreme right). Koenig, the hero of Bir Hakeim, was to comment a few days after the liberation "The worst danger in Paris at the moment are the F.F.I."*

△ Light tanks of the Fighting French drive down the Champs Elysées in a victory parade shared by citizens and soldiers.

▷ A French colour party in an American Dodge command car. The soldiers are from the French North African Army, which served in Italy, France, and Germany. The Germans were to pay tribute to its fighting spirit and the quality of the leadership, which came as a bitter surprise after the easy victories of 1940. Like the British Indian Army it attracted men dedicated to soldiering, for even in the peace-time years before the war, there were skirmishes and fire fights with warring tribes.

◁ Smiling for the camera. Part of the crowds that turned out to greet the American forces entering Paris.

CHAPTER 126
Across the Seine

In late August 1944 the Franco-American victory in Provence thus usefully complemented the Anglo-American victory in Normandy. All those who followed the progress of the war on wall maps and every day moved the little blue flags representing the Allied forces further north, north-east, and east, must have thought that on the Western Front the Germans were on the point of final collapse and the Third Reich on the eve of invasion. On August 26, the 21st Army Group had the left of its Canadian 1st Army in the area of Honfleur and linked up with the British 2nd Army around Louviers; the right of the British 2nd Army was in Vernon, where it had a bridgehead on the north bank of the Seine. Between Mantes and Saint Nazaire,

the American 12th Army Group formed an immense hairpin including the Seine crossings at Mantes, Paris, Melun, and Troyes, then through Saint Florentin and Joigny, back to the Loire at Gien. In the south, whilst the 7th Army Group (U.S. 7th and French 1st Armies) was mopping up in Toulon and Marseilles, the American VI Corps had liberated Grenoble and was trying to cut off the retreat of the German 19th Army in the area of Montélimar.

By September 10 the Germans had only three fortresses in the north of France: Boulogne, Calais, and Dunkirk. Montgomery, newly appointed a Field-Marshal, occupied Bruges, Ghent, and Antwerp whilst his 2nd Army, down river from Hasselt, was on the north bank of

▽ An M10 tank destroyer crosses a pontoon bridge over the Seine on August 24, 1944. On the far bank three cranes, used in the assembly of the pneumatic pontoons and bridging bays, bear witness to the wealth of equipment available to the U.S. forces in Europe.

the Albert Canal. The American 12th Army Group was in Liège, Bastogne, and Luxembourg, and on the outskirts of Thionville, Metz, and Nancy. Until its XV Corps came back into the line, the 3rd Army had its right flank exposed in the area of Neufchâteau, but by September 11 it was in contact at Sambernon with the French II Corps, which formed the left wing of the Franco-American 7th Army Group. The right flank of this army group was in Pont-de-Roide near the Swiss border. Finally, between Mont Blanc and the Mediterranean Kesselring still held on to Modane and Briançon for a few days, but Savoy, the Dauphiné, Provence, and the Alpes Maritimes were virtually free.

This exceptionally rapid progress and the capture of 402,000 prisoners reported in the Allied communiqué of September 15 caused wild optimism at S.H.A.E.F. and at the headquarters of the 21st and 12th Army Groups. Between June 6 and September 11, Allied losses in killed and wounded were no greater than 40,000 and 20,000 respectively. Eisenhower now had 49 divisions in the field.

It is not surprising that the editor of the information bulletin at S.H.A.E.F. should blow the victory trumpet and write:

"Two and a half months of bitter fighting, culminating for the Germans in a bloodbath big enough even for their extravagant tastes, have brought the end of the war in Europe within sight, almost within reach. The strength of the German Armies in the West has been shattered, Paris belongs to France again, and the Allied armies are streaming towards the frontiers of the Reich." A few days later he concluded:

"The only way the enemy can prevent our advance into Germany will be by reinforcing his retreating forces by divisions from Germany and other fronts and manning the more important sectors of the Siegfried Line with these forces. It is doubtful whether he can do this in time and in sufficient strength."

Montgomery suggests a "concentrated effort" . . .

Montgomery agreed with this forecast and desired S.H.A.E.F. to come to a quick decision about the form and direction to be given to the pursuit. Indeed on August 17 he had put to General Bradley an outline plan of operations which was, in essence:

1. After crossing the Seine, the 12th and 21st Army Groups would form a "solid mass of some forty divisions" which would move north of the Ardennes and put a pincer round the Ruhr, the 12th to the south and the 21st to the

△ *A stone railway bridge blown by the retreating Germans. The charges had been placed in the arches of the bridge, which means that the piers remained intact and could be used as a foundation for a Bailey bridge. Europe suffered severe dislocation to its communications as a result of Allied air attacks and systematic German demolitions.*

△ *An American white
phosphorus shell lands in a
village in Lorraine.
Euphemistically designated a
smoke shell, phosphorus was a
terrifying anti-personnel
weapon, particularly when used
against troops in confined
conditions.*

north.

2. South of the Ardennes a "strong American force" would be "positioned in the general area Orléans–Troyes–Châlons–Reims–Laon with its right flank thrown back along the R. Loire to Nantes".

3. The American 7th Army Group would be directed from Lyons to Nancy and the Saar. But, Montgomery remarked: "We ourselves must not reach out with our right to join it and thus unbalance our strategy." He concluded: "The basic object of the movement would be to establish a powerful air force in Belgium to secure bridgeheads over the Rhine before the winter began and to seize the Ruhr quickly."

According to Montgomery, Bradley agreed with the plan, whereas in his memoirs the former C.-in-C. 12th Army Group makes no mention of it. It is common knowledge, however, that Eisenhower was unwilling to ratify the suggestions of Montgomery, though the latter returned to the question on August 22 through Major-General Sir de Guingand, his chief-of-staff and, on the following day, in person during talks which took place between the two leaders alone at Condé-sur-Noireau. But, on the

point of taking over the conduct of land operations himself, General Eisenhower rejected the idea with his customary affability. In fact, though Montgomery did not expressly say so, the formation of a "solid mass of some forty divisions" to operate north of the Ardennes would have meant the inclusion of the whole American 1st Army. In a note which he sent to his chief-of-staff on August 22, moreover, he implicitly excluded Bradley from any part in the race for the Ruhr, even attempting to dissuade Eisenhower from his intention of effectively controlling land operations. This can be read between the lines of paragraphs 3, 4, and 5 of Montgomery's note which de Guingand handed to Eisenhower:

"3. Single control and direction of the land operations is vital for success. This is a WHOLE TIME JOB for one man.

4. The great victory in N.W. France has been won by personal command. Only in this way will future victories be won. If staff control of operations is allowed to creep in, then quick success becomes endangered.

5. To change the system of command now, after having won a great victory, would be to prolong the war."

Eisenhower was in no way inclined to support a plan contrary to the agreement of the preceding winter. But neither did he intend to accept the plan which reduced Bradley and his 12th Army Group to some ten divisions, invited to mark time on the outskirts of the Argonne – for that is what the "strong American force" would have amounted to. Even if he had fallen in with Montgomery's ideas, he would probably have been caught between the discontent of Patton, Hodges, and Bradley and the repudiation of his action by the Pentagon.

By preferring to the concentrated effort proposed by Montgomery a wide-front pursuit aimed at both the Ruhr and the Saar, did Eisenhower nullify the Anglo-American victory in Normandy? Montgomery's memoirs, finished in September 1958, do suggest this. Certainly, the Allied advance began to slow down: by December 15 Hodges was bogged down before the Roer and Patton was only just approaching the Saar.

The Eisenhower-Montgomery controversy

It must not be assumed that the "concentrated effort" would have brought the Allies out-and-out victory before the first snows fell. If Patton had been halted on the Troyes – Châlons – Rheims front, Model and Rundstedt would not have lost the forces he trapped and decimated between the Marne and the Moselle, with a loss to the Germans of 22,600 prisoners, 474 tanks, and 482 guns. Also, if

the inner flanks of Patton and Patch had not linked up, it would not have been possible to trap the 19,600 Germans whose capture Major-General Elster reported to U.S. 81st Division H.Q. at Beaugency on September 8.

When Montgomery's memoirs appeared, Eisenhower was President of the United States and thus not in a position to answer them. Even after he had left the White House he still remained silent. He would appear to have stuck throughout to his original opinion as expressed in 1949 in *Crusade in Europe* when, denying that the Allies could have overrun the enemy, he concluded: "General Montgomery was acquainted only with the situation in his own sector. He understood that to support his proposal would have meant stopping dead for weeks all units except the Twenty-first Army Group. But he did not understand the impossible situation that would have developed along the rest of our great front when he, having outrun the possibility of maintenance, was forced to stop and withdraw."

A very pertinent remark, we would suggest, as on the right bank of the Rhine, somewhere between Wesel and Munster, it is difficult to imagine what chances of success the 21st Army Group would have had if the 12th had been stuck back at Châlons-sur-Marne through lack of fuel and ammunition. Instead of a "reverse Schlieffen plan" such as Montgomery had envisaged, we might have seen Rundstedt manoeuvring between Montgomery and Bradley as Hindenburg had done 30 years before between Rennenkampf and Samsonov at Tannenberg.

△ Covered with autumn leaves, U.S. soldiers wait in an abandoned German trench.

▽ A Sherman tank rumbles across a newly-completed pontoon bridge over the Seine at Vulaines-sur-Seine. Construction bridging techniques and light-weight equipment used by the Allies have ended the image of the military engineer as a soldier shoulder deep in a river struggling with timber and rope.

The German Focke-Wulf Fw 190D-9 fighter

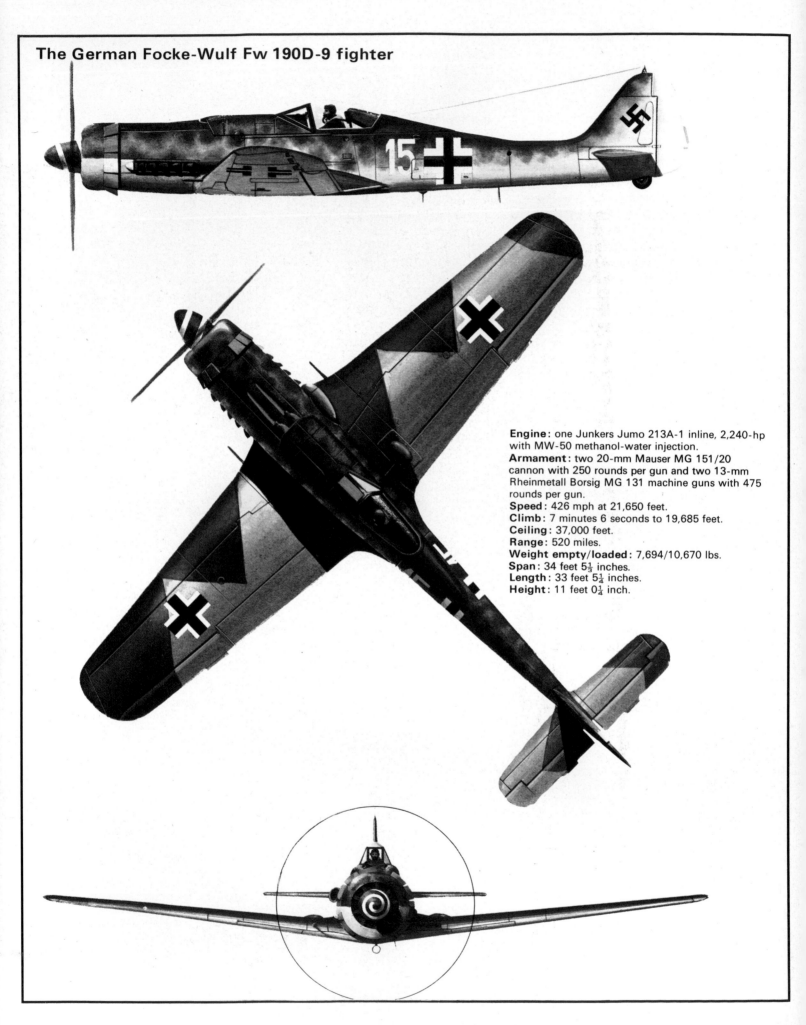

Engine: one Junkers Jumo 213A-1 inline, 2,240-hp with MW-50 methanol-water injection.
Armament: two 20-mm Mauser MG 151/20 cannon with 250 rounds per gun and two 13-mm Rheinmetall Borsig MG 131 machine guns with 475 rounds per gun.
Speed: 426 mph at 21,650 feet.
Climb: 7 minutes 6 seconds to 19,685 feet.
Ceiling: 37,000 feet.
Range: 520 miles.
Weight empty/loaded: 7,694/10,670 lbs.
Span: 34 feet $5\frac{1}{3}$ inches.
Length: 33 feet $5\frac{1}{4}$ inches.
Height: 11 feet $0\frac{1}{4}$ inch.

Logistics: a crisis for General Eisenhower

The Allies were clearly winning. In spite of their spectacular progress, however, between August 25 and September 10 a number of mishaps and strokes of bad luck, combined with shortages on the logistic side which got worse after the Seine had been crossed, brought Eisenhower to a virtual standstill at the end of September, whereas the Wehrmacht was recovering with astonishing speed.

Was this crisis in supplies the fault of Lieutenant-General J. C. H. Lee, Quartermaster-General at S.H.A.E.F., whom Bradley called "brilliant but niggling"? It was he who controlled the organisation and the running of transport. It must be remembered that Patch in front of Belfort, Patton at Nancy, Hodges at Aix-la-Chapelle, Dempsey on the Albert Canal, and Crerar between Boulogne and Zeebrugge were all being supplied via the beaches of Provence and Normandy. But when the German engineers withdrew, they had carried out 4,000 demolitions over and above the damage caused by Allied bombing in the first six months of the year. The French national railway network was in ribbons and its rolling stock reduced to practically nothing after German requisitioning and Allied air attacks. It is not, therefore, surprising that supplies had not been able to keep up with the advancing troops, in spite of the so-called "Red Ball Highways", major one-way roads along which the heavy lorries rolled for 20 hours a day each.

The Allied forces press on into France

Certain mishaps also occurred in Allied strategy. The American 7th Army failed in its attempt to cut the retreat of the German 19th Army. The Germans did, it is true, leave 5,000 prisoners, including Lieutenant-General Richter, commander of the 198th Division, at Montélimar, and had only 64 guns left out of the 1,480 of the preceding August 15. But, General de Lattre tells us, Wiese "knew his job" and, moreover, the French and the Americans were always running out of petrol.

On the left the French II Corps (General de Monsabert: 1st Free French Infantry and 1st Armoured Divisions), which crossed the Rhône at Avignon on August 29, liberated Lyons on September 2 and won a brilliant victory over a detachment of the German 1st Army in the area of Autun on September 9. This gave it Dijon 48 hours later. In the centre the U.S. VI Corps, operating along the axis Bourg en Bresse–Besançon, was held up at Luxeuil and Lure. Finally, on the right was a French group, consisting mainly of the 3rd Algerian Division, the 9th Colonial having had to be stopped when it reached the Swiss frontier between Geneva and Pont-de-Roide. On September 6 General de Lattre formed this group into the French I Corps and put it under the command of General Béthouart. The following day it was held up for lack of ammunition. It held on to its position on top of le Lomont, where the old fort had been captured by the F.F.I at the end of July and from which the Germans had been unable to dislodge them. This was an exploit which, de Lattre says, "gives us an incomparable observation post over the plain of Montbéliard and

A U.S. 75-mm pack howitzer in action. The mainstay of both the British and U.S. airborne forces, this weapon was also used in the Far East where it was stripped down for animal pack as well as parachute dropping. Possibly the most unusual employment of this versatile weapon was its mounting in U.S. Boston and Mitchell medium bombers in a ground attack and anti-submarine rôle.

△ *The David and Goliath bridges at Vernon on the Seine, built by Sappers of the 43rd (Wessex) Division. The heavy girder bridge in the foreground is being manoeuvred into position by a tug, while a bay (two pontoons attached by panels) can be seen anchored to the assault bridge. With the light assault bridge completed, work on "Goliath" could be started from both banks of the river.*
▷ *Eisenhower begins to batter down Germany's protective gate.*

the 'watchdog' of the Belfort gap. The 3rd Algerian Division is in sight of the promised land, but it is out of breath after its terrific run and can't get in.''

We now go over to the American 12th Army Group. The chapter of Patton's war memoirs dealing with this part of the campaign is entitled *Touring with an Army in France.* He could also have adapted the message Colonel-General von Kleist is supposed to have sent to Field-Marshal List in the race for the Caucasus in July 1942: "In front of us, no enemy; behind us, no supplies." On August 25, Patton had been ordered to reach in one bound the line Vitry-le-François–Châlons–Rheims; he was then to move off from there, on the orders of army group, to take the Rhine bridges between Mannheim and Koblenz.

Patton still had under his command U.S. VIII Corps, then occupied in taking

Brest. His other units were two corps and six divisions: at Troyes was XII Corps under Major-General Manton S. Eddy, who had just relieved General Cook, evacuated after a heart attack; in the bridgehead at Montereau XX Corps was eager and ready for the chase.

On August 28, XII Corps crossed the Marne at Châlons where 80th Infantry and 4th Armoured Divisions filled up with petrol thanks to a captured German dump of 88,000 gallons. On the following day XX Corps passed through Epernay and Château-Thierry, then occupied Rheims without any difficulty.

In spite of the threat of petrol supplies running out, Patton had got Bradley's agreement that he should push on from the Marne to the Meuse, and Eddy captured the river crossings at Vaucouleurs, Commercy, and Saint Mihiel on the last day of the month. On his left, Major-

General W. H. Walker, after an advance of some 75 miles, occupied Verdun and crossed the river, the bridges being still intact thanks to the F.F.I. But, writes Martin Blumenson, "in possession of Meuse River bridge-heads between Verdun and Commercy, Patton was in position to attack toward the Moselle between Metz and Nancy, and from there the Rhine River was barely a hundred miles away. This was his intention, but by then his supply lines were drawn to the breaking point. Soldiers in the forward echelons needed shoes, heavy underwear, and socks, and these items could not move fast enough to reach the advancing spearheads. The mechanical beasts of burden needed spare parts and maintenance. Still the most critical shortage was gasoline . . . By then the army was virtually bone dry. Individual tanks were dropping out of combat formations for lack of gasoline. The chance of speedy resumption of the pursuit east of the Meuse, a hope that depended on motorised columns, appeared nil."

Eisenhower puts the brake on Patton

Patton tried to get Eisenhower to change his point of view, urging that the way to the Rhine between Mannheim and Koblenz was virtually wide open to his tanks, the Siegfried Line not being strongly held. His eloquence failed to move Eisenhower.

By September 15 the enemy was considerably reinforced and, though Patton had liberated Nancy, he had lost any hope he might have had of breaking the *Westwall* in his stride or even taking Metz

△ *Three Sherman flail tanks cross a Bailey pontoon bridge at Elbeuf on the Seine. The bridge was destroyed by the R.A.F., who also sank the barge seen in the foreground. The use of Bailey bridges kept up the momentum of the Allied advance, and the bridges also helped in the reconstruction of post-war Europe.*

and Thionville on the way. XV Corps, given to him somewhat late in the day, was engaged on his right in the area Chaumont–Neufchâteau. This gave rise to a battle on September 13 between Vittel and Epinal during which the "Langlade" Combat Command of the French 2nd Armoured Division, sharing equally the honours with the 406th Group, U.S. 9th Air Force from Rennes (365 miles away), severely trounced the newly-formed 112th Panzer Brigade, destroying 34 Panther and 26 Pzkw IV tanks out of the 96 it had set out with.

As we have seen, the U.S. 1st Army, with its right in Melun and its left in Mantes, though not entirely under the command of the Anglo-Canadian 21st Army Group, was given the rôle of supporting, along the Aix-la-Chapelle–Cologne axis, Montgomery's drive through the north of the Ruhr. And so, in the matter of fuel and transport, General Hodges was relatively well supplied.

On the right, U.S. VII Corps with its 3rd Armoured Division (Major-General Maurice Rose) in the lead, broke out of the Melun bridgehead, passed through Laon on August 30, and crossed the Franco-Belgian frontier from Avesnes and Maubeuge, getting into Mons at dusk on September 2.

On the left of the U.S. 1st Army, XIX Corps advanced at the same speed along the axis Mantes–Montdidier–Cambrai–Tournai. 25,000 Germans from 20 different divisions were trapped between the two advancing American columns between Mons and Cambrai and surrendered to VII Corps by order of General Straube, commanding LXXIV Corps.

From Mons and Tournai VII and XIX Corps then changed direction from north to north-east, the former towards Liège, which it reached on September 8, the latter towards the Albert Canal, where it made contact with the 21st Army Group. V Corps, having left Paris, had only got as

The American M4A3E8 Sherman medium tank

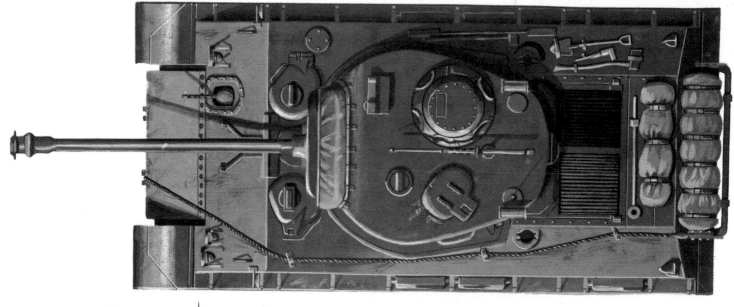

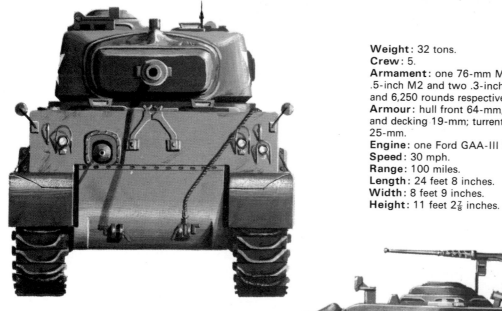

Weight: 32 tons.
Crew: 5.
Armament: one 76-mm M1A2 gun with 71 rounds, plus one
.5-inch M2 and two .3-inch M1919A4 machine guns with 600
and 6,250 rounds respectively.
Armour: hull front 64-mm, sides and rear 38-mm, belly 25-mm,
and decking 19-mm; turrent front and sides 64-mm and roof
25-mm.
Engine: one Ford GAA-III inline, 450-hp.
Speed: 30 mph.
Range: 100 miles.
Length: 24 feet 8 inches.
Width: 8 feet 9 inches.
Height: 11 feet $2\frac{7}{8}$ inches.

far as Landrecies. General Bradley, hoping to get Patton out of his supply difficulties, moved it over behind VII Corps and sent it through the Ardennes. On September 9 his 5th Armoured Division (Major-General Lumsford E. Oliver) liberated Luxembourg and, better still, as part of the same advance, crossed the Sûre at Wallendorf (seven miles east of Diekirch) thus making a breach in the Siegfried Line.

At Koblenz, where on September 5 Field-Marshal von Rundstedt had just relieved Model as C.-in-C. West, this news, according to his chief-of-staff Lieutenant-General Westphal, not one inclined to panic, "burst like a bombshell".

"All available forces, all that could be pulled out from other sectors," he added, "were thrown into the breach. Overcoming the most serious hesitations, we went so far as to denude the Trier sector completely. After a week of pitched battles, the enemy went back over the west bank of the Sûre. A gigantic catastrophe was thus averted. If the enemy command had thrown in greater strength at this point,

not only the defensive organisation we were trying to build in the Eifel, but the whole Western Front, which had no reserves worthy of the name, would have crumbled."

This shows that the Koblenz H.Q. had simply no idea of the logistic crisis already affecting the U.S. 7th and 3rd Armies and now extending to the 1st. Nor did they know that Bradley had no reserves with which to exploit Oliver's success. It is true that, according to Westphal, C.-in-C. West's Intelligence services thought that Eisenhower had 60 divisions, whereas the figure was actually 50.

The Pas-de-Calais cleared

As his notes of August 17 and 23 show, Montgomery claimed for his reinforced 21st Army Group the distinction of inflicting the final blow on the enemy by a "concentrated push" north of the Ruhr. Yet he had only 18 divisions and six or seven independent brigades, and the

Canadian 1st Army had been given (by him) a job which was to divert it from his ultimate objective. Using six divisions and two brigades, it liberated the ports of Le Havre, Dieppe, Boulogne, Calais, and Dunkirk, captured the V-rocket launching-sites and mopped up the Cape Gris-Nez shore batteries, which used to harass the English coast between North Foreland and Dungeness.

Thus only the British 2nd Army was left to continue the thrust northwards, but by August 30 it had only two of its three corps across the Seine. These had altogether five divisions, including three armoured, two brigades of tanks, and General Piron's Belgian motorised brigade. This was a long way from the "concentrated push" (40 divisions) mentioned the previous week.

Montgomery, usually so cautious towards overweening displays of ill-considered optimism, seems to have yielded to the feeling of euphoria evident at all levels of the Allied high command. And yet the "great encirclement" west of the Seine, for which Patton had been halted in front of Falaise, had not come up to expectations. And, though now reduced to three corps and six divisions, the German 15th Army in the Pas-de-Calais was still a considerable fighting force. On August 23 its new C.-in-C. was Zangen, who took over from Salmuth. Sir Brian Horrocks, C.-in-C. British XXX Corps (11th Armoured, Guards Armoured, and 50th Infantry Divisions and 2nd Armoured Brigade), left the Vernon bridgehead with 600 tanks and made such good progress that 36 hours later his 11th Armoured Division took Amiens by surprise during the night of August 30-31, capturing General Eberbach, who had replaced the wounded Hausser as C.-in-C. 7th Army. The F.F.I. had seized the bridges in the town and the 11th Armoured was thus able to push on to the area of Lens, which it reached on September 11.

On Horrocks's right the Guards, who had crossed the Somme at Bray, were at Douai by nightfall on the same day. On September 3 they were off again and by 1400 hours, having done over 70 miles, got into the outer suburbs of Brussels, accompanied by the Piron brigade, amidst great popular rejoicing. That same evening General Horrocks, who set up his H.Q. in Laeken Park, invited Queen Elisabeth of the Belgians to dinner in his tent.

At the same time 11th Armoured Division had reached Alost and been given the

task of seizing the port of Antwerp to prevent the destruction of its installations. In this it was admirably seconded by the Belgian resistance so that on September 4 its quays (34 miles of them!), docks, and locks, its equipment and the tunnel under the Scheldt all fell intact into Allied hands. In 1960, however, General Horrocks said he thought that the order given to 11th Armoured to go straight for Antwerp was a mistake:

"My excuse is that my eyes were fixed entirely on the Rhine, and everywhere else seemed of subsidiary importance. It never entered my head that the Scheldt would be mined, and that we should not be able to use Antwerp port until the channel had been swept and the Germans cleared from the coastline on either side. Nor did I realise that the Germans would be able to evacuate a large number of the troops trapped in the coastal areas across the mouth of the Scheldt estuary from Breskens to Flushing."

He also wrote that it would have been much wiser to have ordered his division to by-pass Antwerp and go on across the

△ *Three Canadian gunners inspect one of the 14-inch guns at Boulogne used to bombard the Channel and south coast ports of England. The gun emplacement has a curtain of chain mail, which bears marks of some of the attempts to silence the guns. They stopped firing on September 22 when the garrison commander, Lieutenant-General Heim, surrendered to the Canadians.*

△ ◁ *French civilians start the work of reconstruction. In the background lie the remains of one of the Marne bridges.*

◁ *Two U.S. soldiers put some scanty camouflage on their machine gun nest. When leaves or underbrush were used to conceal a position, care had to be taken to replace them when they wilted, for a heap of yellowing leaves in a green wood was a danger signal to a wise soldier.*

▷ *After the slogging match in Normandy, the break-out and Seine crossings seemed to go at break-neck speed. The Channel ports were isolated and reduced, and there were optimistic predictions that the war could be over by Christmas. The optimists had not considered that as they fell back towards their own country, the Germans would fight harder.*

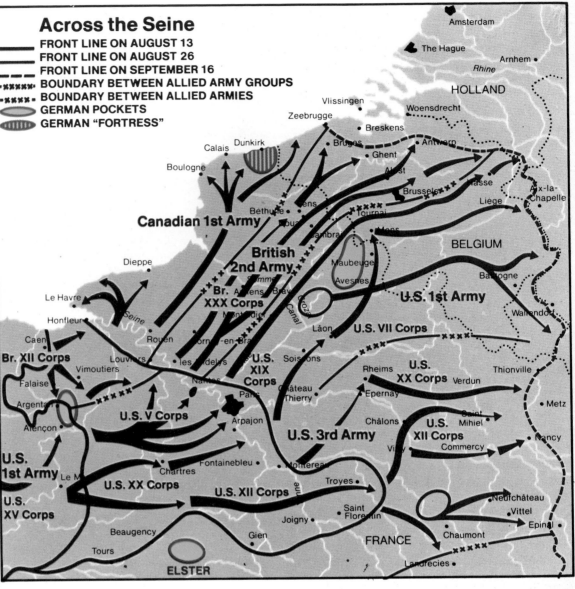

Across the Seine

▬▬▬	FRONT LINE ON AUGUST 13
────	FRONT LINE ON AUGUST 26
─ ─ ─	FRONT LINE ON SEPTEMBER 16
·××××	BOUNDARY BETWEEN ALLIED ARMY GROUPS
·××××	BOUNDARY BETWEEN ALLIED ARMIES
⬭	GERMAN POCKETS
⬭	GERMAN "FORTRESS"

▽ *General Dwight D. Eisenhower with Major-General E. H. Brooks, commander of the 2nd Armoured Division. By the end of the war Brooks commanded VI Corps and in the follow up to the Ardennes offensive his soldiers broke through the Siegfried Line.*

Albert Canal in one solid mass, then make for the Woensdrecht isthmus (15 miles north-east of Antwerp) which has the only metalled road linking the Zeeland archipelago to the mainland. This would have cut off the Germans left behind in the Scheldt estuary and freed the port within a few days.

Horrocks must have had in mind the memoirs of Field-Marshal Montgomery, published two years earlier, which maintained that the "free use of the port of Antwerp" was not the only way of bringing the war to a speedy end; it was necessary at the same time to strike a "violent decisive blow" against Germany. It is significant that Horrocks does not dwell on his former commander's opinion. Colonel Stacey, the official historian of the Canadian Army, concluded, as did Horrocks, but in stronger and more vivid terms: it was "a considerable Allied misfortune". It would seem that the blame for this mishap must lie largely with

Montgomery, for Eisenhower had been urging the importance of opening the port of Antwerp since the third week of August. Indeed, his reason for refusing a thrust north of the Ruhr was the need to open Antwerp first.

On Horrocks's left Lieutenant-General Ritchie's XII Corps (7th Armoured and 53rd Infantry Divisions, with 4th Armoured Brigade) avenged its commander's defeats in Libya. Though it had a harder task, as it was manoeuvring in the rear of the German 15th Army, it drove forwards along the axis les Andelys–Gournay–Saint Pol–Béthune and freed Ghent on September 5. In the Bruges area it made contact with the Canadian 1st Army busy mopping up the Channel ports.

As we can see, General Dempsey had driven forward at top speed and the British 2nd Army had equalled the best records of the American 3rd, though to get the fuel for XXX and XII Corps, VIII Corps had had to be immobilised.

Airborne war: learning the trade

1. *The first use of airborne troops in World War II: a German paratrooper collapses the canopy of his parachute after landing in Norway during the invasion of April 1940. The daring, and in the event successful, use of such airborne forces in the invasion of Denmark and Norway should have warned the Allies of what could happen in the West – such as the audacious glider landing on Eben-Emaël.*

Airborne re-supply to troops in the field was successfully attempted at the end of World War I, but it was the Russians who pioneered paratroop training in the early 1930's.

The foreign observers at the manoeuvres near Kiev in 1936 saw two battalions with light weapons land in eight minutes and occupy the town which was their objective. There was some interest and experiments by the

western countries, but only the Germans and Italians considered vertical envelopment as a valuable tactic.

The German paratroops were trained by the Luftwaffe, and from the beginning were picked troops. In 1940 they saw action in Denmark and Norway, where they were involved in heavy fighting. In the West, a team of airborne sappers neutralised the Belgian fort of Eben-Emaël, and

paratroops attacked airfields and bridges in Holland.

The following year paratroops seized the bridge over the Corinth canal, a vital bottleneck in the British escape route from Greece. It was on the island of Crete, however, that on May 20, 1941 the *Fallschirmjäger* achieved their greatest success. Despite heavy losses they secured Maleme airfield and Ju 52's started to fly in Major-General Julius Ringel's

2
German paratroopers in training, from a German history of airborne forces published in 1940.
2. Trainees learn how to fall after reaching the ground. The failure to do this properly usually meant at least a sprained ankle if not a broken one. Note the parachutes hanging up behind the trainees.
3. Getting the feeling of swinging under the canopy.
4. A German paratrooper in full jumping kit. In his left hand he is holding the static line, which was clipped to a wire in the aircraft before the jump. As the man left the aircraft, the static line pulled open the pack, allowing the parachute to blossom out once the jumper was clear of the aircraft.
5. The German paratrooper's badge, a diving eagle in a wreath of oak and laurel.
6. The paratrooper's cuff title, silver thread on green: "Fallschirm-Jäger-Rgt." (Parachute Regiment).

mountain division. Attacked by fresh troops with heavy weapons, the British were doomed and by May 27 the island was firmly occupied. The losses from Operation "Mercury" were very heavy, the paratroops and assault troops suffering over 4,500 casualties in all, with about 100 Ju 52's destroyed. Though they were used as élite ground troops throughout the war, the *Fallschirmjäger* made only limited drops at Catania in Sicily in July 1943, at Leros later that year, and a final disorganised jump during the Ardennes offensive in December 1944.

The Russians made some landings during the first winter offensive of 1941-42, and another attack, on September 24, 1943, was made in support of an assault crossing of the Dniepr loop between Kiev and Kanev. The operation was a disaster as many aircraft were lost or shot down, and the troops scattered. But the chief reason for the failure was that the dropping zone was in the path of 10th *Panzergrenadier* Division and other units moving up to the front.

The Japanese employed paratroops in their attacks on the Dutch East Indies in 1942 and other island hopping operations, but they served more for infiltration than exploitation.

The British and Americans were not slow to learn from the German successes, and at Ring-

way in Great Britain and Fort Benning in the U.S.A. the Allies began training and developing drills for mass parachute drops.

The first British operation was on February 10, 1941, when 38 men were dropped to attack the Tragino Aqueduct in southern Italy. Though the target was attacked, the damage was negligible and soon repaired.

On February 27 and 28, 1942, the Parachute Regiment won its first battle honour in the Bruneval Raid. Operation "Biting" was carried out by "C" Company, 2nd Parachute Battalion. At the cost of three killed and six missing the raid on the French coast secured a German radar set.

At the end of the year, British paratroops captured Bône airfield, Tunisia, in their first battalion-strength operation.

In July 1943 the 1st Air Landing Brigade and the 1st Parachute Brigade were in action in Sicily capturing the Ponte Grande Bridge and the Primosole Bridge.

D-Day saw the 6th Airborne Division covering the left flank of the Allied landings. In this rôle it captured the Merville Battery and the Pegasus Bridge.

Meanwhile in the south, the 2nd Independent Brigade Group made up part of the 1st Airborne Task Force in the landings of Operation "Dragoon" on August 15.

At the end of 1944, as the Allies thrust through France and Bel-

gium to the borders of Germany, General Montgomery launched Operation "Market Garden", and the 1st Airborne Division jumped over Arnhem.

The American experience was similar to that of the British. In the early 1930's there were theoretical discussions, but it was the successful employment of paratroops in war that started practical training. Lieutenant-

6

7

8

10

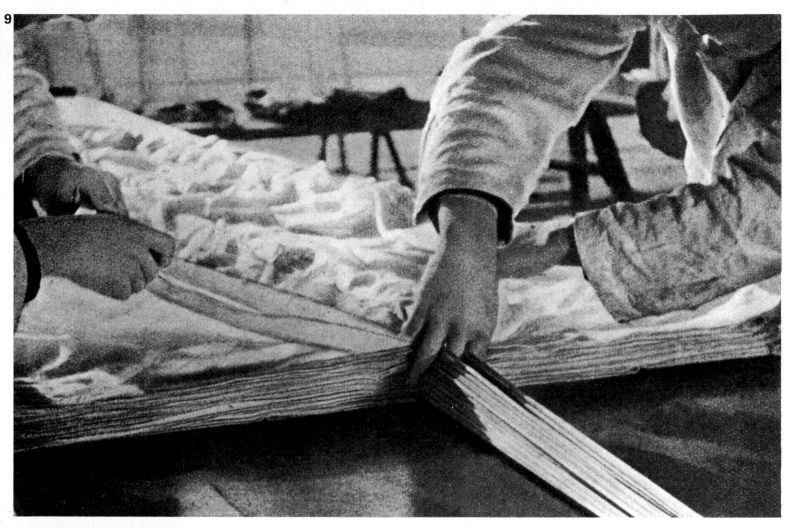

9

Colonel William C. Lee, who commanded the Provisional Parachute Group at Fort Benning, Georgia, pioneered the training.

Like the British, U.S. paratroops had a distinctive uniform and extra pay, but they also suffered from a similar lack of equipment and insufficient aircraft.

U.S. paratroops went into action at Oran and Youks-les-Bains in North Africa during the "Torch" landings. These operations, and a demolition raid on El Djem in Tunisia, showed that sufficient time for detailed planning was essential.

Tragically, Sicily again proved that planning was inadequate. In two drops soldiers were so scattered that only one-eighth landed in front of the 1st Division beaches at Gela. The plan to drop the 504th Regimental Combat Team to reinforce the 82nd Airborne Division at Gela suffered badly after the transports came under fire from the invasion fleet: 23 aircraft were shot down, among them six with troops still on board. As the paratroops jumped they came under Allied fire, and some were even fired at after they had reached the ground.

However, though the Allies were disappointed with the attacks in Sicily, the Germans considered them a success. The scattered soldiers dislocated the enemy rear, and Italian prisoners estimated the number of American paratroops as between 20,000 and 30,000, whereas only about 5,000 men were involved.

The airborne assault on Normandy by the 82nd and the 101st Airborne Divisions was again scattered, but this worked to the Americans' advantage. With no battalion concentrations there was no target to counter-attack, and German patrols sent out to mop up the enemy found themselves involved in hundreds of local fire-fights.

In southern France the Americans achieved their most accurate mass combat drop to date. Nearly 60 per cent of the troops landed on the three assigned drop zones in Operation "Dragoon". But when the 3rd Division approached St. Tropez, one of its objectives, it found that airborne troops had already occupied the area and captured the garrison of 240 Germans, an anti-aircraft battery,

7. Part of a stick of German paratroopers leaves its Junkers Ju 52 transport aircraft. Note the weapons container on the extreme left. Until they could reach this, when they landed the paratroops would be entirely dependent on personal weapons.
8. Before emplaning. The special helmet was a cut-down version of the standard German helmet.
9. The delicate work of parachute packing. Unless the canopy was folded correctly and the rigging lines kept untangled, there was every possibility of the parachute twisting up, or "Roman candling", causing the paratrooper to plummet to his death.
10. Practice in leaving the aircraft.

11. *After ground training and short drops from a practice tower, British paratroopers next moved on to drops from a static balloon. Note the basket, with a circular hatch to simulate that on the underneath of the converted bombers used as Great Britain's first paratroop-dropping aircraft.*

12. *A drop from an Armstrong-Whitworth Whitley II of the 1st Parachute Training School.*

14

13. *British paratroopers make a last careful inspection of their own and their comrades' kit before emplaning. Note the special smock and helmets. The aircraft in the background is a Whitley.*

14. *Ready to go. Note the quick release device on the harness (turn to unlock and press to release) and the Sten sub-machine gun carried by the man second from the left.*

After the success of German parachute troops in 1940, the United States and Great Britain began to train airborne forces. In America, a school was established at Hightstown, New Jersey, under Major-General George A. Lynch, where an initial cadre of 48 men was trained to serve as instructors.

15. A novice begins his training with a jump from a 125-foot practice tower.

16. A year later, in June 1941, the practice tower had been improved, and training had intensified as the war in Europe expanded.

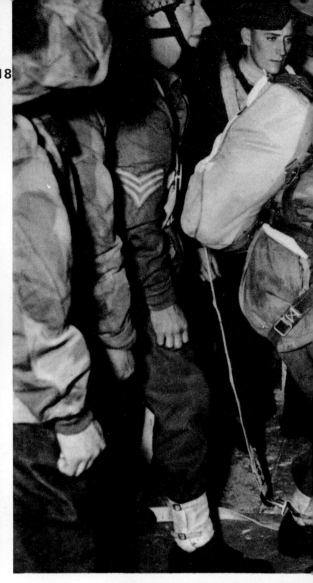

17. *A final check as each man clips his static line before the jump.*

18. *Under the concerned eyes of an R.A.F. dispatcher, a Colour Sergeant prepares to jump.*

19. *A paratrooper in mid exit as he hits the slipstream of the aircraft.*

20. *In near perfect conditions the stick reforms after the jump. Even a slight wind could scatter the men and weapons containers over a wide area and prevent the formation of an effective force.*

21. *Overleaf. The skies over Arnhem fill with parachutes in the opening stages of the operation.*

and two coastal batteries—the airborne troops were those from 20 planes who had jumped prematurely on the red signal light.

The day-light drop by the U.S. 82nd and 101st Airborne Divisions in Operation "Market Garden" proved, contrary to the grim predictions of some planners, to be a spectacular success. Men of the 101st seized their objectives, though one bridge was found to be destroyed. The Guards Armoured Division built a replacement and pressed on towards the 82nd, holding Grave and the ground south-east of Nijmegen. The 82nd had been driven back from the bridge over the Waal. In a joint attack the U.S. 504th Parachute Regiment and the Guards captured the Nijmegen bridge.

For the Americans the operation showed that a day-light drop gave a greater concentration, and could be achieved at low cost, providing there was complete air superiority and sufficient aircraft to fly *Flak* suppression missions.

In the Far East, the Chindit operations in Burma during 1944 further demonstrated what could be achieved with air superiority.

With gliders and transport aircraft, the British placed the 3rd Indian Division behind the Japanese lines. The troops were supplied with stores to build a series of "strongholds" as a base for operations against the Japanese lines of communication. Light aircraft were used for liaison and to evacuate wounded from the airstrips constructed near the strongholds. When the Japanese at last diverted men from the front to attack the strongholds, they suffered very heavy losses in the attacks on the Chindit stronghold known as "White City". Despite mass attacks with artillery and air support the Japanese failed to penetrate the British defences.

Yet paratroops and an airlanding capacity were an arm which, with the exception of selected raids on local targets, and the operations in Burma and Crete, were used as an expensive luxury by planners and ground commanders. For, however, impressive airborne operations may appear, many of the objectives secured by vertical envelopment could have been reached by conventional forces.

CHAPTER 127
ARNHEM: Monty's gamble fails

General Bradley was to describe his stupefaction on learning of Operation "Market Garden" which Montgomery had got Eisenhower to approve and with which Bradley did not agree:

"Had the pious teetotaling Montgomery wobbled into S.H.A.E.F. with a hangover, I could not have been more astonished than I was by the daring adventure he proposed. For in contrast to the conservative tactics Montgomery ordinarily chose, the Arnhem attack was to be made over a 60-mile carpet of airborne troops. Although I never reconciled myself to the venture, I nevertheless freely concede that Monty's plan for Arnhem was one of the most imaginative of the war."

In effect the "carpet" over which XXX Corps was to advance towards the northern outskirts of Arnhem was 60 miles long

and criss-crossed six times by canals and watercourses. Eisenhower had put at Montgomery's disposal the 1st Airborne Army. Commanded by U.S. Lieutenant-General L. H. Brereton, it engaged its I Airborne Corps (Lieutenant-General F. A. M. Browning) as follows:

1. U.S. 101st Airborne Division (Major-General Maxwell D. Taylor) would take Eindhoven by surprise and seize the bridges on the Wilhelmina Canal, the Dommel, and the Willems Canal;
2. U.S. 82nd Airborne Division (Major-General James M. Gavin) would take the Grave bridge over the Maas and the Nijmegen bridge over the Waal (the southern arm of the Rhine); and
3. British 1st Airborne Division (Major-General R. E. Urquhart) would take the bridges over the Neder Rijn (the

△ *Part of the human cargo of an Airspeed Horsa glider waits in the sunshine on an airfield in England before the start of operation "Market Garden". Gliders offered the advantage of putting down a platoon of men in one spot, whereas paratroops could be scattered and take time to form into an effective force.*

Operation "Market Garden"

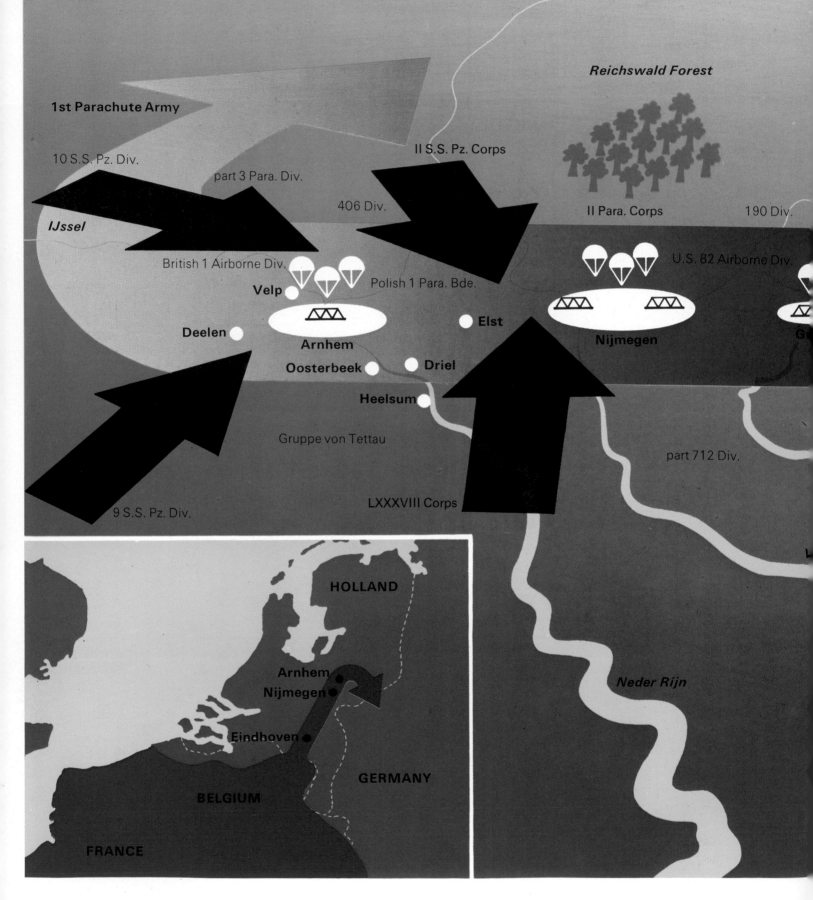

Reichswald Forest

1st Parachute Army

10 S.S. Pz. Div.

part 3 Para. Div.

II S.S. Pz. Corps

406 Div.

II Para. Corps

190 Div.

IJssel

British 1 Airborne Div.

U.S. 82 Airborne Div.

Velp

Polish 1 Para. Bde.

Deelen

Elst

Arnhem

Nijmegen

Oosterbeek

Driel

Heelsum

Gruppe von Tettau

part 712 Div.

LXXXVIII Corps

9 S.S. Pz. Div.

HOLLAND

Arnhem

Nijmegen

Neder Rijn

Eindhoven

GERMANY

BELGIUM

FRANCE

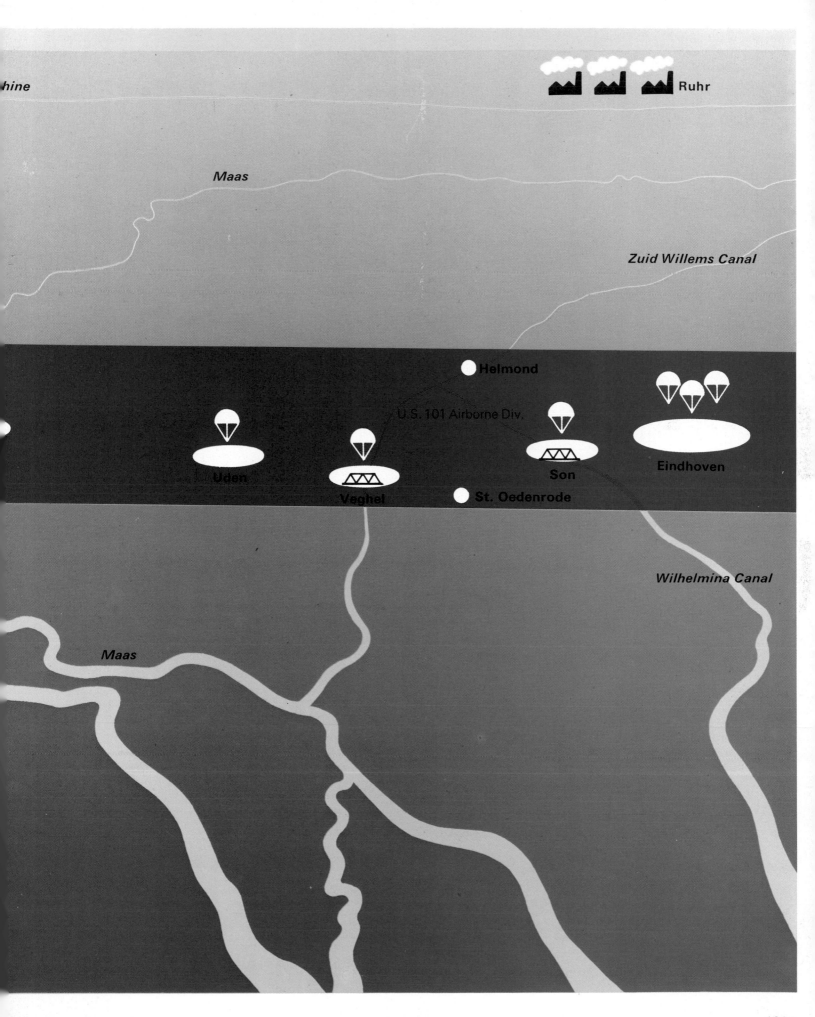

Rhine

Ruhr

Maas

Zuid Willems Canal

Helmond

U.S. 101 Airborne Div.

Uden

Veghel

Son

Eindhoven

St. Oedenrode

Maas

Wilhelmina Canal

1803

△△ *Two film cameramen, part of the team that gave extensive press coverage to the operation. They were to record the struggle in some of the most vivid film and photographs of the war.*

△ *Two paratroopers of the 82nd Airborne Division check their kit before emplaning. The 82nd Airborne jumped at Nijmegen and captured bridges over the Maas and Maas-Waal canal, but failed to reach the Nijmegen bridges. These were later taken in a joint assault with XXX Corps.*

▷ *The interior of a Dakota; the soldiers carry their weapons, with their kit packed in leg bags, or worn under their smocks to prevent it catching in the parachute harness.*

northern arm of the Rhine) at Arnhem. It would then establish a bridgehead around the town and be reinforced by the Polish 1st Parachute Brigade, then by the British 52nd (Airportable) Division.

It was along the corridor opened up by these forces that the three divisions of the British XXX Corps (the Guards Armoured, the 43rd, and the 50th Divisions) under Horrocks were to advance towards Arnhem and, breaking out of the bridgehead, drive on at full speed to the Zuiderzee, a final run of about 37 miles.

Allied Intelligence misses II Panzer Corps

All things considered, it does seem that Operation "Market Garden" relied heavily on what Frederick the Great called "Her Sacred Majesty Chance" and the expectation that she would favour Generals Browning and Horrocks for several days and under all circumstances. Even had she favoured them throughout, however, it is unlikely that XXX Corps could have made the run to Berlin all alone, as Eisenhower had no strategic reserves or logistic resources to exploit fully any initial success of this risky enterprise.

Yet XXX Corps' advance had to take place up a single road flanked by low-lying country, covered with a network of drainage ditches. This was to provide ideal terrain for the Germans to slow down or even halt the advance with a tenacious anti-tank defence, while launching flank attacks against XXX Corps' own communications. And this, in fact, was what was to happen.

Although Montgomery knew from intelligence reports that two Panzer divisions (part of the II S.S. Panzer Corps)

The British Airspeed Horsa I assault glider

Capacity: 2 crew and 25 troops.
Towing Speed: 150 mph.
Gliding speed: 100 mph.
Weight empty/loaded:
8,370/15,500 lbs.
Span: 88 feet.
Length: 67 feet.
Height: 19 feet 6 inches.

△ *Parachutes litter the ground on a dropping zone outside Arnhem.*

▷ △ *Men of the headquarters group of the 1st Airborne Division's artillery start unloading from the first two Horsas to land.*

▷ *The fatal delay. Between four and six hours elapsed before the troops could arrive at the bridge. Some were slowed down by enthusiastic Dutch civilians, who greeted them as liberators.*

▷ ▷ *Landing Zone "Z" covered with gliders, some of which have been broken in half for unloading.*

were refitting just north of Arnhem, he believed them incapable of effective action and Horrocks, the commander of XXX Corps, was not even informed that these German forces lay so close to the battle area.

In fact, these forces also included the 1st Parachute Army which was being built up in the region of 's Hertogenbosch under the command of Colonel-General Kurt Student, the victor of Crete. The Allied forces, with their limited resources, had little chance of success. Additionally, it is arguable that the objectives of "Market Garden" were beyond the Allies' capabilities. The

plan would clearly involve a great deal of risk; and it seemed a highly dangerous operation to informed critics such as Bradley, who wrote later:

". . . as soon as I learned of Monty's plan, I telephoned Ike and objected strenuously to it. For in abandoning the joint offensive, Monty would slip off on a tangent and leave us holding the bag. But Ike silenced my objections; he thought the plan a fair gamble. It might enable us to outflank the Siegfried Line, perhaps even snatch a Rhine bridgehead."

Events were to prove Bradley all too right.

continued on page 1812

AMERICA'S WAR EFFORT

By the end of 1944 the contribution to the war effort of "The Great Arsenal of Democracy" was already legendary. It was seen in manpower. It was seen in financial aid. It was seen in munitions production. And it was the biggest single factor in the Allies' favour as they ground painfully eastward towards the Rhine and the decisive invasion of Germany.

In the Battle of the Atlantic the vast output of America's shipyards had been as potent a weapon in the defeat of the U-boats as sonar detection, air cover, or the depth charge. American transports, shipped to Russia via the agonising "blackout" route to Murmansk and Archangel, had put the Red Army on wheels for the first time in its history – a fact freely and

generously admitted by Soviet commanders. And the financial aid of Lend-Lease constituted the war chest of the Allied war effort against Germany and Japan.

Axis propaganda made ceaseless play against the corroding power of the American dollar. This was hardly surprising. Even without the contributions made by American banks, 100 billion

1. *The colossus of American war production. Thirty years before World War II, Sir Edward Grey had likened the U.S.A. to a gigantic boiler, with limitless energy once the fire was lighted beneath it. Now his prophecy was proved true with a vengeance.*
2. *Fuselage components for Flying Fortress heavy bombers on the production line.*

2

3. Sonorous patriotism with pious religious undertones: an appeal for 100 per cent national war effort in the factory and in the field.

4. For the benefit of the worker. Despite the agreement of the unions not to strike during the war, there were 15,000 work stoppages in the United States between 1941 and 1945. Congress decided to retaliate by passing an act requiring unions to observe a 30-day pause before striking, and empowering the President to seize striking war plants.

5. Mass-production in the shipyards: "pre-fab" American transports take shape.

6. The intense tempo of the American warship-building schedule. As one sub-chaser takes to the water, the keel assembly for its replacement is lowered into position on the stocks.

3 Strong in the strength of the Lord
we who fight in the people's cause
will never stop until that cause is won

dollars' worth of war bonds were bought by American investors. U.S. war-time taxes netted 138 billion dollars; and the American national debt rocketed from 49 billion dollars in 1941 to 259 billion dollars in 1945.

Yet the American war machine did not function with 100 per cent efficiency. Labour disputes remained a problem. The main unions undertook not to strike while the war was still in progress—yet between 1941 and 1945 there were 15,000 work stoppages. Governmental repression quickly followed, and Congress passed an act which required the unions to observe a 30-day respite before striking. And the President was given powers to seize striking war plants.

Sacrifice at home was lower than any of the Allied powers. This was inevitable. The war was so far away. Rationing was imposed in the U.S.A., but with nothing like as much severity as in Britain. Even so, war bonds, salvage, and economy drives remained a constant feature of life in war-time America and enabled the civilian to feel—in the World War I catchphrase—that he was "doing his bit" for democracy and the western way of life.

The American Douglas C-47 Skytrain transport and glider tug

Engines: two Pratt & Whitney R-1830
Twin Wasp radials, 1,200-hp each.
Speed: 230 mph at 8,800 feet.
Ceiling: 24,100 feet.
Range: 2,125 miles.
Weight empty/loaded:
16,865/31,000 lbs.
Capacity: 7,500 lbs, 28 troops, or a
towed glider.
Span: 95 feet.
Length: 64 feet 6 inches.
Height: 16 feet 11 inches.
Crew: 4.

continued from page 1807

Operation "Market Garden"

On Sunday September 17, 1944, zero hour struck at 1430. Under the near or distant cover of 1,200 fighters the first elements of Lieutenant-General Browning's three airborne divisions, which had been packed into 2,800 aircraft and 1,600 gliders, jumped or landed as close as possible to their objectives without undue losses.

For the 101st Airborne Division all went well, except for the Son bridge over the Wilhelmina Canal which it could not save from destruction. The 82nd managed to surprise the Grave bridge, but in the evening, when the Germans had got over the shock, it failed in its first attempt on Nijmegen. By this time General Student had got the plans for "Market Garden" which had been found on board an American glider shot down behind the German lines. Because of heavy A.A. fire round Arnhem it had been decided that the first echelon of the British 1st Airborne Division would drop in heath-land seven miles from the Neder Rijn bridges. Moreover there were not enough aircraft to carry the whole division in one lift, so that three successive drops were necessary.

Field-Marshal Model, commander of Army Group "B" at Oosterbeek, alerted General Bittrich, commanding II S.S. Panzer Corps, and counter-attacked with the 9th *"Hohenstaufen"* Panzer Division through

▽ *A German soldier surrenders to the Guards Armoured Division during the vain dash towards Arnhem.*

1813

△ *Major-General Urquhart,
G.O.C. 1st Airborne Division,
with the Pegasus pennant
outside his H.Q. at the
Hartenstein Hotel.*
▷ *House clearing in Oosterbeek.
Each side used snipers, and
while the British found that they
had to be careful moving in the
open, Sturmbannführer Sepp
Kraft described the British tree
and ground snipers as "the very
devil".*
▽▷ *A casualty is brought into
the Hartenstein Hotel. By the
end of the nine days' fighting,
only 3,000 of the 10,095 men who
landed (including glider pilots)
were capable of crossing to the
Allied lines.*
▽▷▷ *Paratroopers adopt
all-round defence at a cross
roads. In the foreground is a
P.I.A.T. anti-tank weapon.
Supported by some glider-borne
6-pdr anti-tank guns, it was to be
the chief weapon to combat the
German tanks and assault guns.
Despite its crude appearance, it
was an effective weapon, though
it had a powerful recoil. Its 3-lb
projectile could pierce four inches
of armour at short ranges.*

◁ *The Arnhem road bridge. On the ramp at the northern end are the remains of a German armoured column destroyed by the 2nd Parachute Battalion under Lieutenant-Colonel Frost.*

▽ *A contrast in military élites. Prisoners from the 9th "Hohenstaufen" S.S. Panzer Division with their British captors.*
▽ ▽ *Men of the 1st Battalion, The Border Regiment await an attack at Oosterbeek.*

△ *A 6-pdr anti-tank gun in ambush. The crew are about to fire on an assault gun which is only 80 yards away.*

▷ △ *A 75-mm pack howitzer of the 1st Airlanding Light Regiment in action. They were used as anti-tank weapons to supplement the 1st and 2nd Anti-Tank Batteries, but were a poor substitute with their low muzzle velocity and slow cross-axle traverse.*

Arnhem and the 10th *"Frundsberg"* along the left bank of the Neder Rijn.

The British outpaced

The British no longer had surprise, and now problems mounted as for technical and topographical reasons, their radio communications broke down. The divisional commander, Urquhart, decided to go up to the front himself, and within minutes he had lost all means of co-ordinating the movements of his division. Towards 2000 hours Lieutenant-Colonel Frost's battalion, whose commander had led the raid on Bruneval in 1942, had reached a point opposite the road bridge at Arnhem, but was almost surrounded.

Supported on the left by XII Corps and on the right by VIII Corps (Lieutenant-General Evelyn H. Baring), XXX Corps got off to a good start. Admirably supported, as its commander said, by No. 83 Group, Tactical Air Force (Air Vice-Marshal H. Broadhurst), it reached Valkenswaard at the end of the day. A day later its Guards Armoured Division was at Son, where the bridge over the canal was repaired by dawn on the 19th. There was good contact with the 82nd Airborne Division, which had resumed its attack on Nijmegen, but without much success.

By now it had begun to rain. "Market Garden", in fact, enjoyed only one day of blue skies out of ten. Were the weather forecasts ignored? There were consequential delays in the reinforcement of the airborne divisions and a notable drop in efficiency of the ground support. XXX Corps had only one axis along which to advance its 23,000 vehicles. During the 19th, Horrocks was able to get his tanks from Son to Nijmegen (36 miles), but it was not until the evening of the following day that the British and the Americans, fighting side by side, succeeded in crossing the Waal and seizing the road and rail bridges which Model had ordered to be left intact for a counter-attack.

When he had been given his orders the day before "Market Garden" was launched, Browning asked Montgomery how long he would have to hold the Arnhem bridge.

"Two days" said Monty briskly. "They'll be up with you by then."

"We can hold it for four." Browning replied. "But I think we might be going a bridge too far."

The British driven back

The operation was now in its fifth day, and during the night of September 19-20 Urquhart had had to resign himself to abandoning Frost to his fate and to pulling his unit into the district of Oosterbeek with its back to the Neder Rijn. The bad weather continued, air supplies were

The German 3.7-cm *Flak* 36 (Sf) *auf Zugkraftwagen* 5t A.A. mounting

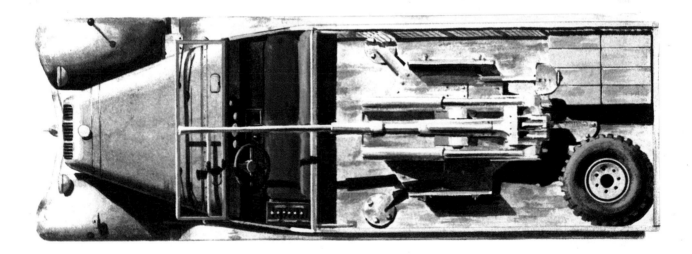

Weight: 10.4 tons.
Crew: 7.
Armament: one 3.7-cm *Flak* 36 L/98 gun.
Engine: one Maybach NL 38 TUKRM inline, 90-hp.
Speed: 25 mph.
Range: 150 miles.
Length: 19 feet 9 inches.
Width: 7 feet 3 inches.
Height: 8 feet 2 inches (vehicle).

reduced to practically nothing, and what was dropped fell equally amongst the Germans and the Allies. In the evening of the 21st, Lieutenant-Colonel Frost was seriously wounded and his battalion, now reduced to about 100 men, was captured by the Germans. On the 21st and 22nd the Polish 1st Parachute Brigade (Major-General Sosabowski) landed almost opposite Oosterbeek, whilst the Guards (Major-General Allan Adair) and the 43rd Division (Major-General Ivor Thomas) were caught in flank by the 10th *"Frundsberg"* S.S. Panzer Division as they tried to cover the ten miles between the Waal and the Neder Rijn. XXX Corps' forward positions, now sticking out like a finger in the German lines, risked being cut off at any moment from either east or west.

The survivors of the British 1st Airborne Division now received the order to pull back to the left bank of the Neder Rijn. 2,163 of them got across during the night of September 25-26 out of a total of 8,905 officers, N.C.O.s, and men and the 1,100 glider-pilots who had held off the attacks of II S.S. Panzer Corps for the last ten days. The Poles left behind 1,000 of their men and the U.S. 82nd and 101st Airborne Divisions lost respectively 1,669 and 2,074 killed, wounded, and missing. Between September 17 and 30, then, about one-third of the 34,876 men who fought between Eindhoven and Arnhem were lost. The people of Arnhem showed admirable devotion and courage in hiding 250 British paratroopers and helping them to escape: among these were Brigadiers J. W. Hackett and G. W. Lathbury.

Major-General Urquhart's epic at Arnhem

In a letter dated September 28 and written in his own hand, Field-Marshal Montgomery expressed the admiration he felt at the bearing of Major-General Urquhart's division. Recalling the centuries-old roll-call of famous deeds by British arms, he wrote to him:

"There can be few episodes more glorious than the epic of Arnhem, and those that follow after will find it hard to live up to the high standards that you have set.

"So long as we have in the armies of the British Empire officers and men who

will do as you have done, then we can indeed look forward with complete confidence to the future. In years to come it will be a great thing for a man to be able to say 'I fought at Arnhem!'"

"Market Garden" a failure

History will bear out this judgement. It is not certain, however, that it will also ratify Montgomery's conclusions on the glorious and tragic episode. In his opinion, if the success of the undertaking was not as great as had been expected, this was because the supply services, contrary to Eisenhower's orders, refused to cut down on rations for the American 3rd Army. General Bradley thought otherwise and wrote to the C.-in-C. on September 21: ". . . all plans for the future operations always lead back to the fact that in order to supply an operation of any size beyond the Rhine, the port of Antwerp is essential."

On September 4 the Scheldt estuary could have been cleared within a few days, and the rapidity of this success would have been a real shot in the arm to the Allied supply problem. Instead, the operation started on September 29 by the 21st Army Group dragged on for a whole month. By November 3 it was all over, but the Germans had profited from the delay by mining the canal, and clearing operations took another three weeks of dangerous and intensive work. Antwerp's major port facilities thus went unused from September 4 to November 23, whilst less than 90 miles away to the south-west the U.S. 1st Army was reduced to cutting down on petrol and ammunition. There were, of course, the "Red Ball Highways". The American historian Robert W. Merrian, writing of these roads, organised from August 25 onwards by Lieutenant-General J. C. H. Lee, says of the service:

"The Red Ball supply high road grew and grew, like Topsy, until it stretched over 700 well-marked miles, thoroughly equipped with fast wreckage and servicing stations manned twenty-four hours a day. The Red Ball began operating on August 25 with 5,400 vehicles, hauled a daily average of about 5,000 tons of supplies for the eighty-one days of its operation. On its peak day of operation, over 12,000 tons of supplies were hauled to the front, more than enough for twelve fighting divisions. Operating on a circle route,

▷ *U.S. paratroopers, caught in the open by German artillery fire, duck and sprint for cover.*
▷ ▷ ▽ *A 3-inch mortar crew in action. Note the two striped rods resting against the parapet of the weapons pit. These were used in aiming, and here they probably define the arc of fire.*
▷ ▽ *Some of the re-supply which reached the British. In the operation, only ten per cent of the supplies reached the 1st Airborne Division, because the Germans had captured the dropping zones. The paratroopers watched helplessly as the Dakotas braved heavy flak to drop their cargoes to the enemy.*
▽ *Field-Marshal Walther Model. His aggressive reaction, and the presence of the 9th and 10th Divisions of II S.S. Panzer Corps north of Arnhem, were to unhinge "Market Garden" before it could begin.*

△ △ *Survivors from the Border Regiment raise a smile for the camera.*

△ *An S.S. officer interrogates two captured soldiers. On the night of September 25/26 the survivors of the Arnhem "Cauldron" had been ordered to withdraw across the Rhine.*

▷ △ *Walking wounded. Over 300 wounded were taken prisoner in the perimeter. Almost ten times that number had already been captured, and were in Dutch hospitals and German dressing stations. Over 1,200 British soldiers were dead, and 3,400 Germans were dead or wounded.*

it was a vast one-way traffic circle, along which raced the life blood of the advancing troops. The driving was hard, the roads merciless on the vehicles, the turnover of equipment staggering, but the supplies were pushed through."

If Operation "Market Garden" proved Allied logistics to have been at fault, it also prejudiced the build-up of a 100-mile salient which was necessary to support Bradley's offensive towards Bonn and Cologne. As Bradley had feared, the British 2nd Army's northwards push ended up between Maastricht, Nijmegen, and Breda. When Antwerp finally got priority Bradley had had to lend two divisions temporarily to 21st Army Group

to help in its capture.

Meanwhile the Canadian 1st Army had seized Le Havre (September 12), Boulogne (September 22), and Calais (October 1), capturing more than 28,000 prisoners. The combined effects of Allied bombardment and German destruction meant that it took longer than expected to get the ports working again. Le Havre in particular had had nearly 10,000 tons of bombs dropped on it and by late October was down to 15 per cent of its capacity. The day after the capture of Boulogne, however, the Allies were able to lay between this port and Dungeness a second 16-tube pipeline, which greatly alleviated the Allied petrol problem.

BRITAIN'S COMMANDOS

Britain's Commandos were born as an act of military defiance in the grim months after Dunkirk.

Churchill had first envisaged them as storm troops to spearhead counter-attacks against the expected German invasion in 1940. But Lieutenant-Colonel Dudley Clark, Military Assistant to the C.I.G.S., suggested that they could be used offensively.

By June 1940, 12 army commandos had been formed. Initially they consisted of ten troops of 50 men, but this was too cumbersome. In October 1940 pairs of commandos were grouped into Special Service Battalions.

Early in 1941 there was a final reorganisation: each commando was to consist of five troops of three officers and 62 men, with a heavy weapons troop of about 40.

The War Office had sent out a circular to commands in the U.K. asking for volunteers for special service of an undefined and hazardous nature. They had to be fully trained soldiers, physically fit, able to swim, and quite incapable of being sea-sick. "Courage, physical endurance, initiative and resource, activity, marksmanship, self-reliance, and an aggressive spirit towards the war" were demanded.

The men came from a wide cross section of the army. Some were Regulars, others Reservists, and Numbers 1 and 2 Commandos had men from the territorial battalions who had operated as independent companies in Norway.

The first Commando raid took place less than three weeks after the force had been conceived. On the night of June 23-24, 120 men landed near Boulogne. There was a brief fire fight and they withdrew.

A raid on Guernsey proved abortive and Churchill growled "Let there be no more silly fiascos like that perpetrated at Guernsey."

Scepticism about the value of the commandos grew in the service ministries. The men themselves began to feel frustrated.

Then on March 4, 1941, Numbers 3 and 4 Commando, with 52 Royal Engineers, conducted the first big raid of the war on the Lofoten Islands off Norway.

It was a complete success; for one casualty the commandos took 216 prisoners, demolished factories and fuel supplies, and captured 11 ships.

Commandos and Combined Operations were now accepted as a lethal and effective weapon.

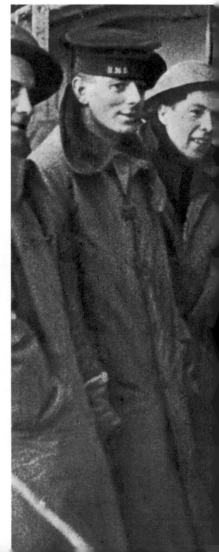

The strategic object of the Vaagsö raid, which was to prompt the Germans to deploy more men in Norway, fulfilled its aim beyond the planners' most optimistic hopes.

The naval forces consisted of a cruiser, four destroyers and two infantry assault ships. The Commandos totalled 590 officers and men.

The raid on December 27, 1941, achieved total surprise. Though the mainland garrison reacted quickly, the battery on Maalöy island was captured in eight minutes.

Fierce street fighting in Vaagsö caused most of the Commando casualties, but the Germans were overwhelmed and the demolition teams completed their work with fire and explosives.

Operation "Archery" yielded 98 prisoners. The raiders lost 20 killed and 57 wounded.

In Hitler's mind "Archery" conjured up images of Norway as a future target for an Allied landing in strength. "Norway is a zone of destiny in this war," he said, and sent reinforcements for the army and navy. By June 1944 the garrison stood at 372,000 men, and they had a very quiet war.

△ ◁ ◁ *Priming hand grenades on the voyage to Vaagsö and Maalöy. The sergeant on the right has his Fairburn knife held in his teeth.*

△ ◁ *Vaagsö seen from Maalöy. In the fighting wooden buildings were burned down to flush out some of the more determined German soldiers.*

△ *Two Commandos assist a wounded comrade to a landing craft. The British lost 20 killed and 57 wounded, while the German losses were never fully confirmed. There were 98 prisoners taken, plus four field guns (Belgian 75-mm guns), an anti-aircraft gun, and a tank destroyed. The Royal Navy disposed of 16,000 tons of shipping.*

◁ ◁ *Soldiers watch as the herring oil factory at Mortenes collapses blazing into Ulversundfjord. Every installation of value to the enemy was destroyed, including the lighthouse and the canning factory on south Vaagsö.*

◁ *Sailors pose with a captured Nazi battle ensign.*

Previous page: *Over the top, 1941-style: the assault party on Maalöy, caught in the glare of a phosphorus bomb.*

1823

Attack at St. Nazaire

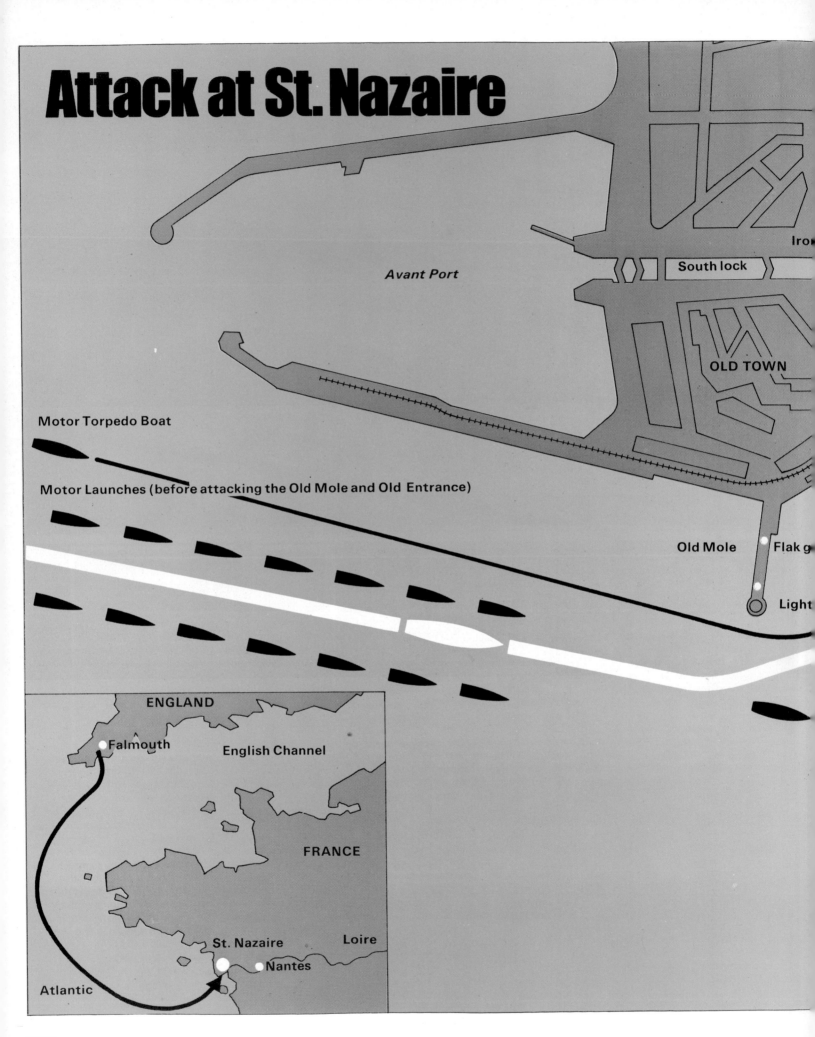

Avant Port

South lock

Iro[n]

OLD TOWN

Motor Torpedo Boat

Motor Launches (before attacking the Old Mole and Old Entrance)

Old Mole

Flak g[un]

Light

ENGLAND

Falmouth

English Channel

FRANCE

St. Nazaire

Loire

Nantes

Atlantic

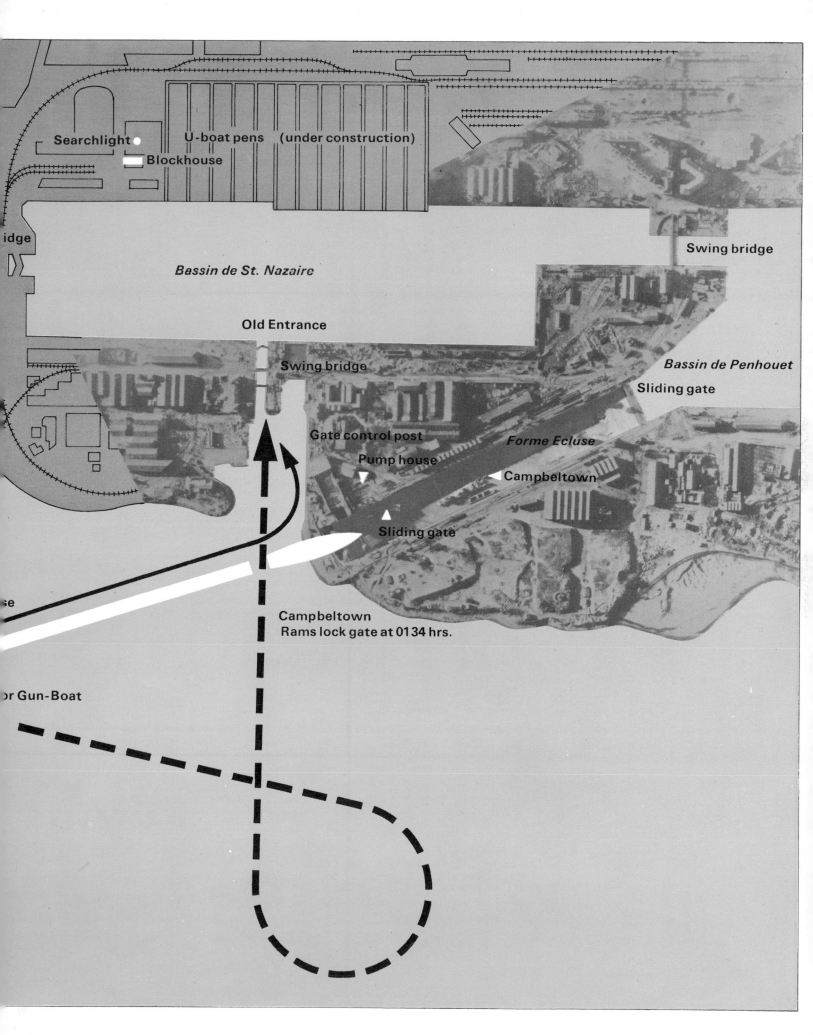

Searchlight

U-boat pens   (under construction)

Blockhouse

idge

Bassin de St. Nazaire

Old Entrance

Swing bridge

Swing bridge

Bassin de Penhouet

Sliding gate

Gate control post

Forme Ecluse

Pump house

Campbeltown

Sliding gate

Campbeltown
Rams lock gate at 01 34 hrs.

se

or Gun-Boat

St. Nazaire: the aftermath

▷ Soldiers and naval personnel are escorted away from the docks.
▷ ▷ A sergeant gives a smart "eyes right" as he leads a file of soldiers past the grave of one of the raiders. The Germans were amazed at the ferocity of the raid, but treated their prisoners generously. At a special parade organised at Lieutenant-Commander Beattie's P.O.W. camp, the German commandant read out the citation for Beattie's V.C.

▽ Campbeltown, *wedged tight in the lock gates of the* Forme Ecluse. *Her funnels had been cut down to resemble a torpedo boat of the* Möwe *class. German officers can be seen on the bows, where five tons of explosive were soon to go up.*
▽ ▷ *A German soldier glances at a dead British sergeant as a patrol moves through the docks.*
▽ ▷ ▷ *The end of the round-up: a German sailor brings in two soldiers. The Germans remained nervous long after the raid, and Organisation Todt workers in their brown uniforms were shot down when they were mistaken for the khaki of British raiders.*

Operation "Chariot", the raid on the docks at St. Nazaire in March 1942, had as its chief target the destruction of the *Forme Ecluse*.

This was the only Atlantic dry dock big enough to take the German battleship *Tirpitz*. If it was neutralised it could reduce the chances of that ship venturing from her moorings in Norway to attack shipping in the Atlantic. Commandos in Britain furnished 80 men as demolition experts, while No. 2 Commando served as a covering force with about 100 men. The naval force consisted of a destroyer, the *Campbeltown* (loaded with five tons of explosives she would ram the lock gates) and light surface craft to transport the Commandos. The date was fixed for March 28.

The last stage of the journey up the Loire was made under German colours. Signals were sent to the shore batteries in German saying that the ships had been damaged and requesting permission to proceed to St. Nazaire.

In five tense minutes they passed the main batteries without receiving any damage. At 0127 hours the Germans opened fire in earnest, the *Campbeltown* hauled down the false colours, hoisted the White Ensign and returned the fire.

At 0134 she crashed into the lock gates. The main part of the operation was complete.

Then the Commandos went into action. They attacked the two control posts for the dry dock gates, and demolished the pump house and a bridge at the northern end of the docks. Two tugs were attacked with charges below the water line.

Throughout these operations the naval force had been exchanging heavy fire at close range with the ships in the port and shore emplacements.

Of the 18 craft which had entered the Loire estuary, only two launches returned safely to England. Only five men managed to return home overland, while 169 of their comrades were killed. The rest were sent into prison camps.

Some time after 1000 hours the charges on the *Campbeltown* exploded, demolishing the lock gate.

The *Tirpitz* never ventured from her Norwegian lair, for the *Forme Ecluse* was out of action for the rest of the war.

COMMANDO

R.N. COMMANDO

COMMANDO

3 COMMANDO

SPECIAL IV SERVICE

4 COMMANDO

1830

The first Commandos were formed in June 1940, each consisting of ten troops of 50 men. Later, in 1941, they were reorganised into five troops of 65, with a heavy weapons platoon of 40. The original name suggested by the War Office was Special Service Battalions, but the initials "S.S." smacked too much of the Nazi Schutzstaffel so the units were later named after the Boer troops commanded by such men as General Smuts. The Commandos were drawn from men of all the Allied nations fighting with the British. They attended a gruelling 12 week course at the depot at Achnacarry Castle 14 miles from Fort William. The titles (the shoulder badge with the corps or regiment's name) and the flashes (the badge with the unit insignia) and the cap badges of the British Army and Marine Commando units are shown in this montage.

1. The Salamander flash of Number 1 Commando. 2. The Fairburn knife of No. 2 Commando, which featured both as a flash and a cap badge. 3. The Combined Operations sign, which depicts the three fighting arms in one flash. 4. The crossed daggers of 5 Commando. 5. The Dolphin flash of 101 Troop 6 Commando. 6. The skull insignia of the depot unit. 7. A representation of the black hackle of 9 Commando. 8. 5 Troop flash. 9. H.Q. Special Service Brigade. 10. Knuckle-duster knife cap badge of the Middle East Commandos. 11. Special Boat Service. 12. Parachute wings worn by parachute troop of 12 Commando. 13. Cap badge of Free French Commandos attached to 4 Commando. 14. The Commando flash. 15. Cap badge of the Royal Marines worn by Marine Commandos.

Skorzeny: Hitler's ace com

The discreet arrest of Mussolini, following his interview with King Victor Emmanuel on July 25, 1943, left the Germans with a double problem: find the former Duce, and having found him, rescue him.

The task fell to Otto Skorzeny, a *Waffen*-S.S. officer running a commando training school at Friedenthal, near Berlin.

When he began his search, Italy was still an ally of Germany. But if the Italians could hold Mussolini until their surrender to the Allies, he could be a trump card in the negotiations.

Skorzeny traced Mussolini to an island prison near Sardinia. He laid careful plans, took aerial photographs, and was about to launch the operation when a final check showed that the Duce had gone. It was a lucky discovery, for Hitler had warned him that failure would mean dismissal and a public repudiation.

Back in Rome Skorzeny intercepted a code message to the Italian Ministry of Interior; it read: "SECURITY MEASURES AROUND GRAN SASSO COMPLETED. CUELI" Skorzeny had discovered that General Cueli was the official responsible for the Duce's safety.

The only place in Gran Sasso, a mountainous part of the Apennines, which could house a state prisoner with his guards, was the winter sports hotel of Campo Imperatore. Built on a 6,000-foot crag, it could only be reached by a funicular railway.

On September 8, Italy surrendered. The operation was now military rather than diplomatic.

Skorzeny established that there was at least a battalion of *Carabinieri* in the area and a further 250 men in the hotel.

His reconnaisance photographs showed a triangular patch of land near the hotel. Paratroops could not land there (the air was too thin), but gliders might.

The Luftwaffe eventually agreed to provide gliders for the 90 Luftwaffe troops and the 20 men from Skorzeny's unit.

On the afternoon of September 12 they set off.

The landing zone proved to be a sloping, rock-studded, shelf. But risking destruction Skorzeny shouted to his pilot, "Dive—crash land! As near the hotel as you can."

With a shuddering, bouncing skid and a rending crash the glider came to a halt.

The soldiers leapt out and raced the 20 yards across to the hotel.

Skorzeny recognised a familiar shaved head at an upper window. "Get back!" he yelled at Mussolini, "Get back from the window."

By sheer surprise and aggressiveness they over-

whelmed the guards without firing a shot.

The *Carabinieri* crowded in the corridors were too close to shoot, and the Germans barged past them and pushed further into the hotel.

Skorzeny burst into a room, and there, with two Italian officers, was the Duce. As the Germans came through the door, two more climbed up the lightning conductor and through the window.

Skorzeny now summoned the Italian colonel who had been the Duce's gaoler.

"I ask your immediate surrender. Mussolini is already in our hands. We hold the building. If you want to avert senseless bloodshed you have 60 seconds to go and reflect."

The bluff worked and the colonel returned with a goblet of wine, for "a gallant victor".

The return trip was no less

mando

hazardous. Captain Gerlach landed a Fieseler *Storch* on a strip cleared on the narrow landing zone.

Then loaded with the substantial bulk of Skorzeny and Mussolini the *Storch* took off. It was held by 12 men as its engine revved to a high pitch, but even then the take-off was only achieved after the *Storch* lurched across the mountain side and plunged headlong over the edge of a ravine.

They landed at Rome and transferred to a transport plane. Skorzeny had completed his mission – overnight he had changed from an obscure S.S. officer to a national hero.

Dr. Goebbels, the Reich Propaganda Minister, noted in his diary: "Even upon the enemy the effect of this melodramatic deliverance is enormous . . . We are able to celebrate a first-class moral victory."

▷ *Otto Skorzeny, photographed on his surrender in 1945. His rescue of Mussolini from the Gran Sasso and use of German troops dressed as Americans during the "Battle of the Bulge" gave him considerable notoriety with the Allies.*
▽ ◁ *Paratroopers race across the rocky plateau, which was later to serve as a hazardous landing strip for the Fieseler* Storch *which would fly Mussolini to "freedom".*
▽ *Skorzeny, on the extreme left, with Mussolini. With words deemed suitable for the dramatic rescue he had greeted the latter: "Duce, I have been sent by the Führer to set you free."*
Mussolini replied: "I knew my friend Adolf Hitler would not abandon me. I embrace my liberator."

◁ A shabby 60-year old Italian struggles into a German spotter plane. It is hard to recognise Italy's Duce in the last months of his life.

▷ With Mussolini in the cramped cockpit, Skorzeny squeezes in, his 6 feet 4 inches frame further congesting the overcrowded space. Twelve men hung on to the Storch while it ran its engine up fully, and then when they let go it raced across the scree, buckled its port wheel, and only became airborne when it had plunged over a ravine.

▽ Kaltenbrunner watches, at the left, as Hitler greets Skorzeny at the Wolfsschanze. Earlier on the telephone Hitler had said: "Skorzeny, you are a man after my own heart. You have gained the day and crowned our mission with success. Your Führer thanks you!"

Desert freelancers':
"Popski's Private Army"

Vladimir Peniakoff, born 1897 in Belgium, became a sugar manufacturer in Egypt in the inter-war years. Here he developed desert navigation skills which he would employ leading a raiding force known as "Popski's Private Army". Popski was a great admirer of the British way of life and had been an undergraduate at Cambridge before joining the French Army in World War I. In World War II he joined the British Army and wanted to become a member of the Long Range Desert Group, but he was persuaded to form his own group, which was first known as No. 1 Long Range Demolition Squadron, though it soon earned the un-official title Popski's Private Army. It created its own style of reconnaissance and demolition in North Africa and Italy, attacking petrol dumps and other installations.

1. *The astrolabe badge of Popski's Private Army. The early badges were made of brass, but some white metal and silver versions were made later in Italy.*
2. *Vladimir Peniakoff, Belgian adventurer of Russian origin, who led his raiding force in Africa and Italy.*
3. *Popski's jeep.*
4. *Popski, with a hook for a left hand, and Cpl. Cokes, with 50 skin grafts on his legs, near the end of the war.*

△ *P.P.A. jeeps laager up in the Apennines. The men have pitched their bivouac tents by their jeeps and found time for some washing.*
Previous page: (Above) Jeeps of Popski's Private Army move cautiously along a country lane in the Apennines.
(Below) P.P.A. jeeps pull off the road into a defensive position. The vehicle in the foreground is armed with a .5-inch Browning M2 heavy machine gun and a .3-inch Browning M1919A4 machine gun. All the P.P.A. vehicles carried a heavy fire power, some being armed with two M2's. Popski's Private Army was over 100 strong, and though it had the reputation of being a dare-devil unit, Popski asserted that all his operations were based on careful planning and he took few risks.

"No. 1 Demolition Squadron", better known as "Popski's Private Army" was one of several reconnaissance and raiding units spawned by the 8th Army in Africa.

Vladimir Peniakoff (his name was changed by British signallers to Popski) was a Belgian of Russian origin. He had settled in Cairo before the war and developed a taste for desert travel.

He volunteered for service in the British Army, and in 1942 formed a commando of 23 Arabs with a British sergeant.

With this force he collected intelligence, attacked an Italian petrol dump, and arranged escape routes for prisoners-of-war.

At the end of 1942 he served in an L.R.D.G. patrol and lost a finger in a raid on the strategically important Barce airfield.

He wanted to remain with the L.R.D.G., who had taught him desert skills and shown him equipment like the sun compass, condenser, and sand channels, but was persuaded by Colonel Hackett of the Middle East Headquarters to form his own special long-range unit.

The name was Hackett's invention: he suggested it as a joke, but the title Popski's Private Army was accepted by the Middle East H.Q.

Popski set out with 23 men in four armed jeeps and two three-ton trucks. This first venture was unsuccessful for most of the vehicles were captured or destroyed by the Germans.

Drawing new jeeps from the 8th Army, he moved into southern Tunisia. In operations south of the Mareth Line his jeeps were destroyed by fighters, and his unit marched 115 miles in the desert before being picked up by friendly forces.

Popski conducted some further limited operations in Africa before the Axis surrender in May 1943.

P.P.A. landed at Taranto soon after the Italian armistice in 1943. Its mission was to ascertain German strength in southern Italy.

This was accomplished through the public telephone system: Italian officers, now new allies, rang their colleagues, who gave a situation report on German moves in their area, telephone communications still being intact after the invasion and armistice.

Popski's major coup came when, dressed in British khaki drill, he passed himself off as an Italian and called at the German headquarters in Gravina. Here he stole a list of all the men on the

ration strength of the 1st Parachute Division, a premier German formation operating in southern Italy.

P.P.A. expanded and began to operate in separate patrols. They consisted of five or six jeeps each mounting a .3-inch and a .5-inch machine gun. The latter fired in succession tracer, armour-piercing, and incendiary rounds. With stowed fuel the jeeps had a range of 600 miles. The patrols carried mines and explosives and their own water and rations.

Near Salerno Italian peasants brought him Brigadier Klopper, who had been captured at Tobruk with the 2nd South African Division. He had escaped in Italy after the armistice.

Besides enlarging their conventional forces (they numbered 118 by the end of the war) P.P.A. collected two Russian P.O.W.'s, Ivan and Nikolai.

Popski's Private Army cooperated with Italian partisans, harried small German garrisons and the lines of communication, and reconnoitred routes for the Allied armies.

In a local counter-attack in 1944 in northern Italy Popski lost his left hand.

After a spell in hospital, Popski led patrols which made contact with Russians in Austria in 1945.

SAS:the winged sword

The Special Air Service was conceived by a young Commando officer as he was recovering from a training accident in North Africa in 1941.

Lieutenant David Stirling felt that the commando principle of large forces being launched on a single raid was wasteful. A third of the force had to be used to hold the beach-head while the remainder conducted the assault and demolitions.

His scheme would employ about six men, who would place charges with delay fuses on targets like aircraft. By the time the charges exploded the raiders would be far away. Sixty men with 12 charges each could destroy the Axis air force on the ground in simultaneous raids.

In an audacious "raid" in July 1941, Stirling visited the Middle East Headquarters. He had no permit to enter the building, and had to worm his way through a small gap in the barbed-wire fence. Risking arrest he tried doors in the building and found General Ritchie, Deputy Chief-of-Staff, Middle East Forces. His idea was forwarded to General Auchinleck, who gave it his approval. It was economical; six officers and 60 men were not a vast loss to the 8th Army, and if they succeeded the effects of the raid could be dramatic.

The name of the force, "L Detachment of the Special Air Service Brigade" was a staff office invention to deceive the enemy into the belief that there were paratroops in North Africa.

The first operation, on November 17, 1941, was a parachute attack on five forward fighter and bomber airfields at Tmimi and Gazala. Unfortunately heavy sand storms caused the force to be dropped in the wrong area and the operation was a complete failure, only 22 of the original 63 men surviving.

The S.A.S. launched no more parachute attacks in the Middle East. Instead they used the Long Range Desert Group for transport and between December 1941 and March 1942 made about 20 raids behind the enemy lines, destroying 115 aircraft and numerous vehicles.

Having proved its worth, "L Detachment" was expanded. Rommel was later to pay it the compliment that it "caused us more damage than any other unit of equal strength".

The S.A.S. insignia was adopted about this time. A winged sword, it symbolised King Arthur's sword Excalibur, the weapon which would win freedom from the invader. Its colours, dark and light blue, were chosen because the original unit had had a number from both the Oxford

continued on page 1846

▽ *Lieutenant-Colonel David Stirling with some of his desert raiders. Rommel paid tribute to Stirling and the S.A.S. in his diary. "These Commandos, working from Kufra and the Qattara Depression, sometimes operated right up into Cyrenaica, where they caused considerable havoc and seriously disquieted the Italians." He described Stirling as the "very able and adaptable commander of the desert group which had caused us more damage than any other unit of equal strength".*

R. B. "Paddy" Mayne, a pre-war Irish rugby football international, succeeded Stirling as the commanding officer of the S.A.S. By the end of the war Mayne had destroyed more aircraft than any man alive and had been awarded the D.S.O. and three bars, becoming the most decorated soldier in the British Army. An enthusiast for action, he was unhappy when he was ordered to run recruit training at the S.A.S. base at Kabrit, where he proved a poor administrator.

David Stirling was born in 1915 and joined the Commandos in 1940, serving with "Layforce" in the Middle East. In July he presented plans to Generals Ritchie and Auchinleck for a special force to attack enemy airfields. In December, operating from Jalo, they destroyed 90 aircraft in two weeks and Stirling was given permission to expand the unit. To the Germans he was known as the "Phantom Major". On January 10, 1943 he was captured by German soldiers who had been brought in to track down the S.A.S. As a persistent escaper he was sent to Colditz Castle.

◄ *An S.A.S. jeep in desert guise. It is fitted with twin Vickers K machine guns, a condenser on the radiator grill, and carries fuel in a collection of American and German petrol cans. The crew wear caps bearing the S.A.S. badge, the winged sword with the motto "Who Dares Wins".*

▷ *S.A.S. jeep in the European theatre. At the wheel is Major Ian Fenwick, who led a group from 1st S.A.S. in Operation "Gain". Ten men were killed, including Major Fenwick, in the operation, which cut rail communications between Rambouillet, Provins, Gien, Orléans, and Chartres.*

▽ *A Vickers machine gun crew in northern Italy. The man on the left carries the 50-lb tripod, the one in the centre the 33-lb gun, and the man on the right the 7½ pints of water to cool the barrel. Over long ranges the curving trajectory of the weapon could be used for a plunging fire effect.*

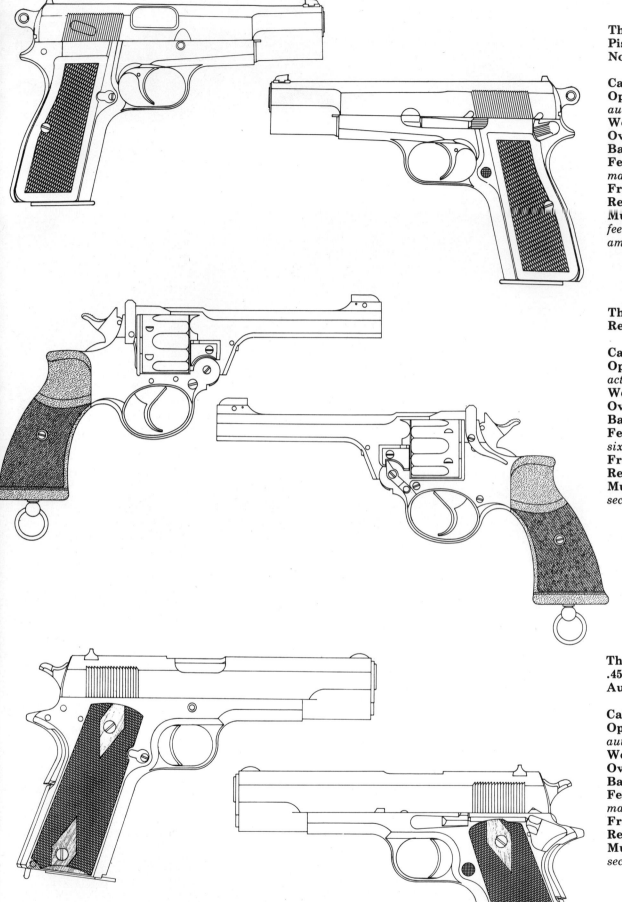

The Canadian Inglis 9-mm Pistol, Browning, Hi-Power, No. 2 Mark 1

Calibre: *9-mm Parabellum.*
Operation: *recoil, semi-automatic.*
Weight: *1.9 lbs.*
Overall length: *8 inches.*
Barrel length: *4.75 inches.*
Feed: *detachable double-row box magazine with 13 rounds.*
Front sight: *blade.*
Rear sight: *vee notch.*
Muzzle velocity: *1040 to 1500 feet per second depending on ammunition.*

The British Enfield .38-inch Revolver No. 2 Mark 1

Calibre: *.38-inch.*
Operation: *single or double action.*
Weight: *1.58 lbs.*
Overall length: *10.25 inches.*
Barrel length: *5 inches.*
Feed: *revolving cylinder with six chambers.*
Front sight: *blade.*
Rear sight: *square notch.*
Muzzle velocity: *600 feet per second.*

The American Colt Calibre .45-inch Model 1911 Automatic Pistol

Calibre: *.45-inch.*
Operation: *recoil, semi-automatic.*
Weight: *2.43 lbs.*
Overall length: *8.62 inches.*
Barrel length: *5 inches.*
Feed: *detachable inline box magazine with seven rounds.*
Front sight: *blade.*
Rear sight: *square notch.*
Muzzle velocity: *830 feet per second.*

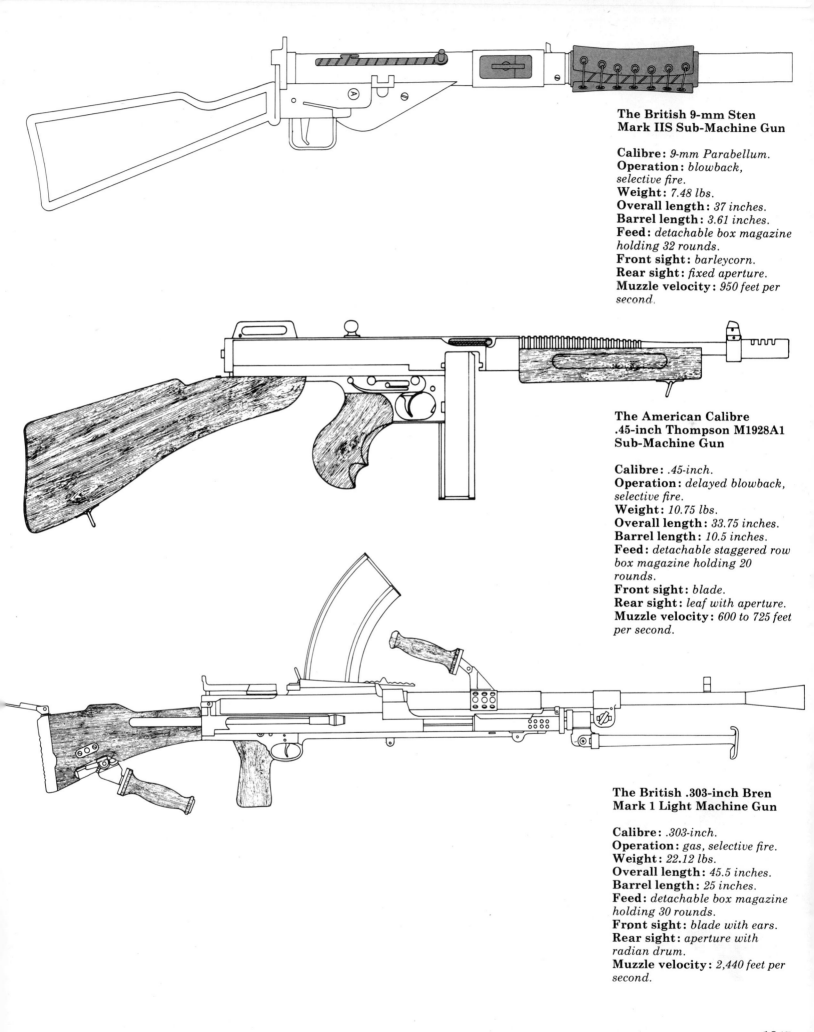

The British 9-mm Sten Mark IIS Sub-Machine Gun

Calibre: *9-mm Parabellum.*
Operation: *blowback, selective fire.*
Weight: *7.48 lbs.*
Overall length: *37 inches.*
Barrel length: *3.61 inches.*
Feed: *detachable box magazine holding 32 rounds.*
Front sight: *barleycorn.*
Rear sight: *fixed aperture.*
Muzzle velocity: *950 feet per second.*

The American Calibre .45-inch Thompson M1928A1 Sub-Machine Gun

Calibre: *.45-inch.*
Operation: *delayed blowback, selective fire.*
Weight: *10.75 lbs.*
Overall length: *33.75 inches.*
Barrel length: *10.5 inches.*
Feed: *detachable staggered row box magazine holding 20 rounds.*
Front sight: *blade.*
Rear sight: *leaf with aperture.*
Muzzle velocity: *600 to 725 feet per second.*

The British .303-inch Bren Mark 1 Light Machine Gun

Calibre: *.303-inch.*
Operation: *gas, selective fire.*
Weight: *22.12 lbs.*
Overall length: *45.5 inches.*
Barrel length: *25 inches.*
Feed: *detachable box magazine holding 30 rounds.*
Front sight: *blade with ears.*
Rear sight: *aperture with radian drum.*
Muzzle velocity: *2,440 feet per second.*

▷ A resupply drop in France in 1944. In 1944 there were British, French, and Belgian S.A.S. contingents operating in northern Europe.

△ Men of the French S.A.S. battalions marching down the Champs Elysées in 1944. They operated in the Brittany area and the Vosges during the summer of 1944, attacking German convoys, mining roads and supporting Maquis groups. The units in the Brittany area suffered heavy casualties in a vigorous German counter-attack, but though lightly armed they were better soldiers with local support and knowledge, and so for the loss of 32 men they killed 155 of the enemy. In fighting near Orléans, French S.A.S. units linked up to attack the German lines of communication, and in late August and early September captured 18,000 Germans. Lacking the facilities to handle such large numbers they presented them to an officer of an advanced American unit— to his considerable surprise. After the liberation of Paris the companies were withdrawn for a rest and refit. They were later employed in Belgium and in the follow-up to Operation "Varsity".

continued from page 1841

and Cambridge University boat race crews.

The S.A.S. evolved a style of warfare in the desert which, with some alterations, would typify their operations throughout the war.

The jeep, which was becoming available through Lend-Lease sources, served as their steed. Loaded with ammunition and fuel, and stripped of excess fittings, it was equipped with a variety of automatic weapons. The Vickers K machine gun, formerly fitted in Gloster Gladiator fighters, was adapted to a ground rôle. Mounted in pairs, with a rate of fire of 1,200 rounds a minute, they were effective against men, soft-skinned vehicles, and parked aircraft. Later the jeeps were fitted with .5-inch Brownings, in addition to the personal weapons of the crew. In France and Italy they supplemented this with a variety of mortars and anti-tank weapons, and even sometimes a 75-mm pack howitzer.

By April 1942 the S.A.S. had expanded to include French and Greek soldiers, and at the beginning of 1943 the establishment stood at about 1,100 officers and men. Of these a high proportion were officers and N.C.O.s. Though the S.A.S. has been criticised

for the large numbers of first-class men it absorbed, it is arguable that they did more damage to the enemy in this force than they could if they had been in a conventional unit.

As the war in North Africa drew to a close the nature of S.A.S. operations changed. The 1st S.A.S. Regiment (formed from the original "L Detachment") was split into the Special Raiding Squadron and a Special Boat Squadron. In May 1943 it was joined by the 2nd S.A.S. Regiment, and together they raided Crete, Sardinia, and the Greek islands, and took part in the invasion of Sicily and Italy.

At the end of 1943 the regiments returned to Britain in preparation for the invasion of Europe. They now consisted of the 1st and 2nd Regiments and 3rd and 4th French Parachute Battalions and a Belgian Independent Parachute Squadron.

From June 6 to October 31, 1944, the S.A.S. Brigade carried out 43 operations, delivered and supplied by Nos. 38 and 46 Groups of the R.A.F.

Using Brittany as a base they attacked the communications to the Normandy bridgehead. When the Allies broke out, the S.A.S. turned to harrying the retreating enemy. Losses were heavy in

these operations, however.

In secret directives, Hitler paid the S.A.S. and Commandos a dubious compliment – German commanders were to "slaughter to the last man all those who take part in Commando engagements" and S.A.S. troops "must be handed over at once to the nearest Gestapo unit. These men are very dangerous and the presence of S.A.S. troops in any area must be immediately reported. They must be ruthlessly exterminated."

S.A.S. forces expanded after the landings in Normandy and took their war to central and southern France, Belgium, and Holland.

Late in 1944 when the fighting had been stabilised along the Rhine, the 3rd Squadron, 2nd S.A.S. Regiment, was sent to Italy to co-operate with Italian partisans.

With the break-out over the Rhine, the S.A.S. spearheaded the final offensive, capturing key bridges and airfields in Holland and Germany. In Norway, 1 and 2 S.A.S. had a share in the surrender of the German garrison held by 300,000 men.

At the end of the war the French and Belgian regiments became part of their respective armies, while the British regiments were disbanded.

1847

The American/British L.R.D.G. Chevrolet 30-cwt 4 x 2 truck

Wheelbase: 134 inches.
Engine: one Chevrolet 6-cylinder inline, 85-hp.
Range: over 1,000 miles.
Capacity: 2 tons of stores.
Armament: one .303-inch Vickers machine gun and the crew's personal weapons.

CHAPTER 128
Finland drops out

The dramatic circumstances in which Field-Marshal Model just managed to hold the Soviet push between the Niemen and the Carpathians have already been noted. On August 16 he was recalled to replace Kluge as C.-in-C. West, and handed over command of Army Group "Centre" to Colonel-General Reinhardt, while Army Group "North Ukraine" passed from his hands into those of Colonel-General Harpe, under the title of Army Group "A".

Until the end of December, Marshal Rokossovsky and General Zakharov, commanders respectively of the 1st and 2nd Belorussian Fronts, restricted themselves to operations with limited objectives. Halfway through September Rokossovsky, with 70 divisions, had taken his revenge for the check he had received six weeks previously on the approach to Warsaw. He had fallen back to Wołomin and reoccupied Praga, on the outskirts of the Polish capital. The German defenders were at the end of their tether. Further north, Rokossovsky had pushed as far as Modlin at the confluence of the Bug and the Vistula.

On his right, Zakharov, at the head of 71 infantry divisions and five tank corps, had penetrated the corridor between the Bug and the Narew. On the right bank of the latter he had taken a wide bridge-head around Pułtusk from the German 2nd Army (Colonel-General Weiss). And so, between the 2nd and 3rd Belorussian Fronts—the latter still under the command of Colonel-General Chernyakhovsky—the outline of the pincer movement which would lead to the encirclement and then the conquest of East Prussia was forming.

Puppet government

Meanwhile, behind the Polish front, a series of events of great importance for the future was taking place. First of all, east of the Curzon Line the Russians established—or purely and simply restored—their own authority. Moreover, a "Polish Committee of National Liberation" was set up in Lublin under the Communist E. B. Osóbka-Morawski,

▽ *Finnish infantry in 1944. Although they had managed to hold the Russians in the terrible winter of 1939-1940, the Finns now had good weather, as well as battle-hardened Russian troops, to struggle against. It was to be an impossible task.*

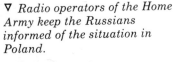

△ *Russian infantry double over a pontoon bridge across the Bug, under cover of a smoke screen. Despite its enormous numerical superiority, however, the Red Army was still finding considerable difficulty in forcing the Germans back.*

▽ *Radio operators of the Home Army keep the Russians informed of the situation in Poland.*

who was so totally submissive to the Kremlin that he made no protest when the Russians systematically organised a persecution of the Polish Home Army fighters on Polish soil.

The Baltic states overrun

At Tukums, as has been described, the 1st Baltic Front (General Bagramyan) had cut the last land contact between Army Group "North" (Colonel-General Schörner) and the other armies of the Reich. But Bagramyan was himself attacked on August 16 and his flank turned by the 3rd *Panzerarmee*, now under Colonel-General Raus after Reinhardt's promotion. It had been reinforced to the strength of two Panzer corps, with five Panzer divisions and the *"Grossdeutschland" Panzergrenadier* Division. It launched its attack from the region north of Taurage and met few difficulties other than the natural ones of terrain. By August 20, it had covered 125 miles and had established a solid link with the right wing of the 16th Army near Tukums.

Guderian clashes with Hitler

This new Russian success led to a clash between Hitler and the new Chief-of-Staff of O.K.H., Colonel-General Guderian. Guderian tried in vain to impress upon the Führer that he should use this temporary respite to evacuate Estonia and the eastern part of Lithuania as quickly as possible, though maintaining a bridgehead around Riga. In this way, more solidity would be given to Army Group "North", which would then have some chance of success in checking the Russians. The Führer cut him short sharply. To abandon Tallinn and Paldiski, he said, would automatically provoke the "defection" of Finland.

Was he unaware that this was as good as complete already? In any event he

was informed of the Finno-Soviet armistice on September 3, 1944, and this cut away the ground from his argument. Nevertheless, he refused to send new orders to Colonel-General Schörner. This time he lyingly claimed the support of Grand-Admiral Dönitz when he spoke to Guderian. But by now Army Group "North" had only 32 divisions to put into the field against 130 Russian ones of the Leningrad and three Baltic Fronts.

Estonia invaded

Overwhelming *Armeegruppe* "Narva" by September 24, Marshal Govorov's Leningrad Front had occupied Estonia almost completely. Then his 8th Army (General Paern), using American landing-craft, began, first with Moon and Dagö, to take the islands in the Gulf of Riga defended by the 23rd and 218th Divisions. With the aid of a naval force under Vice-Admiral Thiele, including the pocket-battleships *Lützow* and *Scheer* and the cruisers that Hitler had wanted to send to the scrapyard, these two divisions managed to hold out on the Sworbe peninsula against six Soviet divisions until November 23 and then cross over to Kurland without too many losses. This was the first example on the Eastern Front of those amphibious retreats which the Kriegsmarine would effect, saving the Army serious losses of men and equipment.

Riga falls to Eremenko

On October 13, the advance parties of General A. I. Eremenko's 3rd Baltic Front had entered Riga. The day after Colonel-General Raus's success, Guderian had obtained Hitler's approval for a directive requiring Army Group "North" to transfer the 3rd *Panzerarmee* from the south to halt the Russian drive on Memel. But Schörner did nothing about it, for he did not believe that Memel was in danger.

While Guderian vainly pleaded with

▽ *The commander of a Polish armoured unit serving with the Red Army gives his orders. Note the predominantly Russian uniform worn.*

The German Heinkel He 111H-20/R3 bomber

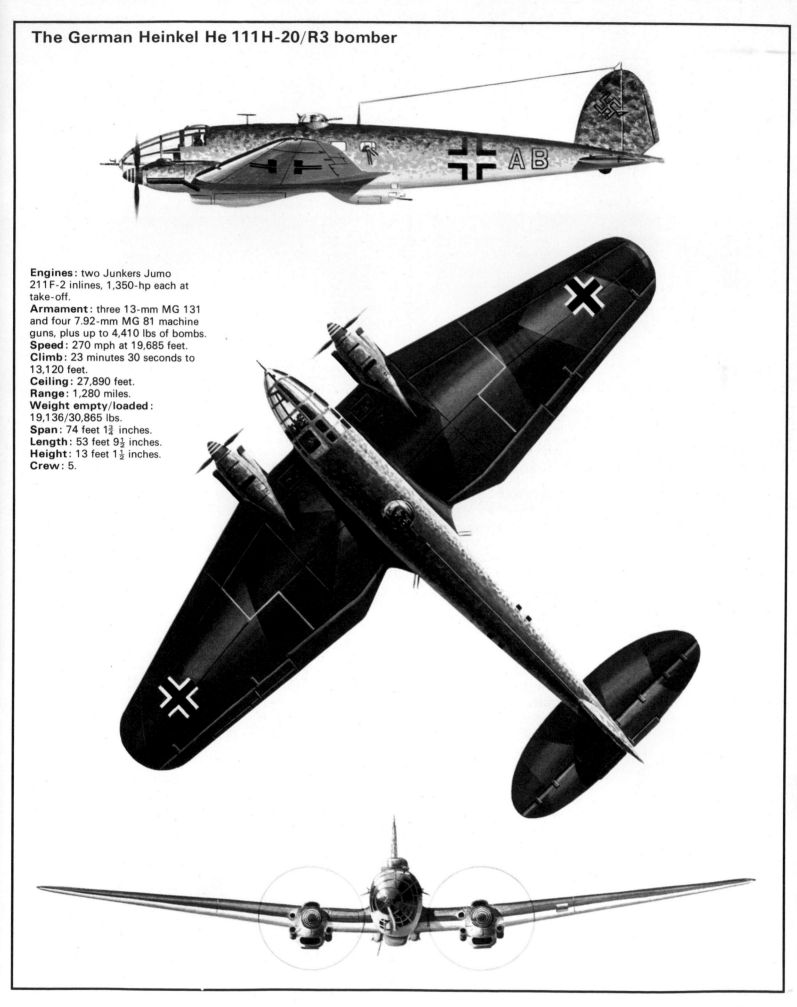

Engines: two Junkers Jumo 211F-2 inlines, 1,350-hp each at take-off.
Armament: three 13-mm MG 131 and four 7.92-mm MG 81 machine guns, plus up to 4,410 lbs of bombs.
Speed: 270 mph at 19,685 feet.
Climb: 23 minutes 30 seconds to 13,120 feet.
Ceiling: 27,890 feet.
Range: 1,280 miles.
Weight empty/loaded: 19,136/30,865 lbs.
Span: 74 feet 1¾ inches.
Length: 53 feet 9½ inches.
Height: 13 feet 1½ inches.
Crew: 5.

Schörner, the *Stavka* had discovered that the road to Memel was very weakly held by the Germans. And so, on September 24, General Bagramyan received the order to transfer the centre of gravity of the 1st Baltic Front without delay from the Mitau area to the Siauliai region, exactly where Guderian wanted to place the 3rd *Panzerarmee*, and to break the German line at that point.

Communications cut

The attack began on October 5. On the first day 14 divisions and four armoured corps (more than 500 tanks) breached Schörner's defensive screen. Covering a distance of 90 miles in five days, Bagramyan reached the Baltic at Palanga, 15 miles north of Memel. For the second time, Army Group "North" which, on October 10, had 26 divisions, including two Panzer, found itself cut off. It is true that it received supplies by sea and that the Kurland pocket, along the Tukums–Auce–Weinoden–south of Liepāja

line, was about half the size of Belgium. In spite of this, once Bagramyan had made his drive, there was no way of maintaining the German 18th Army around Riga.

In contrast, Colonel-General Chernyakhovsky received a bloody check on his first attempt to invade East Prussia. And yet the 3rd Belorussian Front put about 40 divisions into the line, strongly backed by armour and aircraft, over a front of 90 miles, while the German 4th Army could muster only 15 on a front of 220 miles between the Niemen and the Narew at Nowogród.

But the defence was commanded by a resolute leader, General F. Hossbach, and had the advantages of permanent fortifications. Moreover, the Soviet attack did not enjoy the benefit of surprise. At the beginning (October 16-19) the 11th Guards Army, which formed Chernyakhovsky's spearhead,

managed to break General Matzky's XXVI Corps and advance 30 miles over the same east-west line that had been followed by the Russian forces under General Rennenkampf in August 1914. Meanwhile, further to the south, the 31st Army took Gołdap.

Withdrawing five or six divisions from his less threatened sectors, Hossbach managed to seal the breaches. Later, with the aid of armoured formations placed at his disposal by O.K.H. he was able to counter-attack. On October 21 and 22, trying to force a passage over the River Angerapp, the 11th Guards Army was assailed from the north and south and thrown back in disorder onto the right bank of the Rominte. Chernyakhovsky left behind him 1,000-odd tanks and more than 300 guns. He also left clear traces of atrocities of all kinds committed by his troops against the inhabitants of some 300 villages. As may

▽ *Even in the forests of East Prussia the tank/infantry tactics developed by the Russians proved quite effective.*

well be imagined, Goebbels made great play with these atrocities. The result of his propaganda was that, three months later, five or six million Germans fled before the Soviet invasion, in temperatures of 20 degrees below zero.

Among the causes of the check of the Russian 3rd Belorussian Front on the Kaunas–Königsberg line should be mentioned the inability of the 2nd Belorussian Front to move out of its bridgeheads on the Narew and thus catch Hossbach in a pincer movement. This would have imitated the manoeuvre

△ △ *President R. H. Ryti of Finland inspects an artillery command post. Within a few weeks he was to be made the "scapegoat" of the breach between Finland and Russia.*
△ *Russian artillerymen with their gun behind a camouflage screen of branches.*

attempted by Samsonov as he marched to meet Rennenkampf in August 1914. Should the dismissal of General Zakharov be considered as a punishment for this lack of success? Whether or not this was the reason, at the turn of the year, General Zakharov was called upon to hand over his command to Marshal Rokossovsky.

Mannerheim called to power

In Helsinki, on August 1, acting out a previously-prepared drama, President Ryti resigned as head of state and the Finnish parliament appointed Marshal Mannerheim as his successor. This 75-year-old soldier would have to pilot the nation out of the war. For this purpose, he held a trump card in the performance of the Finnish Army during the recent battle of Karelia. So much heroism, spirit, and tenacity could effectively have shown the Kremlin that Finland's unconditional surrender could only be bought at a price much greater than any benefit that might be obtained from it. But before negotiating with Moscow, Finland could not wait for the Red Army to settle itself solidly in Tallinn and Paltiski, which would allow it to launch an amphibious operation across the Gulf of Finland and to use its crushing superiority in men and *matériel* to the best advantage.

In his task Mannerheim had to take into account the German 20th Army. This possessed three corps (ten mountain divisions) and faced Russia between the Arctic Circle and the Rybachiy peninsula on the frozen Arctic Ocean. This force, including the naval gunners in the many coastal batteries and the air force, totalled 204,000 men under the command of Colonel-General Dr. Rendulic.

The consequences of Finland's "defection" . . .

O.K.W. had envisaged the possibility of a Finnish defection since the spring. It had prepared two operations to counteract its effects. Operation *"Birke"* (Birch tree) provided for the 20th Army to retreat on the Finno-Norwegian frontier, while Operation *"Tanne"* (Pine tree) would require the army and the navy to prepare to occupy the Åland Islands, in the south of the Gulf of Bothnia, and the island of Sur Sari or Hogland in the Gulf of Finland.

Meanwhile on June 26, with the Soviet offensive at full force in the Karelian Isthmus, Ribbentrop had agreed to supply arms to the Finns only if they bound themselves unconditionally to the Third Reich. Trapped, President Ryti, with the verbal approval of his ministers, had agreed to this in writing. Therefore his resignation could imply a tacit rejection of the signature as being put on the agreement entirely on his own responsibility. Such a subterfuge was absolutely justified in view of Germany's blackmail.

. . . and Germany's contingency plans

That was how Blücher, Germany's minister in Helsinki, and General Erfurth, O.K.W.'s liaison officer attached to Marshal Mannerheim, interpreted the crisis of August 1 and the solution adopted. Rendulic, for his part, pointed out that the Finnish Minister of War, General Walden, had made no reference to Finno-German military partnership during that interview. And so the staff of the 20th Army began to prepare Operation *"Birke"* with all speed.

To clarify the situation, Hitler sent the O.K.W. chief-of-staff to see the new President of the Finnish Republic. Keitel was received by Mannerheim on August 17 and had the arrogance or the tactlessness to tell the latter that the people of the Greater Reich would maintain their war effort for another ten years if it were necessary. This swagger was received coldly and politely with the answer that "it was probably true for a nation of 90 million people".

As may be well imagined, Mannerheim did not express his thoughts too openly. All the same, he did not conceal the fact that Ryti's resignation had come because "in view of circumstances beyond his control, the ex-President had not been able to maintain his freedom of action", and that Mannerheim himself had agreed to combine in his person the supreme military and civil power in order that "in their precarious situation the Finnish

people could rely on having the freedom to act within their own interests".

Though he put a brave face on this, Keitel did not fail for a moment to realise the meaning and the importance of these prudent statements. Mannerheim was going to begin to "guide" Finland out of the war.

◁ *Inhabitants of Helsinki emerge from their air-raid shelters to survey the damage caused by Russian bombers.*
△ *With a raid imminent, a Finnish policeman orders pedestrians into the shelters.*

▽ *While his parents arrange transport out of the city, this Helsinki boy guards what his family have recovered from their bombed-out home.*

Relations with Russia renewed

And, in fact, on August 25, the Soviet minister in Stockholm, Mme. Kollontai, was surprised by a message from the Finnish Government, asking her what the Soviet conditions would be for re-opening the peace talks which had been broken off on April 18 at Finland's request. The Soviet reply arrived at Helsinki in record time and included only two conditions:

△ *Finnish soldiers rest in a northern town.*

▷ *Women auxiliaries of the Finnish Army in an observation post.*

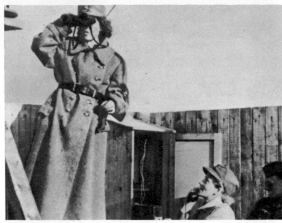

▽ *Mealtime for Finnish troops at a camp staffed by young girls.*

1. Immediate breaking-off of diplomatic relations between the Republic of Finland and the Third Reich.
2. Evacuation in two weeks, the absolutely final date fixed for September 14, of all Wehrmacht forces stationed in Finnish territory, after which the Helsinki Government agreed to intern any men left behind.

Great Britain associated herself with these conditions and the United States, who had not declared war on Finland, made it known that they approved. On September 2, after a session behind locked doors, the Finnish parliament authorised the government to begin discussions on the basis of the above conditions.

In consequence there was a cease-fire between the Russians and the Finns at 0700 hours on September 5.

Mannerheim informs Hitler

As Minister Blücher was receiving his passports on September 2, Mannerheim had a handwritten letter given to General Erfurth to be passed on to the Führer.

It was, Mannerheim wrote, first of all the general development of the war which "more and more prevents Germany from providing us, in the precarious situations which will doubtless arise and at the right time and in sufficient quantity, the aid of which we shall have urgent need and which Germany, as I sincerely believe, would be willing to grant us".

Moreover, if the worst occurred, the risks run by both countries, as Mannerheim told Keitel, were far from equal. Here, he added, "I must point out that even if fate did not favour German arms, Germany could continue to exist. Nobody could say the same for Finland."

And, at the same time as he heaped praises on the behaviour of "our German brothers-in-arms" towards the Finnish population, he declared that he cherished the hope that "even if you disapprove of my letter you will want, as do I and all Finns, to control the present situation and avoid any worsening of it".

However, the implementation of the second condition imposed by Moscow on Helsinki would set the Finns and Germans against each other—and for good reason, for it could not be done in the time allowed. Both Marshal Mannerheim and Colonel-General Rendulic agree on this in their memoirs.

Evacuation of Finland

Considerable German forces would be left stranded by the Finnish Government's decision to withdraw from the fighting. Though XIX Mountain Corps (General Ferdinand Jodl), whose left faced the Rybachiy peninsula, could get over the Norwegian frontier in a few days' march, this did not apply to the right wing of the 20th Army, consisting of XXXVI Mountain Corps (General Vogel); in action halfway between the White Sea and the Russo-Finnish frontier in the south, in a fortnight he would have to cross a good 625 miles before he left Finnish territory. That is why, from September 3, Mannerheim began to study the means at his disposal to keep his word regarding the internment of his ex-comrades in arms.

Hitler was the first to make a move. Though he ordered Rendulic to carry on with Operation "Birke" and abandoned the idea of a landing on the Åland Islands for fear of possible Swedish reaction, he nevertheless maintained his decision to put Sur Sari under firm Wehrmacht control, in spite of the objections of Vice-Admiral Buchardi, commander of the Kriegsmarine in that part of the Baltic.

The expedition was launched in the night of September 14-15 and resulted in total defeat for the Germans. Colonel Mietinnen, under whose command the island's garrison had been placed, conducted a spirited defence and then counter-attacked with such energy that the following evening the Germans had lost 330 killed and wounded, and surrendered a good 1,000 of their men.

The news of this unpardonable act of aggression and its defeat was welcomed in official circles in Helsinki with certain relief. From now on there was no need to bother about an ally of that sort.

In any case, even if Hitler had restrained himself from committing this act of brutal stupidity, events would not have taken a very different course. A few days later, it would have been known in Helsinki that Rendulic had received

△ A member of the Russian armistice commission on the day of his arrival in Helsinki on September 22, 1944. Behind him to the left are three Swedish newspapermen.

▽ German soldiers in Helsinki just prior to their evacuation from the country.

orders to stay in Finnish Lappland so as to keep the base at Petsamo and the precious nickel mines of Kolosjoki for the Third Reich.

Mannerheim now transferred his III Corps into the region of Oulu on the Gulf of Bothnia. This corps was commanded by General Siilasvuo, who had distinguished himself during the campaign of the winter of 1939-40. But the Germans did not permit a breakthrough, although their new enemies tried to cut them off by an unexpected landing at Kemi, close to the Finno-Swedish frontier.

On October 15, the Germans evacuated the little town of Rovaniemi after having reduced it to ashes. Then they slipped into Norwegian territory along the route they had prepared between Rovaniemi and Pôrsangerfjord. It was difficult to pursue the retreating Germans because they methodically destroyed all bridges, and also because of the season and the fact that the Finnish Army was due to complete its demobilisation by December 5, 1944.

On October 4, O.K.W. ordered Colonel-General Rendulic to abandon Petsamo and to fall back on Lyngenfjord. His preparations for the retreat were almost complete when, on October 7, XIX Corps was attacked in great strength and most energetically by the Karelian Front troops under General K. A. Meretskov. The 20th Army met this Soviet offensive with delaying tactics, using the many

rivers in the region. On October 9, XIX Corps was on the point of being surrounded but the danger was averted by the fast 400 mile transfer of the 163rd Division, which hurled itself into Salmijärvi, and then by the rest of XXXVI Mountain Corps.

Petsamo was occupied on October 15 by the Russians, who then pushed on as far as Kirkenes, on Norwegian soil. This battle, fought above the Arctic Circle, earned Meretskov the title of Marshal of the Soviet Union. In spite of this, it is strange that Soviet accounts, normally so rich in detail, make no mention of trophies or prisoners when they speak of this battle.

The Lyngenfjord base included the fjord of that name, half-way between the North Cape and Tromsö, and also the salient of Finnish territory which protrudes into the region. This meant the sacrifice of the Norwegian province of Finnmark, whose population was evacuated while the Germans burnt Lyngenfjord and Hammerfest. After its retreat, the 20th Army was dissolved. Three of its divisions were given to O.B.W., and a fourth was put at the disposal of O.K.W. Colonel-General Rendulic received the command of the "Norway" Army.

On September 19, 1944, the new Finnish minister, Enckell, was in Moscow to sign an "armistice treaty" which can be taken as a real preliminary and whose clauses regarding territory and payments

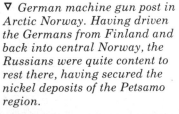

▽ *German machine gun post in Arctic Norway. Having driven the Germans from Finland and back into central Norway, the Russians were quite content to rest there, having secured the nickel deposits of the Petsamo region.*

were reproduced in the definitive peace treaty.

△ *Germans at work digging a trench from the frozen earth above the Arctic Circle.*

Finland's peace

In addition to the loss of territory which Finland had had to suffer by the treaty of March 7, 1940, she now had to witness the amputation of the Petsamo region, thus losing her access to the Atlantic as well as the advantages she gained through the export of nickel from Kolosjoki.

In exchange for the lease of the Hangö peninsula, which the first Treaty of Moscow had granted Russia for 50 years, in the second treaty the Soviet Union obtained the same rights over the Porkkala promontory on the Gulf of Finland, less than 25 miles from Helsinki.

Out of a population of four million, the valiant little nation had lost 55,000 dead and 47,500 wounded.

RUSSIA'S WAR EFFORT

1. After an evacuation of plant, still not fully comprehended in the Western world, at the beginning of the war, the Russians started afresh behind the Urals, and by the last year of the war were turning out huge quantities of basic, but perfectly adequate, weapons, such as the 76.2-mm guns seen here. This weapon was the standard divisional ordnance.
2. Soviet might advances to victory, which was won, at great cost, by the effective combined action of infantry, armour, and ground-attack aircraft.

Soviet Russia was the country which made the biggest land contribution to the Allied cause in World War II—an obvious fact which is often overlooked. By 1945 the Red Army's total strength—deployed on all fronts from Siberia and Manchuria to Persia and Europe—amounted to some 500 divisions. To equip and supply this immense host was a superb achievement, rendered even more impressive by the fact that the bulk of the work had been accomplished in the "crisis year" of 1941-42.

Draconian measures had been adopted to evacuate as much industrial material as possible to the east—but draconian measures alone could never have achieved such fantastic results without the wholesale co-operation of the Soviet workers. This was,

quite simply, the biggest integration of the civilian population with national war effort in the whole of World War II. Reams of figures have been quoted with justifiable pride by Soviet historians. The following are a few examples.

All records were broken when it came to setting up new blast furnaces in the Urals and getting them into operation. Before the war it had taken two and a half years to build a new blast furnace. But at the great war production centre at Magnitogorsk in the Urals two new furnaces were set up in eight months, a time sliced to seven months at Chusovaya. Whisked lock, stock, and barrel from Zaporozh'ye on the Dniepr, the Engels plant was going full blast a mere 20 days after arriving at its new site.

And at Moscow the military plant of the Armaments Commissariat was loaded *en masse* on to 12 trains in the middle of October 1941—the month when the capital was declared to be in a state of siege—travelled east for 11 days, and was in production by the end of the first week in December—with an output 50 per cent higher than it had been before the evacuation.

Bear in mind that these feats were achieved in the Russian winter, on completely new sites as often as not, where the workers had to build their own camps in temperatures of −40 degrees C. With a new mass call-up for the Red Army, this necessitated a complete overhaul of the Soviet labour force. In 1942 alone 4,400,000 workers were either trained or "re-educated", and

1

ПО ВРАЖЬЕЙ ЗЕМЛЕ,
ВПЕРЕД К ПОБЕДЕ!

3

4

the number of women workers rose dramatically. And this was for heavy work. Women driving steam-engines rose in number from six per cent at the beginning of 1941 to 33 per cent by the end of 1942. For women operating forging and press machines the increase was from 11 per cent to 50 per cent, and for compressors the numbers rose from 27 per cent to 44 per cent.

In the 12 months between July 1941 and July 1942, 15,198 tanks were produced in the Soviet Union, helping to explain the Red Army's crushing "comeback" under Zhukov in the Stalingrad counter-offensive. The same applied to the aircraft industry—in particular to the mass production of the superb Il-2 "Shturmovik"—and to artillery. This did not merely apply to field artillery but to "infantry artillery"—mortars. Here again the initial German superiority was soon dwarfed by Soviet mass production.

Standardisation and mass production, it must be emphasised, were not the whole answer. It was an immense national effort, with civilian defence funds and collective farms clubbing together to buy "their" tanks for the army, much as happened in Britain and America. None of the figures or statistics can paint the full picture of the human side of this phenomenon, which had no parallel in world history down to 1945 and has only been matched since the end of World War II by the efforts of Communist China.

3. *Food for Russia's god of war. Major Soviet offensives were normally heralded by artillery barrages that rendered World War I barrages pale in comparison, and these consumed enormous quantities of ammunition. This photograph was taken in a Urals factory in 1943.*

4. *A T-34/76 tank assembly line in Leningrad. After standardising a simple but sound design, the Russians were able to turn out quantities of this vehicle that German tank production just could not hope to match.*

5. *A Russian shell factory. Visible is ammunition for light field artillery, ranging up to some for super-heavy guns.*

5

CHAPTER 129
Defeat in the Balkans

On August 20, 1944, the troops of the 2nd Ukrainian Front attacked Iaşi, capital of Moldavia. On Christmas Eve, acting in concert with the 3rd Ukrainian Front, it laid siege to Budapest, while the Soviet Union took complete control over Bulgaria. It exercised no less strong an influence over those provinces of Yugoslavia liberated by Marshal Tito, as well as over the ex-kingdom of Albania.

Not only had the "New Order" instituted by Hitler and Mussolini been upset, but also the old European balance, established in these parts in the 19th Century. On June 22, 1944, Army Group "South Ukraine", which had responsibility for the 400-mile front running between the mouth of the Danube and the Carpathian range, included 23 Rumanian and 33 German divisions, nine of which were Panzer or *Panzergrenadier*. But the defeat in Belorussia, the rout in the western Ukraine, and the invasion of Poland had forced O.K.H. to remove six Panzer and seven infantry divisions from this army group. They had only been partially replaced by units of lesser worth. With everything included, when Colonel-General Hans Friessner succeeded Schörner at the head of Army Group "South Ukraine" at the beginning of August, he took over 52 divisions, 24 of which were German. What made the circumstances more serious was that he had only four Panzer divisions.

Antonescu recommends retreat

It had become evident that the Russians had two formidable bridgeheads on the Dniestr, at Tiraspol and Grigoriopol, and that between the Dniestr and the Prut the position of the front favoured one of those pincer movements so liked by the Russians. So Marshal Antonescu, the Rumanian *Conducator,* summoned to

◁ *Cheerful Rumanian musicians welcome the Russians to Rumania.*
▽ ◁ *The Axis begins to dissolve. The* St. Paul Dispatch *of Minnesota poses the pertinent question "Who'll jump first?" It was in fact to be Finland, closely followed by Rumania and then Bulgaria.*
▽ *German comment on the "liquidation" of the Axis satellites. Stalin, as auctioneer, offers: "Here's another lot of little countries: Rumania, Bulgaria, and Finland. No one wants them? I'll take them then . . ."*

△ *Cossack cavalry move up through a Rumanian village, to the apparent delight of its inhabitants.*

O.K.W. on August 5, offered as his advice that Army Group "South Ukraine" should be pulled back along a line running from the northern arm of the Danube, through Galaţi to the right bank of the Siretul and then the Carpathians. This line had been surveyed and partially fortified by the Belgian General Brialmont at a time when fear of the Russians had caused Rumania to flirt with the Triple Alliance. Strategically sound, this solution nevertheless required the evacuation of the southern districts of Bessarabia and Moldavia, a serious sacrifice for Rumania that Antonescu nevertheless made.

Rumanian peace overtures

The day after the last interview between the Führer and Antonescu, the latter summoned Colonel-General Guderian to go over the political and military scene with him. Guderian wrote:

"He soon came to talk about the assassination attempt of July 20, without hiding his horror at it. 'Believe me,' he said, 'I could trust any of my generals with my life. In Rumania, it would be inconceivable for any officer to take part in a *coup d'état!*' There and then, I was not in a position to answer his grave reproaches. A fortnight later, Antonescu would find himself in a very different situation, and so should we."

It seems, therefore, that the Rumanian dictator had not the slightest idea of the plot led by King Michael I and the leaders of the main political parties, who were preparing to seize power from his hands. As was seen earlier, following the battle of Stalingrad, Rumanian diplomats had attempted to re-establish contact with Great Britain and the United States. In 1944, Alexander Creziano, the Rumanian minister in Ankara, contacted the representatives of the two Western powers while the embassies in Madrid and Stockholm went forward with other soundings. Finally, with the consent of the King, the leader of the National Peasants' Party, Julius Maniu, who was the principal conspirator, sent two emissaries to Cairo in the persons of

Constantin Visoïano and Prince Stirbey. But neither Washington nor London was disposed to reply to these overtures before Bucharest had reached agreement with Moscow on the conditions for a cease-fire.

Now, on April 2, Antonescu's adversaries noted a statement by Molotov that they interpreted as an encouraging overture.

"The Soviet Union," proclaimed Stalin's Foreign Minister, "in no way seeks to acquire any part of Rumanian territory or to change the present social order. Russian troops have entered Rumania solely as a result of military necessity."

Certainly, when Molotov spoke of "Rumanian territory", he excluded the provinces of Bessarabia and Bukovina, which the ultimatum of June 26, 1940 had placed under Soviet control. All the same, Julius Maniu informed the Allies that he was ready to enter discussions on this basis and to consent to substantial reparations being paid to Moscow. It is also true that Rumania had been assured that, as soon as she left the German camp, she would be able to get back the part of Transylvania that the Vienna agreement of August 30, 1940 had transferred to Hungary.

The Rumanian dictator was more or

▽ *The Rumanian high command: King Michael (bare-headed, in the background) and Marshal Antonescu (bare-headed, in the foreground). Soon afterwards, a coup headed by King Michael ousted Antonescu and threw Rumania's lot in with the Allies.*

The German Panzerjäger IV/70 tank destroyer

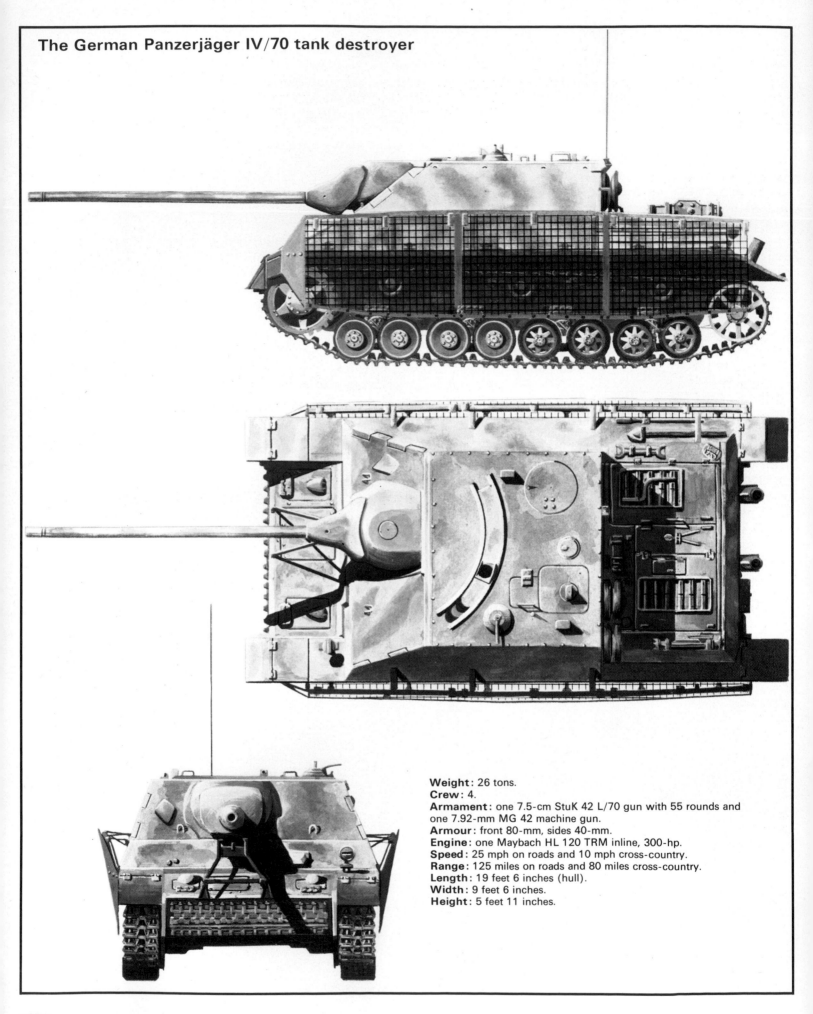

Weight: 26 tons.
Crew: 4.
Armament: one 7.5-cm StuK 42 L/70 gun with 55 rounds and one 7.92-mm MG 42 machine gun.
Armour: front 80-mm, sides 40-mm.
Engine: one Maybach HL 120 TRM inline, 300-hp.
Speed: 25 mph on roads and 10 mph cross-country.
Range: 125 miles on roads and 80 miles cross-country.
Length: 19 feet 6 inches (hull).
Width: 9 feet 6 inches.
Height: 5 feet 11 inches.

less aware of these dealings, but did not forbid them absolutely. He merely refused to agree to them, considering that his honour bound him to the Wehrmacht. Moreover, he did not feel personally threatened, ignoring the fact that it was not to him but to the sovereign that the officer corps had sworn loyalty.

The Rumanian situation caused great puzzlement in Hitler's circle for the reports being received were in disagreement with each other.

On August 3, Friessner had sounded the alarm and indicated how little confidence he felt in his Rumanian subordinates, particularly the senior officers. Hence his conclusion:

"If these symptoms of insecurity among the Rumanian troops go on being noted for long, it will be necessary to order an immediate retreat on the front behind the Prut on the Galati–Focşani–Carpathians line."

But General Hansen, who had been the "German General in Rumania" since October 1940, held a diametrically opposed opinion. The representative of the Third Reich in Bucharest, Ambassador von Killinger, telegraphed Ribbentrop on August 10: "Situation absolutely stable. King Michael guarantees the alliance with Germany."

Certainly this diplomat was not very highly thought of by Ribbentrop, but Marshal Antonescu had the entire con-

△ Russian air superiority. With the few Axis aircraft left swept out of the skies by Russian fighters (the patrol is composed of Lavochkin La-5's), Soviet close support aircraft could blast open a path for the tanks and infantry.
◁ Russian armour moves into Bucharest in August 1944 to the acclaim of the Rumanian public.

fidence of Hitler. That is why, in view of Hitler's optimism, nothing was prepared by the Germans to ease the consequences of a "defection"

Rumanian collapse

On the vital day, that is at dawn on August 20, Army Group "South Ukraine" was divided into two sections:

1. From the Black Sea to Korneshty, *Armeegruppe* "Dumitrescu" included the Rumanian 3rd Army (General Dumitrescu) and the German 6th Army (General Fretter-Pico).
2. From Korneshty to the Yablonitse pass (contact on the right with Army Group "North Ukraine") *Armeegruppe* "Wöhler" put the German 8th Army (General Wöhler) and the Rumanian 4th Army (General Steflea) into the field.

So, of 250 miles of front, 100 were

defended by Rumanian troops but, for reasons of security, "integration" as it is now called, of the Axis forces had gone as far as army level and, in some places, down to corps level. The system, which in his jargon Hitler had curiously named "whalebone stays", was at its height here. It was – ignoring for the moment the plans of King Michael and the suspicions of Colonel-General Friessner – to ignore the wisdom of the old saying that a chain is only as strong as its weakest link.

As usual, the Soviet sources say nothing of the numbers of men which the *Stavka* put at the disposal of Generals Malinovsky and Tolbukhin; the Germans, for their part, calculate them as 90 or 94 infantry divisions and seven tank corps. In armoured strength alone, this gave the attackers an advantage of at least five to one. In his centre of gravity, which pivoted on Iaşi, Malinovsky had massed 125 guns and mortars per mile. Tolbukhin's advance from the Tiraspol

bridgehead was, in addition, aided by 7,800 guns. Soviet aircraft dominated the skies and, during the preparation of the attack, the Red Air Force co-operated with the artillery in attacking enemy positions, then transferred its effort along the lines taken by the Germans' reserve armour.

By the evening of August 20, both Malinovsky and Tolbukhin had already gained victory. In the German 8th Army, IV Corps (General Mieth) resisted fiercely in the outskirts of Iaşi, but the Rumanian IV Corps on its left foundered in spite of the help of the 76th Division. *Armeegruppe* "Dumitrescu" had been attacked at the link-point between the German 6th Army and the Rumanian 3rd Army, and the rupture was even more decisive after the collapse of the two Rumanian divisions which completed General Brandenberger's XXIX Corps. And while the Russians followed up their advantage, Friessner had already used up his ar-

◁ *Gunboats on the Danube.*
△ *A.A. guns.*
The original caption reads: "The watch on the Danube. Two major tasks have devolved on the Hungarian Army, which is excellently trained and superbly equipped: first the protection of Hungary against foreign threats and occupation; second, by preserving her independence the ensuring of free trade between Central and South-Eastern Europe, between Greater Germany and the Balkan States. This trade, whose main route is the Danube, forms the basis of the New Order in Europe." And it was all crumbling in the autumn of 1944.

moured reserves (13th Panzer Division, 10th *Panzergrenadier* Division, and Rumanian 1st Armoured Division).

In this situation, there was nothing Friessner could do but take the responsibility himself of ordering his army group to retreat without waiting for Hitler's authorisation. He did so that same evening. But, as he himself remarked:

"In spite of the preparations we had made in more leisurely moments, we were naturally unable to disengage ourselves from the enemy methodically. The way the situation was developing, any movement of ours could only be carried out under the enemy's control and only step by step. This was not now a retreat, it was a fighting withdrawal."

▽ *Sofia welcomes the Red Army. On the banner is the slogan "Death to Fascism".*
▽▽ *The Red Navy moves into the Bulgarian Black Sea base of Varna.*

Antonescu overthrown

The *Führerbefehl* reached Friessner on August 22. The following day King Michael summoned Antonescu and his Minister of Foreign Affairs to the palace and ordered them to conclude an immediate armistice with the Allies. The Marshal's reply was vague, and the King immediately had them both arrested. Then, at 2200 hours, Radio Bucharest broadcast the cease-fire order to all Rumanian forces. When the commander of Army Group "South Ukraine" heard the news, he rang up Generals Dumitrescu and Steflea. Both men refused to disobey the oath of loyalty they had sworn to their sovereign. At the same time, Ambassador von Killinger and General Hansen were confined to the German legation.

Hitler was totally surprised by this turn of events and, without even warning Friessner of his intentions, ordered Luftwaffe formations based on Ploieşti to bomb Bucharest, concentrating particularly on the Royal Palace and the Prime Minister's residence. This was a particularly stupid thing to do and the new Prime Minister, General Sanatescu, took advantage of it to declare war on the Third Reich on August 25. As a result, Rumanian troops occupied the Danube, Prut, and Siretul crossings, opening them to the Russians.

△ ◁ *Back in the Reich, all production records for armaments were being smashed as Speer's production plan swung into full speed. Here production workers finish off a batch of 3.7-cm anti-aircraft guns.*

6th Army routed

This was followed by a complete disaster for the German 6th Army. Cut off from the Danube by Tolbukhin's armour, which had pushed through as far as the Prut at Leovo, it could not cross the river higher up because that would have thrown it into the arms of Malinovsky, whose 6th Guards Tank Army (Colonel-General Chistyakov) had pushed on swiftly from Iaşi towards Huşi. Fourteen German divisions were annihilated in the pincers thus formed, and only two divisional commanders escaped death or capture. All four corps commanders were taken prisoner. In the German 8th Army, IV Corps, which had retreated along the right bank of the Prut, was trapped by the Russian 2nd Ukrainian Front, and the remains of its 79th and 376th Divisions were forced to lay down their arms with their commanders, Lieutenant-Generals Weinknecht and Schwarz. General Mieth did not suffer the same humiliation, having succumbed in the meantime to a heart attack. To sum up, of 24 German divisions which he had under his command on August 20, Colonel-General Friessner had lost 16 in the space of a fortnight. The Soviet communiqué of September 5 claimed 105,000 German dead and 106,000 prisoners.

The right course?

Seeing their country subjected to the Communist yoke and enslaved to the U.S.S.R., certain emigré Rumanians see the events of August 23 as the cause of their country's unfortunate fate. In this they do not appear to be correct. In the

1877

Δ *Bulgarian partisans prepare for an ambush on the retreating Germans.*

U.S.S.R., Great Britain, and the U.S.A., but was the only one to sign. What was more serious was that, while Ambassador Bogomolov sat as an equal partner in the organisation charged with carrying out the Italian armistice, the Allied commission set up by Article 18 of that agreement, with the same rôle, had its activity strictly limited; it read:

"The Allied Commission will follow the instructions of the Soviet High Command (Allied) acting in the name of the Allied Powers."

On the military side, it is also worth noting that the armistice of September 12 obliged Rumania to declare war on Germany and Hungary and pursue it with a minimum of 12 divisions, placed under the "Soviet High Command (Allied)". But already, on September 6, the Bucharest Government had declared war against Hungary.

And so it was as on a peace-time route march that Marshal Malinovsky sent 25 divisions of his front from Wallachia to Transylvania, while his left marched towards Turnu Severin on the frontier with Yugoslavia. By September 1, Tolbukhin had reached Giurgiu on the Danube.

The Rumanian cease-fire raised the first place the destruction caused by the war on land stopped at the left bank of the Danube and the Siretul and the cease-fire saved the lives of hundreds of thousands of young Rumanians, for the battle for Moldavia and Bessarabia was already irrevocably lost, and in the worst conditions.

It is also evident that neither King Michael nor those who had advised him could imagine that they would be purely and simply abandoned to the Communist subversion ordered from a distance by Moscow. Having re-established the liberal constitution of 1921, restored political rights, and freed political prisoners, they counted on being granted the benefits of the Atlantic Charter of August 14, 1941 and the principles it had proclaimed in the face of Hitler.

But the fatal process was already under way. The Rumanian emissaries who had arrived in Cairo were sent to Moscow. The British and Americans agreed to appear in the background in the armistice agreement, which was signed on September 12 between King Michael's plenipotentiaries and Marshal Malinovsky, who spoke for the governments of the

question of Bulgaria. The situation in Sofia was as follows. On December 12, 1941 King Boris had declared war against the United States and Great Britain but, for historical reasons, had been careful not to engage in hostilities against the Soviet Union. On his mysterious death, which occurred on August 28, 1943 after a visit to Hitler, a Regency Council, composed of his brother Prince Cyril, Professor Filov, and General Michov, assumed power in the name of King Simon II, who was only a child.

It was thus logical that the Regents should send a delegation to Cairo to enquire about the armistice conditions that London and Washington might be willing to grant them. At the same time they formed a democratic-style government and denounced the Anti-Comintern Pact, which Bulgaria had joined on November 25, 1941.

These peaceful overtures were received by Stalin, on September 5, by a declaration of war. The Bulgarian Government thought it could counter this by declaring war against Germany on September 8. For the Kremlin the important point was to bring the negotiations to Moscow and exclude the British and the Americans. The signing of the armistice took place in Moscow on October 28 and General Maitland Wilson, commander-in-chief of the Allied forces in the Mediterranean, was reduced to the rôle of a mere spectator. Meanwhile, forces of the 3rd Ukrainian Front had penetrated Bulgaria at Silistra and Ruse, amid popular acclaim. Several days later the Gheorghiev government, preponderantly Communist, was formed. Soon the reign of terror began in Bulgaria. Dismissed, imprisoned, dragged before a carefully selected court, all three Regents fell before a firing squad on February 2, 1945. They were naked, as a diplomat at the time posted to Sofia recounted later, because the authorities wanted to preserve their clothes.

Following the declaration of war on September 8, Bulgaria sent its 5th Army against Germany. It was commanded by General Stanchev and had ten divisions equipped by the Wehrmacht, including one armoured division which had just received 88 Pzkw IV tanks and 50 assault guns. Acting as Marshal Tolbukhin's left wing, it was given the task of cutting the Germans' line of retreat as they pulled back from the Balkans. It was only partially successful in this, as we shall see in the next chapter.

△ *Julius Maniu, head of the Rumanian National Peasants' Party.*

▽ *The signing of the Russo-Bulgarian armistice on October 24, 1944. Foreign Minister Molotov is standing seventh from the right.*

The German *Mittlerer Zugkraftwagen* 8t SdKfz 7 half-track carrier

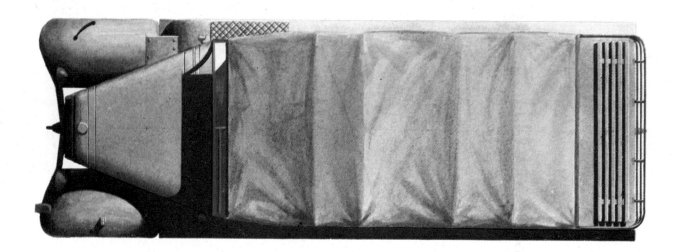

Weight: 11.5 tons.
Crew: 12.
Engine: one Maybach HL 62 TUK inline, 140-hp.
Speed: 31 mph.
Range: 250 miles.
Length: 20 feet 3 inches.
Width: 7 feet 10½ inches.
Height: 8 feet 7 inches.

'For the Motherland,
for Stalin!'

THE RUSSIAN PARTISANS

Despite the splendid reaction of the Soviet people during the months of the German advance into Russia, it was a profound embarrassment to Stalin's régime that the people in the German-occupied regions did not instantly rise in furious rebellion against their alien overlords. There were three clear reasons for this. The first was a genuine sense of bitterness at the speed at which the Red Army had been forced back to the east. There had been far too many scenes of Party officials heading the rush to get back eastwards on "essential" missions–resentment, in short, of the indecent "skedaddle" put up by officials and defenders of the régime. The second was the deceptive but understandable viewpoint that such a complete collapse must mean the defeat of the country; a canny sense of wait-and-see made itself felt. Third and most important was the fact that the Stalinist régime had made no provision whatsoever for emergency resistance measures in the event of the western provinces becoming overrun by enemy forces. Stalin had proclaimed the Soviet people to be "monolithically united", and that was that.

The first step was taken on June 29, 1941, by the Central Committee of the Communist Party (one week after the invasion). This was a directive stating the need for partisan and sabotage activity in the west, and it was amplified by a radio speech by Stalin on July 3. This boiled down to an appeal to the people of Russia "to create unbearable conditions in the occupied areas for the enemy and all who help him, to pursue and destroy them at every step, to disrupt everything they do." But another fortnight of unmitigated disaster went by before the Party issued its first detailed directive on how such partisan activity was to be organised, with at least one resistance unit operating in every former Soviet administrative area. But this did not happen in the chaotic months of the late summer and autumn of 1941. It did not begin to materialise until much later. And in many areas it does not seem to have materialised at all.

To start with, it was obvious that initial partisan activity must be localised to areas where the terrain offered the best opportunities for survival–the Pripet marshes, the forests of Belorussia. In addition, weapons must be supplied or captured in sufficient quantity before any effective activity could begin. As the campaign of 1941 moved to its crisis and turning-point before Moscow, it is clear that the war of the partisans behind the German front line was the least of the Soviet régime's worries.

So for these reasons the Russian partisan war was conducted in a very low key in 1941. Certainly there was no tight Party control; and operations were led by officers cut off by the initial rout who decided to carry on by themselves with what they had–a handful of rifles and hand grenades and local volunteers who felt the same way. Certainly it was not until Zhukov's Moscow counter-offensive that there was any indication that the Soviet Union had a chance of survival, let alone of winning the war. And the Moscow battle saw the first real signs that partisans and regular Red Army forces could work together. In the Moscow–Tula–Kalinin area there were about 10,000 partisans, and although many of these had been sent behind the enemy lines–rather than having operated there from the start of the offensive–they certainly made their presence

2

1. *Partisans return to their hideout after an operation near Pinsk in 1944. Earlier in the war the wounded man might have been shot and left behind, but by 1944 the Belorussian partisans were well equipped even with medical facilities.*

2. *Partisans are sworn in to the Red Army. With thousands of able bodied and willing men and women cut off from the west of Russia by the German advance in 1941, great partisan bands were not difficult to raise. Supplied from the air, these bands tied down considerable German forces.*

Previous Page: *A Russian cavalry charge.*

3

Обявление!

За пойманного бандита „КАТЮ"
Германское Командование
вознаградит поймавшего:
10 марок; 5 пудов соли, а также
чным наделом в 25 гектар

4

felt during the Moscow offensive. Soviet records credit partisan activities during the *whole* of the winter of 1941-42 with having accounted for 18,000 Germans – well over the equivalent of a division. The sources for such statistics remain inscrutable. What is certain is that the Moscow battle saw the first German executions of prominent "partisan terrorist leaders" – Gurianov and Solntsev.

Not until May 30, 1942, did the Soviet High Command *(Stavka)* push through the establishment of a "Central Staff of the Partisan Movement". By this time recruitment was steadily increasing, largely due to the fact that the Germans had already revealed what their policy was going to be like in the occupied territories: brutal in the extreme. Still, any form of central supply system from Moscow remained basic; and it was not until the next crisis, that of September/October 1942, that the partisan "War of the Rails" (officially declared in July of the following year) began to make itself felt. It was instrumental in slowing up the Manstein-Hoth offensive which vainly tried to break through the ring of steel encircling the trapped 6th Army in Stalingrad.

As in so many other different ways, Stalingrad had an immense effect on the partisan movement. Its boost of Russian national morale coincided with an increased flow of armaments from Moscow – more food supplies, rifles and sub-machine guns, mortars, anti-tank guns for use on trains – even some heavy artillery – and medical supplies, which in many ways were the most important item of the lot as far as partisan morale was concerned. Soviet figures for Belorussia in 1943 assess the increase in the partisans' numbers as rising from 65,000 in February to 360,000 in December; for the Ukraine at the end of the year, 220,000.

In July 1943 the Soviet High Command gave its formal order for the launching of the "War of Rails" – the partisan "offensive" aimed at paralysing the German lines of supply. The immediate target was the German Army Group "Centre", which had to cope with the partisans in the Gomel, Orel, and Bryansk regions. Between July and the end of September over 17,000 rails had been blown by the partisans of the three regions, working in co-ordination. Matters were made even worse for the Germans

5

3. *One of the most celebrated Russian partisans was a woman known as "Katya". In their efforts to catch her, the Germans offered several hundred marks, 180 pounds of salt, and about 62 acres of land for any Russian who would turn her in, as in this poster sent out by the district Kommandantur of Dobrush in Belorussia.*
4. *Smolensk partisans, all well armed with PPSh sub-machine guns.*
5. *Not so well equipped: Donbass partisans in 1942, with a motley assortment of captured and indigenous weapons.*
6. *The Smolensk area again. Men of the "Kletnyanskaya" Brigade on parade. By 1944 many of the larger partisan units were in effect proper army formations, lacking only the uniform to complete the transformation.*

6

in Belorussia, where between **7** August and November 200,000 rails were blown, 1,014 trains wrecked or derailed, and 72 railway bridges destroyed or badly damaged. The effect on the German railway net was impressive: two-thirds of the Belorussian lines were effectively put out of action for weeks at a time, and for the space of ten days the key Minsk-Molodechno line was blocked.

Some of the accounts of the partisan war lay excessive stress on its daredevil side–raiding a German H.Q. at Christmas and shattering the Teutonic festivities with hand grenades, or the gruesome fate of High Commissioner Wilhelm Kube of Belorussia, blown to eternity by a time-bomb put under his bed by his (partisan) Belorussian girl friend. But in reality the partisan war served as much to increase Russia's agony as to speed the day of the Germans' departure. German reprisals were heavy-handed and ruthless, with whole villages being wiped out, Lidice-style. As German atrocities were always one of the most compelling sources of partisan recruitment this created a vicious circle which only added to the tragedy.

When the great Red Army advances began, with their paths paved by partisan operations, the partisans found that their war was not over: they were drafted into the Red Army.

Although slow to get under way, Russia's partisan movement grew apace. At its height at least half a million patriots fought in the partisan ranks.

8

7. *In Odessa, the partisans hid in the city's catacombs, from one of which they are here seen emerging.*
8. *A partisan column in southern Russia. Further to the north the partisans had forests and marshes in which to hide, and further to the south mountains, but in the plains, mobility was of the essence in evading the Germans.*
9. *By 1943 many of Russia's provinces were largely in the hands of the partisans, and here they could operate as ordinary troops, as this photograph of partisans in the Pinsk area indicates. Note the DP light machine gun providing covering fire.*

9

1888

Although by 1945 the Red Army, the biggest in the world, could field the greatest concentration of armoured power in the world, it was basically as it had been for centuries: an infantry force. Its masses of "foot-sloggers", plain and simple, were in the long run the basic factor which ground down the resistance of the Wehrmacht.

Four nine-men sections made up a platoon; three platoons, plus a mortar platoon, a machine gun section, and a medical section made up a company. Three companies made up a battalion, which also had a machine gun company, a mortar company, an anti-tank platoon, an anti-tank troop (the platoon being armed with anti-tank rifles and the troop with two 57-mm guns), a medical platoon, and a supply platoon. And

three battalions made up the normal rifle regiment (about 2,500 men, under a colonel or lieutenant-colonel), which was the smallest numbered formation in the Red Army.

Then came the rifle division of three rifle regiments, plus supply, veterinary, and medical services, a divisional staff, an artillery regiment, an anti-tank battalion, an anti-tank rifle company, an A.A. artillery company, and both engineer and signals battalions. Two to four divisions made up a corps; two to four corps made up an army, and anything from three to 14 armies made up a "front" or army group.

In addition to the basic, all-arms army there were the guards armies. "Guards" was an honorific title given to any unit down to regiment which had especially

distinguished itself in action. Then there was the "shock" army, a special formation made up of experienced units, plus more fire-power and artillery, for particularly formidable attacks; and the "tank" army.

In attack the massed Soviet infantry was given lavish artillery, armoured, and air support; but the outcome of the assault inevitably depended on the infantry. Soviet tactics – even those of ace commanders such as Zhukov, Konev, and Rokossovsky – tended to be basic. Eisenhower, in his memoirs, recalls how he met Zhukov after the war and asked him the secret of the Red Army's massive breakthroughs and advances. The Allied Supreme Commander was horrified when Zhukov obliged. Reminding Eisenhower of the faith

10. *In the north, the Russians had learned the lessons of the Winter War against Finland well. Now they had properly trained ski troops and specialised equipment, such as the sledge seen here, for moving supplies and weapons that could not be carried by men. The machine gun is a 7.62-mm SPM, which weighed fractionally under 100 pounds.*
11. *Front line medical aid: Nurse Liza Kozyukova in northern Russia.*
12. *Cold is not the prerogative only of northern Russia, as can be seen in this photograph of a Russian attack in the Ukraine, which can be (and often was in World War II) as cold as areas many hundreds of miles further north.*

13. *More specialised equipment: tank-towed sledges for troops and supplies. In this photograph, Russian ski troops are getting an easy ride up to the front.*

the Germans pitted in extensive minefields, Zhukov said that the Russian way was to send the first wave in *without lifting the mines.* They suffered murderous casualties, it was true, but the second wave had a much easier time. And the third wave . . .

But it is unwise to draw generalisations from this. Soviet tactics varied considerably. One trick used in the attacks on the Baltic front was to plaster the German lines with shellfire but leave regular gaps along the line. While the Germans were still being bombarded and keeping their heads down, the Soviet attack would be launched up the "corridors" between their own shells into these gaps. Given any major inaccuracy in the fire-plan the Soviet infantrymen in the attack were bound to suffer badly from their own shells. But by the time the bombardment lifted and the Germans prepared for an orthodox defence, they would find the Russians as far as a mile behind them already.

Inexhaustible reinforcements of men and machines lay at the disposal of the Soviet commanders and they were never loath to make

full use of them. But by 1945 there were new trends emerging from the traditional, heads-down tactics which had bulldozed the Wehrmacht from the Volga to the gates of Berlin. For a start, the Red Army was becoming mobile. This was largely due to the Western Allies. The tanks they sent to Russia may not have measured up to the gruelling standards of the Eastern Front, but the transport was another matter. By the end of the war Russia had been sent 427,000 trucks, over 2,000 Ordnance vehicles, and 35,000 motor-cycles, and over two million tyres. For the first time in its history the Red Army had been "put on wheels", and began to get the fullest benefit out of the deadly advantages of modern mobile warfare.

This came to full fruition in the very last campaign which the Soviet Union fought in World War II: the attack on the Japanese Kwantung Army in Manchuria. This was an extremely sophisticated affair, using all arms: Army, Air Force, and Marines. Mass parachute drops speeded the advance, which was carried

out with close co-ordination between the various units.

The wheel had indeed come full circle from the first, frantic battles of 1941, when the long brown ranks, arms linked, had charged the German machine guns with roars of *"Urra!"* until the sickened German gunners could hardly bring themselves to keep firing. But even in these disastrous days the Russian soldier had shown his best quality: incredible endurance. This was typified by the almost-forgotten siege of Brest-Litovsk, right on the start-line of "Barbarossa", which held out for an incredible month until July 24.

This was the spirit of Stalingrad, which the Western Allies were proud to honour. By the end of 1941 the Red Army had saved its country from annihilation. By the end of 1942 it had proved itself a match for the Wehrmacht, and that the Soviet Union might well beat Germany without Allied aid, given time. And by the end of 1943 it had gained the initiative, never to lose it, and proved itself the greatest Allied instrument of victory.

CHAPTER 130
Confusion in the Balkans

On August 23, the German forces occupying Albania, mainland Greece, and the Aegean Islands came under Colonel-General Löhr, commanding Army Group "E" with headquarters at Salonika. These forces were subdivided into four corps (Tiranë, Yanina, Athens, and Salonika) totalling ten divisions (seven of which were on the mainland) and six fortress brigades: in all, about 300,000 men, to whom must be added 33,000 sailors (most of whom were attached to the coastal artillery) and 12,000 airmen and anti-aircraft gunners.

The day following the Rumanian cease-fire, Löhr was confronted by an order from O.K.W. ordering him to begin evacuation of the Aegean and Ionian islands and mainland Greece, south of a line running from Corfu to Métsovon and Mt. Olympus. But a few days later Sofia's declaration of war on Berlin forced Hitler to annul this order and to instruct Army Group "E" to retreat to a line running along the line Scutari–Skopje–Bulgarian/Yugoslav frontier of 1939–Iron Gate Pass on the Danube. On the other side of the river he would be in contact with the 2nd *Panzerarmee* (General de Angelis). The latter would relieve Field-Marshal von Weichs's Army Group "F". In this way a continuous front between the Carpathians and the Adriatic would be formed to bar the enemy from the Danube plain.

Time was pressing, and it·was not possible to recover all the 60,000 men who garrisoned the Aegean. Using the very few transport aircraft available and a large number of powered *caiques*, two-thirds of the men were brought back to mainland Greece. The remainder continued to hold Rhodes, Léros, Kos, and Tílos under the command of Major-General Wagner, as well as Crete and the island of Mílos under General Benthak. They remained there until after the end of the war on May 9, 1945.

The evacuation of the Peloponnese gave rise to some clashes between the 41st Division (Lieutenant-General Hauser) and the royalist guerrillas of Napoleon Zervas, opportunely reinforced by the British 2nd Airborne Brigade, which liberated Patras on October 4. All the same, the Germans reached Corinth, then Athens which General Felmy, commanding LXVIII Corps, handed over to the control of its mayor that same day. In Epiros, the troops of XXII Mountain Corps (General Lanz) fought bitter battles

As the Red Army moved deeper into the Balkans, the uneasy anti-Axis truce between the Royalists and the Communists in Greece broke down completely. The latter, in the hope of securing Russian intervention in Greece, started an insurrection in Athens. But Greece fell within the British sphere of influence, and Churchill reacted swiftly. Comprising airborne landings and subsequent amphibious reinforcement, Operation "Manna" was intended to nip the Communist flower in the bud. But soon General Scobie's III Corps found itself embroiled in a full scale civil war.
▽ *British paratroopers in Athens during the E.L.A.S. uprising. Note the weapons carried: a Bren gun, an American M1 carbine, and an American Thompson sub-machine gun.*

with partisans. But, all in all, the evacuation of Greece took place with very few losses and serious delays to the retreating Germans.

Mention should be made here that in 1947, the Greek Government revealed to the United Nations the text of an agreement made between a representative of the 11th Luftwaffe Division and a delegate of the "E.L.A.S." partisans, according to whose terms the men of the "Peoples' Army" agreed not to hinder the German retreat on the condition that they were given a certain quantity of heavy arms and other military equipment for their forthcoming war with the loyalists.

Trouble in Yugoslavia

It was in Yugoslavia that things became difficult for Army Group "E". On October 14, the Bulgarian 5th Army took Niš, on the most practical route for the Germans to reach the Danube. In addition, on October 1, Tolbukhin had crossed the Danube near Turnu Severin and then forced his way over the Morava against the resistance of XXXIV Corps' (General F. W. Müller) two divisions. Then the Russians marched on Belgrade. On October 20, working with Marshal Tito's troops, they overcame the final resistance in the streets of the Yugoslav capital, undertaken by *Armeegruppe* "Felber" (Army Group "F").

The fall of Niš had forced Löhr to think of a way to escape the noose and he decided to follow a route through Skopje, Mitrovica, Novi Pazar, and Višegrad. The Belgrade road would have enabled Tolbukhin to cut Army Group "E"'s last line of retreat if his enemy had not opportunely guarded his flanks around Kraljevo and Užice. In short, Colonel-General Löhr established his headquarters at Sarajevo on November 15, having managed to bring his four corps through

◁ ◁ *E.L.A.S. supporters on the roof of Athens University.*
▽ ◁ *Male and female soldiers of E.L.A.S. With the Germans pulling back towards Yugoslavia, E.L.A.S. now saw its task as leading Greece into the Communist bloc.*
▽ *Loyalists demonstrate in favour of Papandreou and the Western Allies.*

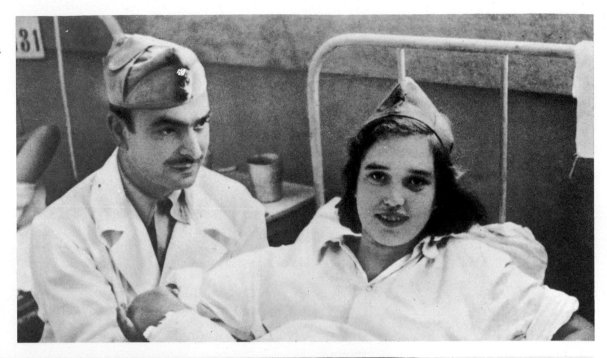

▷ *Doctor Carlo Ubertalli tends Ksenija Kavacic, an 18-year old Yugoslav partisan wounded in an attack on the German-held town of Klis. She finally arrived in Italy for hospital treatment under the care of Doctor Ubertalli, who had sent the partisans medical supplies while serving with the Italian Army and then deserted to the Titoist side.*

▽ *After recovering from their wounds at a hospital in Italy, these Yugoslav partisans are undergoing battle drill before being returned to Yugoslavia.*

without being encircled. Marshal Tito's Yugoslav partisans had failed in their attempts to hinder the retreat of Army Group "E" for long enough to allow Tolbukhin to develop his manoeuvre. All the same the partisans sowed hostility behind the Germans' backs in Bosnia and Hercegovina and increased their activities in Croatia and Slovenia. On the Adriatic Coast they liberated Cattaro (Kotor), Ragusa (Dubrovnik), and Spalato (Split) and, on November 8, occupied the Italian town of Zara (Zadar), which would be "slavicised" by means which Hitler would not have disdained.

Churchill pressures Bulgaria

As has been mentioned, on October 4 a British airborne force had helped to liberate Patras. A few days later, other parachute forces dropped on the aerodromes at Elevsís and Mégara. On October 14, a mixed Greek and British squadron under Rear-Admiral Troubridge dropped anchor in the Piraeus and disembarked most of the British III Corps

under the command of Lieutenant-General R. M. Scobie.

This operation, code-named "Manna", had two aims. Following the terms of the armistice, the Bulgarian Government had agreed to return to the borders of April 6, 1941. But although Tito and Gheorghiev reached immediate understanding, the Bulgarian leader cherished the hope of being able to keep the Greek provinces of Western Thrace and Eastern Macedonia within Communist Bulgaria. These provinces had been granted to King Boris by Hitler. Here he thought he could count on the aid of E.L.A.S. (Greek Peoples' Liberation Army).

Communist *coup* prevented

Furthermore, General Scobie was ordered to prevent, by force if need be, the Peoples' Liberation Army from overturning the established system in Greece by absolutely unconstitutional means. The personality of the prime minister, George Papandreou, gave this régime a liberal, democratic, and social hue despite the fact that it was rabidly right-wing in its political outlook. But the possibility of

▽ *British troops approach Corinth in October 1944.*

CZECHOSLOVAKIA

Brno

4th Ukrainian Front

U.S.S.R.

2nd Ukrainian Front

3rd Ukrainian Front

Army Group "South"
8th Army

Danube
Vienna

Košice

Uzhgorod

Mukachevo

Dniestr

AUSTRIA

Miskolc

Komárom
Eger

Győr

Nyíregyháza

Debrecen

HUNGARY

Siretul

Prut

Rumanian 4th Army

Iaşi

Tiraspol

6th Army

6th Army

Graz

Budapest
Lake Velencei
Székesfehérvár

Lake Balaton

Szolnok

Karcag

Mezőtúr

Oradea

Dunaföldvár
Kecskemét

Salonta

Cluj

8th Army (Wöhler)

Huşi

Leovo

Galaţi

Rumanian 3rd Army (Dumitrescu)

Kaposvár

Csongrád

Szeged

Arad

2nd Panzerarmee

Barcs

Mohács

Pécs

Baja

Alba Iulia

Sibiu

Brasov

Army Group "South Ukraine"

Zagreb

Drava

Sava

Army Group "E"

Belgrade

RUMANIA

Bucharest

Constanţa

Fiume

YUGOSLAVIA

Turnu Severin

IRON GATES

Giurgiu

Danube

Ruse

Silistra

Varna

Zara

Spalato

Sarajevo

Užice

Višegrad

Kraljevo

Niš

Pleven

Burgas

Novi Pazar

Mitrovica

XXI Mountain Corps

XXII Mountain Corps

Bulgarian 5th Army

Sofia

Plovdiv

Ragusa

Cattaro

Scutari

Skopje

BULGARIA

Istanbul

ALBANIA

Durazzo

Tiranë

Vardar

XIC Corps
Salonika

Valona

LXVIII Corps

Metsovon

Yannina

GREECE

ITALY

TURKEY

Patrai

Megara

Athens

Corinth

Kos

Milos

Tilos

Rhodes

Crete

FRONT LINE ON AUGUST 20 1944
FRONT LINE ON OCTOBER 6
FRONT LINE ON OCTOBER 25
FRONT LINE ON NOVEMBER 25
FRONT LINE ON DECEMBER 31
2nd UKRAINIAN FRONT ATTACKS
3rd UKRAINIAN FRONT ATTACKS
4th UKRAINIAN FRONT ATTACKS
FRONT BOUNDARIES
GERMAN COUNTER-ATTACKS AND RETREATS
Crete   ISLANDS HELD BY THE GERMANS UNTIL THE END OF THE WAR
ARMY GROUP BOUNDARIES
ARMY BOUNDARIES
AXIS POCKETS
AREAS HELD BY YUGOSLAV PARTISANS IN JANUARY 1945

1896

subversion was growing day by day and, summoned by a Liberation Committee of Communist inspiration (E.A.M.), units of E.L.A.S. converged on Athens, passing the retreating Germans without clashing.

In spite of the reservations of the White House and the State Department, and the furious onslaughts of the Labour M.P.s Emmanuel Shinwell and Aneurin Bevan, the cold disapproval of *The Times* and the *Manchester Guardian*, everybody knows that Churchill did not hesitate to oppose E.L.A.S. with force, such was his fear of Communism. Nevertheless, it was the beginning of a civil war. It would be waged savagely until the day in June 1948 when the quarrel broke between Tito and Moscow. Deprived of the important aid that Tito provided, the insurrection wavered and then collapsed under the blows struck at it in the following year by Marshal Papagos.

Malinovsky slows down

Marshal Malinovsky was last seen crossing the Wallachian Carpathians and establishing his front along the Braşov–Sibiu–Alba Iulia line. Doubtless his intention was to push straight on north and to strike the German 8th Army in the rear. This German army had established itself along the Moldavian Carpathians. But Colonel-General Friessner foresaw Malinovsky's plan, and counter-attacked from near Cluj (known then as Koloszvar) in a southerly direction, with the Hungarian 2nd Army (General Veress) and III Panzer Corps (General Breith), which had just been attached to his command. He was able to pull his 8th Army out of the Szecklers salient. In spite of this, a breach was opened between the right of the Army Group "South" (ex-"South Ukraine") and the left of Army Group "F". This breach was weakly held by the Hungarian IV and VII Corps. The 6th Guards Army plunged into it and though Friessner had received five divisions as reinforcements, two from Field-Marshal von Weichs and three from O.K.H., he could not stop Malinovsky establishing himself along a line from Oradea (Nagyvárad) through Arad to Timişoara. And so, on Rumanian soil, was fought the prologue to the battle of Hungary.

The fact that, in this duel between the 2nd Ukrainian Front and the German Army Group "South", Malinovsky needed

continued on page 1900

△ *Marshall Rodion Malinovsky.*
◁ *A Soviet Frontier Post re-erected on the Rumanian border.*

▷ *A youthful member of the Waffen S.S. fires an M.G.42 machine-gun.*
▷ ▷ *A Soviet gun in action during street fighting in a Hungarian town.*
▷ ▷ ▷ *Pzkw IV and Tiger tanks of the celebrated "Grossdeutschland" division prepare a counterattack in the Lasi area of Rumania.*
▽ *Hungarian and German troops shelter in a ditch near Budapest.*
▽ ▷ *A long-barrelled Sturmgeschütz III on the Eastern Front, 1944. The German Army increasingly relied upon self-propelled guns of this type, being desperately short of main battle tanks.*

continued from page 1897

△ *With the end of the Third Reich at hand, Nazi propaganda still screamed out defiantly that "At the end stands Victory!"*

between plains and mountains composed of the following:
1. Hungarian 3rd Army (General Heszlenyi);
2. German 6th Army (General Fretter-Pico); and
3. *Armeegruppe* "Wöhler", with the Hungarian 2nd Army and the German 8th Army.

In all there were nine corps and 26 divisions or their equivalent. True, they were at half their establishment strength. But IV Panzer Corps and the 24th Panzer Division would join the force shortly.

Tank clashes

One important point was that in this force there were 14 Hungarian divisions, whose combat performance caused the commander of Army Group "South" some anxiety.

On October 6, the 2nd Ukrainian Front went over to the offensive towards the north-west and the west, and attacked Salonta and south of Arad with the 6th Guards Tank Army and the 53rd and 46th Armies, whose seven tank and mechanised corps gave considerable impetus to the attack. Under the impact, the Hungarian 3rd Army broke, confirming the most pessimistic estimates of Colonel-General Friessner. Even before night had fallen, the Russians were fanning out over the Hungarian plain, some towards Debrecen, some towards Szolnok or Szeged across the Tisza.

Yet the Soviet tanks hurled themselves ahead to exploit their success at a speed that the infantry could not match. Furthermore, the mostly treeless Hungarian plain allowed the Panzers, as in North Africa, to adopt "warship" tactics and seek out the flanks and rear of enemy columns which kept to the roads. On the outskirts of Debrecen on October 10 the 6th Guards Tank Army was trapped in such a manoeuvre by III Panzer Corps while, on its left, the Soviet 27th Army was itself violently halted in front of Mezötúr and Karcag.

This was further proof of the qualitative superiority of Germany's armoured forces, which were now called upon to perform an essentially defensive role. Despite heavy losses, and the growing realisation that the war was inevitably lost, the morale of the German Army was still holding up remarkably well.

four attempts and the aid of Tolbukhin to overcome the Axis forces, when the superiority of forces was entirely to his advantage, speaks highly for the tactical ability of the German command and the standard of training of its officers and men. At the beginning of October, with his right to the south of Timişoara and his left on the Carpathians, Colonel-General Friessner could present a line

8th Army escapes

The Soviet commander, Marshal Malinovsky took Debrecen on October 20 and thus, on the 22nd, the armoured group under General Pliev managed to thrust 47 miles into the Tokay vineyards on the left bank of the Tisza. He profited little by it, for he was caught in a pincer from the east and the west near Myregihaza.

On October 30, an O.K.W. communiqué claimed that Malinovsky had lost close on 12,000 killed and 6,662 prisoners, and suffered the destruction or capture of about 1,000 tanks and more than 900 guns. But the losses of the German 6th Army, the temporary victors, were not small. Its six Panzer divisions now had only 67 tanks and 57 assault guns.

This hard fought success was to be among the last for the German armies. Inevitably, the sheer weight of Russian numbers was to prove too much for the hard pressed Wehrmacht. Scarcity of man-power and *matériel* was an insuperable problem for the German commanders, who found that even the most limited plans were severely circumscribed by shortages of essential material, especially of engine fuel, the life-line of the Panzers.

Colonel-General Friessner, an experienced and able commander, now faced the task of re-organising the tank forces he had sacrificed, in preparation for the next Soviet assault.

It was by paying this price that Friessner had checked Malinovsky for the second time in his attempt to cut off the retreat of the German 8th Army and to drive it into a corner in the Carpathians. Now it could align itself on the west bank of the Tisza, with the 6th Army. Following hard behind it, Colonel-General Petrov's 4th Ukrainian Front penetrated the ancient Czech province of Ruthenia. On October 26, it occupied Mukachevo and the day after, Uzhgorod.

Hungarian armistice

In spite of the occupation of Hungary, Admiral Horthy had managed to maintain his secret contacts with the British and Americans. As the situation grew worse he was obliged to give way to the demands of London and Washington, who directed him towards the Soviet Union. And so,

at the end of September, Lieutenant-Marshal Farago, once a military attaché in Moscow, slipped away from the watching eye of the Gestapo and arrived in the Russian capital. He was, Horthy tells us, authorised to conclude an armistice, if possible under the following conditions:

"Immediate cessation of hostilities. The British and Americans to share in the occupation of Hungary. Unhindered re-

△ *The other side of the coin: a Russian poster bids the "Fascist rabble" a Happy New Year with the cheering thought that this last year of the war would see the Germans so hard pressed that they would not even be able to bury their dead.*

treat of German troops."

And so, on October 11, a preliminary armistice agreement received the signature of both parties. Did Stalin mean to press matters so as to place a *fait accompli* before the Western powers while Washington, through Churchill and Eden (then on a visit to Moscow), protested against being left out of the negotiations?

This is the version that Horthy gives in his memoirs. Eden's contain no suggestion of any such procedure. And Churchill, on October 12, 1944, telegraphed to his colleagues:

"As it is the Soviet armies which are obtaining control of Hungary, it would be natural that a major share of influence should rest with them, subject of course to an agreement with Great Britain and probably the United States, who, though not actually operating in Hungary, must view it as a Central European and not a Balkan State."

From this it is clear that Great Britain, and more so the United States, took little interest in the negotiations in course between Budapest and Moscow.

Meanwhile Admiral Horthy reached full agreement with the Prime Minister, Lakatos, and, at one in the afternoon of October 15, proclaimed an armistice in a broadcast over Budapest radio.

This broadcast was a complete condemnation of Hitler and his policies, and concluded:

"Today for everyone who can see plainly, Germany has lost the war. All governments responsible for the fate of their countries must draw their conclusions from this fact, for, as was said once by the great German statesman Bismarck: 'No nation is forced by its obligations to sacrifice itself on the altar of an alliance.'"

▽ *Russian armour races across the Hungarian puszta. Outnumbered and pressed steadily backwards, all that the German armoured divisions could do was to inflict the occasional heavy tactical reverses on the Russians.*

▷ *Otto Skorzeny, in the uniform of an S.S. Hauptsturmführer or Captain. It was this daring and resourceful man who had led the raid to rescue Mussolini, and he was now called upon to abduct the wavering Horthy.*

Skorzeny's raid

But the secret of the Hungarian-Soviet negotiations had leaked out and Hitler could count on the complicity of the Hungarian Nazis. Everything was ready for a strike. Led by the Ministers Rahn and Weesenmayer, the *Waffen*-S.S. General von dem Bach-Zalewski, and Colonel Skorzeny, it took place with lightning speed. Admiral Horthy was kidnapped in his mansion in Buda and taken under escort to the castle of Weilheim, close to Munich.

Major Szálasi, leader of the "Arrow Cross", was summoned to replace him, but in spite of his fanaticism and his ferocity, it was beyond his powers to breathe new life into the Hungarian Army. General Vörös, the chief-of-staff,

△ *Two Soviet infantrymen, armed with PPS M1943 sub-machine guns, cover three of their comrades during the street fighting for Budapest.*

surrendered at Malinovsky's headquarters. So did General Miklos, commander of the 1st Army and Louis Veress, the latter in the motor car which Guderian had just given him. It is interesting to note that during the rule of the "brown" quisling government in Budapest, a "red" quisling government was organised at Debrecen.

Malinovsky rolls on

The fall of Szeged around October 10 had forced Friessner to organise a defence line between the Tisza at Csongrád and the Danube at Baja, where he was in contact with Army Group "F". This sector was evidently the weakest, and thus it was here that Malinovsky transferred his 6th Guards Tank Army. On October 29, the 6th reopened the offensive. Its attack was directed on the Hungarian 3rd Army, which broke like a reed and opened the road to Budapest to three Soviet tank corps. In one single movement, they reached Kecskemét, only 40 miles from the capital.

But Friessner and Fretter-Pico did not lose a moment in preparing their defence.

In the Budapest bridgeheads III Panzer Corps repelled the attackers and, at the same time, the *"Feldherrnhalle" Panzergrenadier* Division (Colonel Pape) with the four Panzer divisions of LVII Panzer Corps (General Kirchner) caught the enemy columns in the flank as they moved out of Cegléd. The Russians were better organised than before, and held their ground everywhere except between Debrecen and Nyiregyháza. Moreover, the defection of the Hungarian troops in the centre and on the left of the German 6th Army allowed them to obtain several bridgeheads on the west bank of the Tisza. Even so, Malinovsky had to regroup his forces for the drive which, he hoped, would finish the business.

Germans exhausted

The Germans were nearing the end of their tether. There were very few infantry battalions which could muster 200 men. The Panzer divisions, so essential for counter-attack, were no longer more than a shadow of what they had been. The consequences of an insufficient inspection and test programme at the end of the factory assembly-lines were mechanical defects which became more and more frequent in the new machines reaching the front. So the number of tanks available to each division daily was no more than five or six.

Even though it is true that the losses of the 2nd Ukrainian Front since October 6 had not been light, it still maintained an enormous numerical and *matériel* advantage over its adversary.

Faced with this situation, Hitler agreed to send three new Panzer divisions into Hungary. These were the 3rd, 6th, and 8th Panzer Divisions. He also sent three battalions of Panther tanks. But while waiting for these reinforcements to be put into line, Army Group "South" had to fall back from the Tisza above Tokay and dig in on the heights of the Mátra mountains, overlooking Hatvan, Eger, and Miskolc. It had to limit its counter-attacks to local actions only, as a result of the previously mentioned exhaustion of its men and equipment. And so the curtain fell on the third act of this tragedy, the overall direction of which was assumed by Marshal Timoshenko in the name of the *Stavka*.

6th Army forced back by Tolbukhin

The curtain rose again on November 27 with the appearance on the stage of the forces of the 3rd Ukrainian Front, available now that Belgrade had surrendered. On that day, Marshal Tolbukhin unexpectedly forced the Danube at Mohacs. This was 125 miles up river from Belgrade past the confluence of the Drava and the Danube. Brushing aside the weak defences of the 2nd *Panzerarmee*, his 57th Army swept along a line from Pécs to Kaposvár and, by December 5, called a halt after an advance of 75 miles between the south-west tip of Lake Balaton and the River Drava at Barcs.

On December 3, on Tolbukhin's right, the 3rd Guards Army arrived at Duna-földvár, 60 miles north of Mohacs. As a result, in order to avoid its right being rolled up, the German 6th Army could only pull back along a line Lake Balaton–Lake Velencei–Budapest.

Tolbukhin's advance northward allowed his partner Malinovsky to re-arrange his deployment yet again. At the foot of the Mátra mountains, he built up a strategic battering-ram, with the Pliev Group and the 6th Guards Tank Army. Near Hatvan on December 7, the exhausted German 6th Army broke under the force of the attack launched by the Russians and, several days later, Pliev reached the elbow formed by the Danube above the Hungarian capital and could now bring the strings of barges which supplied it under the fire of his artillery. Furthermore, between the Danube and the Mátra mountains, on December 14, Soviet armour captured Ypolisag. And so the Russians had almost completely out-flanked the right of the 8th Army, and were once more threatening to hem it in against the Carpathians.

Last desperate effort

However the 8th Panzer Division, newly arrived, was immediately put under the command of LVII Panzer Corps, and this formation kept disaster at bay. Friessner would have liked to reinforce Kirchner with the 3rd and the 6th Panzer Divisions, which had just been stationed on the isthmus which separates Lakes Balaton and Velencei. If they hurried, he maintained, there was a great opportunity to crush the 6th Guards Tank Army, which was in a salient around Ypolisag. When Hitler received this proposal, he ordered Friessner to attack from the isthmus between the two lakes and to throw Tolbukhin back to the Danube. To which the commander of Army Group "South" retorted that the state of the ground between Lake Balaton and the Danube, after long weeks of sleet and rain, was absolutely impassable.

Wrong compromise

Guderian forced a very poor compromise in this dispute on December 18: the *Führerbefehl* would be carried out when frost had hardened the ground. Meanwhile, the 3rd and 6th Panzer Divisions would cross the Danube at Komarom, carry out Friessner's proposed counter-attack, but leave their tank battalions behind. In vain did Friessner protest that this plan would deprive them of their entire striking power. He was told that he should either obey or resign.

△ △ △ *The pale light of dawn: the Hun surveys the empty seats of the Axis defaulters.*
△ △ *Stalin's lengthening shadow in the south, from the* London Punch.
△ *A "family scene in Central Europe", from the* London Star. *"It's nothing, mother," says Hungary. "I'm opening a second front with Rumania."*

△ A scene typical of the street fighting in which the Russians took Budapest street by street, house by house, reducing it virtually to rubble in the process. Note the "dragon's teeth" anti-tank obstacles in the background.

This is the version that Friessner gives of this episode, and Guderian's silence on it seems to indicate that he agrees.

Tolbukhin's advantage

Forty-eight hours later, Tolbukhin was attacking the sector between the Danube and Lake Balaton defended by III Panzer and LXXII Corps (General August Schmidt) of the 6th Army. In front of him roved a first echelon of about ten divisions which, very cleverly, moved along the roads impassable to tanks because of the soft terrain. Between the river and Lake Velencei, the 217th *Volksgrenadier* Division was crushed on the first day. Between Lake Velencei and Lake Balaton, the 153rd Infantry Division and the 1st and 23rd Panzer Divisions defended the little mediaeval town of Székesfehérvár to the end, without the tanks held in reserve by Guderian's express order being of any help to them. By December 24, all was over and the Kremlin communiqué claimed that the Germans had lost 12,000 dead, 5,468 prisoners, 311 tanks, and 248 guns destroyed or captured.

On the same day Tolbukhin launched his armoured formations through this gap, now over 40 miles wide. On December 27, after an excursion of 55 miles through the rearguard of the Army Group "South", they occupied Esztergom on the right bank of the Danube and, from the other side of the river, recognised the 6th Guards Tank Army that LVII Panzer Corps had been quite unable to dislodge.

"Fortress" Budapest under siege

On December 1, the Führer had proclaimed that the Hungarian capital was a "fortress". This took it out of the authority of Army Group "South". The garrison consisted of the S.S. IX Mountain Corps (General Pfeffer-Wildenbruch). When Friessner realised that the 3rd Ukrainian Front was attacking, he wanted to take it in flank by a counter-attack with this corps, but the manoeuvre would involve the evacuation of Budapest. So, on the night of December 22/23, Friessner was relieved and ordered to hand over to General Wöhler. Fretter-Pico shared his disgrace.

Two S.S. cavalry divisions, the 13th Panzer Division, and the *"Feldherrnhalle" Panzergrenadier* Division were thus caught in the trap. Having got them cut off, Hitler now had to get them out, so without consulting O.K.H., he robbed Army Group "Centre", which was responsible for the defence of East Prussia. He took IV S.S. Panzer Corps (General Gille: 3rd *"Totenkopf"* Panzer Division and 5th *"Wiking"* Panzer Division) and sent them over the Carpathians. This order was made on Christmas Day, and, though Guderian tried to have the units recalled, he wrote:

"All my protests were useless. Hitler thought it was more important to free the city of Budapest than to defend Eastern Germany."

All the same, Hitler was acting more logically than Guderian gives him credit for. The day before, while Guderian tried to draw Hitler's attention to the increasing number of signs pointing to a coming Soviet offensive between the Carpathians and the Niemen, the Führer had riposted:

"Now, my dear General, I do not believe in this Russian attack. It is all a gigantic bluff. The figures produced by your 'Foreign Armies: East' section are far too exaggerated. You worry too much. I am firmly convinced that nothing will happen in the East."

Obsession with the Soviet threat could deceive Major-General Gehlen, head of "Foreign Armies: East" of O.K.H.; it could even impress Colonel-General Guderian. But it had no effect on the far-sightedness and *sang froid* of the Führer!

CHAPTER 131
Eisenhower slows down

On the eve of the German offensive in the Ardennes it was possible to discern on the Allied side a certain degree of frustration similar to that prevailing in Britain and America immediately before the breakthrough at Avranches.

On September 15, victory seemed to be close at hand. Three months later, General Eisenhower could indeed claim to have liberated Mulhouse, Belfort, Strasbourg, and Metz, to have taken Aix-la-Chapelle (Aachen), cleared Antwerp and the Scheldt estuary, and taken more than 150,000 prisoners. Nevertheless, on December 15 the Rhine bridges and Ruhr basin were, if anything, further away from the Allied armies than at the end of the summer. It was clear to everyone that between the present positions and the final objective, there would be more major battles; however, no one suspected that the first would be a defensive one.

The slowing down of the Allied thrust can be explained by a combination of factors: the weather, the terrain, the degrees of determination shown and decisions made by commanders on both sides of a front line that ran from the Swiss frontier to the North Sea. As far as the weather was concerned, persistent rain fell throughout the latter part of the summer and the autumn of 1944, so much so that during the Ardennes offensive Patton required his chaplain to write a prayer for fine weather. The unseasonable climate and the shorter days resulted in a disastrous drop in the number of sorties effected by the tactical air forces in support of the infantry. The figures below relating to the American 3rd Army are typical of the whole front:

August	12,292 missions	(396 per day)
September	7,791 missions	(260 per day)
October	4,790 missions	(154 per day)
November	3,509 missions	(117 per day)
December (1–22)	2,563 missions	(116 per day)

Knowing the use made of their "flying artillery" by the Allies in the battle of Normandy, it is not surprising that such a reduction told heavily on the Allied advance. Furthermore, the terrain was

▽ *Eisenhower, already short of men and supplies, was now further slowed in developing his broad-front offensive towards Germany by the torrential rain and resultant mud that characterised the autumn of 1944.*

now one of forest and mountain, country well-suited to a defensive strategy, in the sense that lines of attack were pressed into comparatively few axes that were easy to block. The Vosges, Hunsrück, and Eifel were such regions, and, in addition, their vast forests made aerial reconnaissance virtually impossible and reduced considerably the feasibility of air support. On the plains of Lorraine, the defence made good use of flooded rivers as natural obstacles, as well as of the system of fortifications round Metz and Thionville. The Roer and the *Westwall* system fulfilled the same rôle in the Aix-la-Chapelle (Aachen) sector.

The British and Canadians soon found themselves obliged to mount amphibious operations.

Manpower shortages

As regards strategic factors behind the hold-up, it should be remarked that in Washington General Marshall had been somewhat over-stringent in calculating the numbers to allocate to American ground forces, and that Eisenhower now found himself short of divisions, although it had seemed improbable that after two months of movement and retreat the enemy would manage to establish himself on a continuous front of some 500 miles,

and thwart some 60 Allied divisions in their hopes of achieving a decisive breakthrough. In these circumstances, the Pentagon was obliged to turn various anti-aircraft units into infantry units, but the inactivity of the Luftwaffe caused no problem here.

Even so, at the time of transferring S.H.A.E.F. from Granville to Versailles, Eisenhower would have been somewhat embarrassed if a miracle had brought him the 30 additional divisions he needed to return to the attack. As it was, the logistic problem of keeping 60 divisions in the field was a major problem for the Allied planners.

The Allied commanders disagree over aims

Clearance of the approaches to Antwerp enabled the Allies to end the vicious circle, although it took Field-Marshal Montgomery one whole month to achieve this; and during the delay two divergent operations, in flagrant disregard of the "concerted thrust" which Montgomery had urged, took place. While the British 2nd Army, its right flank at Grave on the Maas, its left at Eindhoven, mounted an attack north-west towards Tilburg and Breda, the American 1st and 9th Armies

▽ *Japanese American infantry of the 2nd Battalion, 442nd Combat Team, move up a muddy French road towards their bivouac area. At the beginning of the war American Japanese were distrusted by the government and most of the population of the United States, but later on, Japanese units serving in the European theatre proved to be loyal and efficient combat troops.*

were trying to breach the *Westwall* in the Aix-la-Chapelle (Aachen) sector, with the aim of reaching the Rhine below Cologne.

Obviously, Eisenhower's task was not an easy one. To appease Patton, he organised an American 9th Army on September 5 under the command of Lieutenant-General William H. Simpson, with the immediate objective of taking Brest. Once this fortress had fallen, the 9th Army was shifted to the Ardennes front, then on October 23, to the left of the 1st Army, with which it participated in the November offensive on the *Westwall*. Coming under General Bradley's command, it provided the link with the British and Canadian 21st Army Group.

On September 15, at Vittel, Lieutenant-General Jacob L. Devers assumed command of a new Allied 6th Army Group, directly subordinate to S.H.A.E.F. and responsible for the conduct of operations between Epinal and the Swiss frontier. In the course of these changes, Army Detachment "B" was designated as French 1st Army on September 19. Then, to give Generals Patch and de Lattre homogeneous sectors, the French II and American VI Corps were interchanged. On September 29 General Patton was ordered to hand his XV Corps over to the American 7th Army.

Such was the disposition of the Allied armies in preparation for the autumn campaign.

The German forces

On September 4, when Hitler relieved Field-Marshal von Rundstedt as Commander-in-Chief in the West, a document prepared at O.K.W. gave the following situation for the German Army on the Western Front.

	Infantry divisions	Panzer divisions
Completely fit	13	3 (+ 2 brigades)
Partially fit	12	2 (+ 2 brigades)
Totally unfit	14	7
Dissolved	7	–
In process of reorganisation	9	2

Hence Rundstedt was faced with the task of giving battle with 30 divisions (five of them Panzer), these to be joined by 11 divisions being reorganised, thus enabling those qualified as "totally unfit" to be pulled back. Furthermore, Hitler intended to despatch 28 further divisions to the West, these being 28 of the 43 "people's grenadier divisions" *(Volks-grenadierdivisionen),* which Himmler, as commander of the reserves, was hastily preparing for the line. Their standard of training was very poor, their complement was on the small side (10,000 to 12,000), and their equipment was inferior.

Lieutenant-General William "Big Bill" Simpson graduated from the same class at West Point Military Academy as Patton and Hodges in 1909. The three officers served together in World War I and remained life-long friends. Simpson took over command of the 9th Army on September 5, 1944 and led the army in the American counter-offensive after the Ardennes. 9th Army's assault over the Roer was the last American set-piece assault in Europe. Eisenhower described Simpson as a man "who never made a mistake".

The German *Panzerjäger* Panther or *Jagdpanther* tank destroyer

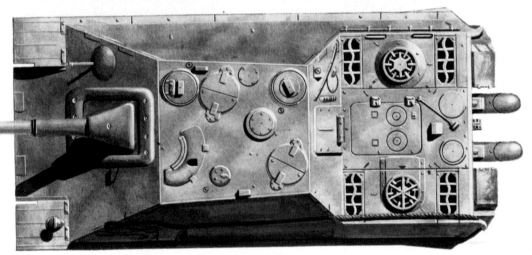

Weight: 46 tons.
Crew: 5.
Armament: one 8.8-cm PaK 43/3 gun with
60 rounds and one 7.92-mm MG 34
machine gun with 600 rounds.
Armour: hull nose 60-mm, front plate
80-mm, upper sides 50-mm, lower sides,
hull rear, and superstructure 40-mm,
decking 17-mm, belly 15-mm, and mantlet
120-mm.
Engine: one Maybach HL 230 P30 inline,
700-hp.
Speed: 28 mph on roads, 15 mph
cross-country.
Range: 100 miles on roads, 50 miles
cross-country.
Length: 33 feet 3 inches.
Width: 10 feet 10 inches.
Height: 8 feet 11 inches.

In addition, three more Panzer brigades were assigned to Rundstedt, each of them comprising a battalion of 68 Panthers. At the same time, ten assault gun brigades, several *Nebelwerfer* brigades, and ten battalions of anti-tank vehicles, some of them equipped with the new and devastating *"Jagdpanther"*, were sent to him. By sacrificing the fully traversing turret, this vehicle combined in its 46 tons the speed of a Panther with the fire-power of a *"Königstiger"*, with an 8.8-cm, 71-calibre gun.

In fact, there was no shortage of new *matériel* in the arsenals of the Third Reich. While it was perfectly true that, at the front, Army Group "B" could only muster 100 operational tanks, factory production during the summer, in spite of air raids, totalled 1,500. At Dompaire, on September 16, it was estab-

lished that some of the tanks belonging to the 112th Panzer Brigade, demolished by the French 2nd Armoured Division, bore the manufacturing date of August 15. At Friesen on November 23, *Jagdpanthers* which were roughly handled by the French 5th Armoured Division during General de Lattre's offensive in upper Alsace, had left Nuremberg only 12 days previously.

Rundstedt's objective

"I must hold on for six weeks," Rundstedt wrote on September 7, 1944 in his first report to O.K.W. But if fortune denied General Weygand the 11-day respite he sought on June 4, 1940, a pause in the fighting of 65 days was granted to

△ *Sherman tank crews of the American 3rd Armoured Division wait at the edge of a forest for their attack to begin. Allied tanks were completely outclassed by such German vehicles as the Jagdpanther, their only advantage being the extra manoeuvrability bestowed on them by powerful engines and low weight.*

"I insist upon the importance of Antwerp... I am prepared to give you everything for the capture of the approaches to Antwerp"

Eisenhower

Walcheren in 1944 was to the British an ill-starred place: in 1809 a landing on the island had met with total disaster, and now in the autumn of World War II it was the final obstacle to the opening of the Scheldt estuary and the port of Antwerp. The Allies had cleared the rest of the estuary, and advanced the 157th Brigade as far as the causeway linking Zuid-Beveland with Walcheren. But the defences of the island, entrusted to the 70th Division, looked formidable, with some 50 7.5- to 22-cm guns and nearly 10,000 men. Rather than launch a frontal attack, 21st Army Group decided that bombers should blow breaches in the sea walls to flood the centre of the island, and then the 155th Brigade should cross from Bres-

kens to land in Flushing while the 4th Special Service Brigade made a landing at Westkapelle.

The operation proved difficult but straightforward. Bombers blew open two breaches in the sea defences on the south-west side of the island and one each on the north-east and south-east sides, flooding most of the interior of the island with the exception of the town of Middelburg. The landings went in with heavy gun-fire and air support at about dawn, and soon took Westkapelle and Flushing, the last resistance in the latter ending on November 4. Meanwhile the "rim" of the Walcheren "saucer" had been secured, and the Allies pushed on to Middelburg, where General Daser surrendered with his last 2,000 men on the 6th.

3

4

1. Rescue for men from a landing craft sunk on the approach to Walcheren.
2. An American light tank is swayed ashore at Antwerp, a vast port just behind the Allied front line.
3. Walcheren: a dismal spot, but one of the keys to the port of Antwerp.
4. American patrol boats in the Scheldt estuary.
5. The Walcheren landings.

▷ *French infantry advance with tank support through a forest in Alsace.*
▽ *A Polish Bren gunner prepares to give covering fire during the battle for Breda in Holland.*
▽▷ *Cromwell cruiser tanks of the Polish 1st Armoured Division move up past a Dutch windmill.*

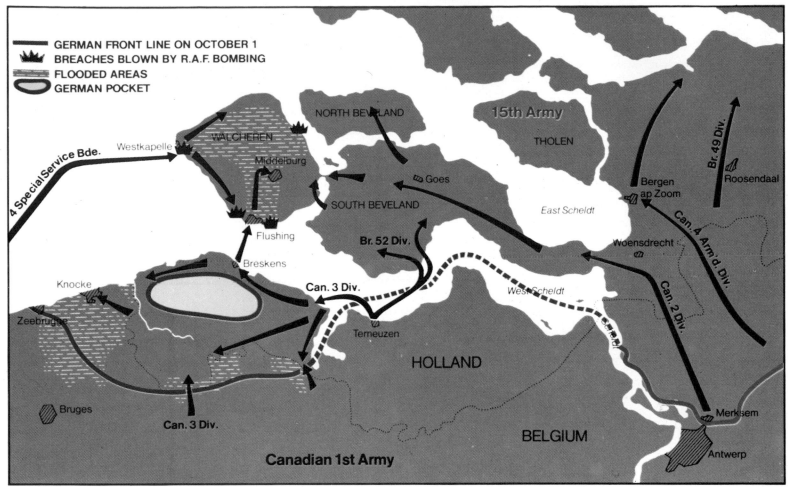

Rundstedt, General Bradley being unable to unleash his armies in the drive for the Saar and the Ruhr until November 8.

On October 1 or thereabouts, O.B.W. was responsible for 41 infantry divisions and ten Panzer or *Panzergrenadier* divisions. On November 26, according to O.K.W. records, these figures were 49 and 14 respectively. Even granted that most of these units were below strength, the effort implicit here in relation to the tricky situation of September 6 was remarkable.

After Arnhem, Rundstedt had two army groups under his command:

1. Army Group "B", in position between the estuary of the Scheldt to a point south of Trier (Treves), still under the command of Field-Marshal Model, Rundstedt's predecessor as Commander-in-Chief in the West.

Under Model's command were the 15th Army (General von Zangen), whose task was to prevent the enemy obtaining access to the Scheldt estuary; the 1st Parachute Army (Colonel-General Student), at the head of the Arnhem salient between the Tilburg and Venlo areas; and the 7th Army, blocking the way to Cologne,

△ An American Gun Motor Carriage M12, a 155-mm "Long Tom" gun on a Sherman chassis, in action near the Moselle. Note the crewman in the foreground with his hands over his ears to avoid concussion, the firer at left holding the lanyard in his right hand, the gun at full recoil, and the spade at the rear of the vehicle dug into the ground to help take up some of the recoil.
▷ An American Sherman blasts a German strongpoint.

Koblenz and Trier, with, at its head, General Brandenberger, who had succeeded General Eberbach when the latter was taken prisoner at Amiens.

2. The area from south of Trier to the Swiss frontier was the responsibility of Army Group "G". On Hitler's orders, Colonel-General Blaskowitz had handed over command on September 22 to General Balck, whose record on the Russian front was a distinguished one. Army Group "G" consisted of the 1st Army, command of which had been assumed by General Schmidt von Knobelsdorff, who had made a name for himself at the head of XLVIII Panzer Corps, on September 6, with the task of blocking the route to Saarbrücken from a point north of Thionville to the Château Salins region; the 5th *Panzerarmee* (General von Manteuffel replacing the wounded General Hausser), blocking the way to Strasbourg from positions in front of the Vosges between Château Salins and Saint Dié; and the 19th Army (General Wiese) holding a position on the upper Moselle and defending the Belfort gap on the Doubs above Montbéliard.

Hitler's grandiose scheme

But the idea of a large-scale and decisive counter-offensive was already in the Führer's mind. As early as September 1, realising the Allies' logistic problems, he urged O.B.W. to hurl the 5th *Panzerarmee* from the Nancy–Neufchâteau area on

▽ *American self-propelled 155-mm guns start their barrage against the* Westwall. *Note that the front of each vehicle has been driven onto a ramp, to allow the guns a higher elevation and hence greater range.*

△ The Allied advance continues: an American Sherman about to cross the Moselle by means of a pontoon bridge. With a few notable exceptions, such as Remagen, the Germans demolished all the bridges they left behind very efficiently. It is greatly to their credit that the Allied engineers managed to bridge the gaps thus left with great speed. It is worth noting, however, that the size and weight restrictions of the standard Allied bridges were to a certain extent responsible for the design of the small, light tanks that proved so inferior to their German counterparts.

Rheims with a view to cutting the American 3rd Army's lines of communication. The scheme was a hopeless one and its failure brought about Blaskowitz's disgrace.

On September 19, Hitler's strategic reflections bore fruit again. He summoned General Balck, commander designate of Army Group "G", and Major-General von Mellenthin, his chief-of-staff, and, in Mellenthin's words, gave them the following appreciation of the situation: "According to the Führer, the British and American advance would come to a standstill on a line running from the mouths of the Scheldt, along the *Westwall* as far as Metz and from there along the Vosges. Supply problems would force the enemy to halt, and Hitler declared that he would make use of this pause to launch a counter-offensive in Belgium. He spoke of mid-November as the proper moment for such an operation."

The longer nights and late autumn mists would provide cover from Allied air reconnaissance and allow the plans to be prepared and carried out, and Hitler had taken the steps of ordering the formation of a 6th *Panzerarmee,* under the command of Colonel-General Sepp Dietrich of the *Waffen*-S.S., and of fetching the May 1940 *"Fall Gelb"* dossier from the archives.

On September 22, while the Battle of Arnhem was at its height, Eisenhower

telegraphed Montgomery as follows: "I insist upon the importance of Antwerp. As I have told you I am prepared to give you everything for the capture of the approaches to Antwerp, including all the air forces and anything else you can support. Warm regard. Ike." The note of urgency detectable here would seem to suggest that Montgomery was so taken up with the vision of a lightning breakthrough towards Westphalia that he had come to give secondary consideration to Eisenhower's orders for the capture of Antwerp. However, failure at Arnhem made Montgomery more prepared to listen to Eisenhower, who this time offered him not only the air strength promised on September 22 but also the American 7th Armoured and 104th Divisions to strengthen the right flank of the 21st Army Group, and free British and Canadian troops for the clearing of the Scheldt. However, not until October 16, did Montgomery give clear and overriding priority to his commanding General's repeated requests for action. But as September was drawing to a close, the German 15th Army, consisting of three corps (seven divisions), had had time to take up strong defensive positions and, even more important, recover morale, which had been badly shaken over the previous weeks.

"When they have taken the Scheldt fortifications, the British will then be able to unload enormous quantities of *matériel* in a large and perfectly protected harbour. With this *matériel* they could deal a deadly blow to the northern German plains and to Berlin before the onset of winter . . . The German people are watching us. At this moment the Scheldt fortifications play a crucial part in our future. Every day in which we can deny access to the port of Antwerp to the enemy and his resources could be vital."

The fighting that followed was thus very bitter. With General Crerar ill, Lieutenant-General Simonds led the Canadian 1st Army's attack. In the first phase, the British I Corps (Lieutenant-General Crocker) moved northwards from Antwerp, and on October 10 closed the Woensdrecht isthmus giving access to the island of Zuid-Beveland, but only with heavy losses. Meanwhile, the Canadian II Corps (Major-General Foulkes) set about cleaning up the bridgehead, where the Germans had been able to hold on, with the help of flooding, between Knocke and a point opposite Terneuzen. This took three weeks (October 6-26), even though two and subsequently three divisions were ranged against the single 64th Division. According to Major Shulman of Canadian Army Intelligence, the German division put up "an admirable piece of defensive fighting.

"Utilising their experience to the full, they took advantage of the flooded terrain in which they fought and forced the Canadians to rely on the narrow roads and dykes for their forward movement. The morale of the defenders heightened with each day they continued to resist, and General Eberding succeeded in instilling in his troops that will to fight which had been lacking in the Channel ports." Breskens, opposite Flushing (Vlissingen) fell on October 22, and on November 1 Eberding was taken prisoner.

On October 22, the left flank of the British 2nd Army (XII Corps) attacked from east to west towards 's Hertogenbosch and Tilburg on a line converging with that taken by the Canadian right flank's thrust towards Breda. A second pincer movement from Woensdrecht and Terneuzen gave Zuid-Beveland to General Simonds on October 31. There remained Walcheren.

The centre of the island is below sea level and the breaching of the sea-dykes (effected with 1,263 tons of bombs) gave it the look of a saucer filled with water,

△ *U.S. infantry advance into the suburbs of Metz.*
◁ *An American bazooka team waits on the Dutch-German border for Panzer prey. The punch of the bazooka was so great that many German tank commanders who had had their vehicles knocked out by one of them thought they had been hit by a 6-inch shell.*

with the defending troops clinging to the rim. These were men of the 70th Division (Lieutenant-General Daser), nicknamed the "White Bread Division", since it comprised men on a special diet for medical reasons.

The Allied assault on Walcheren

▽ An American M10 tank destroyer in action in the streets of Aix-la-Chapelle. The M10 stemmed from the realisation early in the war that towed anti-tank guns would not be able to keep up with armoured formations, which nevertheless needed anti-tank protection. The 3-inch gun had a performance equal to that of the British 17-pounder and German 7.5-cm KwK 42, and was fitted in a new turret on the Sherman chassis. Production started in September 1942.

On November 1, with a sustained barrage of covering fire provided by the battleship *Warspite* and the monitors *Erebus* and *Roberts,* a brigade of Royal Marines landed at Westkapelle, while the British 52nd Division (Major-General E. Hakewill Smith) crossed the Scheldt between Breskens and Flushing. On November 3, resistance on the island was broken. Mopping up operations were completed on November 9, with the capture of Daser. In the meantime, Zangen, assisted by dreadful weather, had succeeded in putting the width of the lower Maas between his troops and the Canadian 1st Army.

It cost the Allies 12,873 casualties altogether to clear Antwerp, many of whom were Canadians; they took 41,043 prisoners. From November 3 on, minesweepers went to work to clear the channel, and on the 28th the first convoy berthed in the great port, though on the previous day V-2s had claimed their first military and civil victims there.

But by then, two months had elapsed since the opportunity to take Antwerp on September 4 had occurred, and one is inclined to endorse Jacques Mordal's conclusion on the subject: "Allowing for 40,000 tons a day, the two months lost represented *matériel* amounting to 2,400,000 tons which, if supplied at the time required, would certainly have cost the Allies fewer disappointments in October. And possibly some might have been spared altogether if the people at S.H.A.E.F. had paid more heed to Admiral Ramsay, when he declared that he could think of nothing more vital than Operation 'Infatuate', the capture of Antwerp."

The whole episode illustrated how important it was for commanders to realise the central role that logistics played in modern warfare.

Struggle for the *Westwall*

Bradley's 12th Army Group was restricted operationally in October and November as a result of the continued serious shortage of fuel and munitions.

As we have seen, on the express instructions of Eisenhower, the American 3rd Army was especially hard hit in this respect. And the 1st Army, to which General Bradley, acting on instructions, had given priority treatment, faced the *Westwall* and found itself attacking the Germans at their strongest points, since Hitler, Rundstedt, and Model were quite prepared to pay any price to block the principal route through to Cologne and the Ruhr.

So it was that the October battle for the *Westwall* took on the aspect of an "updated version of the Battle of the Somme" as foreseen by General Gamelin at the time of Munich. The attack was launched on October 8 on a five-mile front. Entrusted to the American XIX Corps (Major-General Corlett: 30th Infantry and 2nd Armoured Divisions), the attack was opened and supported by 372 105- to 240-mm guns and 396 twin-engined bombers and fighter-bombers, while 1,250 four-engined bombers operating on the edge of the sector pounded rail junctions and marshalling yards at Kassel, Hamm, and Cologne.

The attack proceeded slowly across the Wurm which, in the vicinity of Maastricht, constitutes the Dutch-German frontier. In five days, Corlett advanced five miles against the German defences. However, this somewhat moderate success enabled General Hodges, commander of the 1st Army, to push his VII Corps (Major-General J. L. Collins) south-east, and by reaching Stolberg on October 10, he managed to complete the encirclement of Aachen, which had been started in September. The town, with its 4,000 defenders, was reduced by the 1st Division after a week's street fighting.

On the same date, the American 1st Army announced that it had taken 10,000 prisoners since D-Day. During the same period, it had fired more than 300,000 105- and 155-mm shells, but the munitions crisis now forced it to call a halt.

The 3rd Army, reduced to XII and XX Corps, was marking time in front of Metz. On the right, XII Corps advanced from the area of Grand Couronné to the Seille above and below Nomény; on the left, XX Corps had reached the Moselle between Metz and Thionville, but in the centre its repeated attempts to take *"Kronprinz"* fort, commanding the Nancy–Metz road at Ars-sur-Moselle, failed in spite of the use of napalm, flame-throwers, and machine guns. Detachments of the 5th Division which had found their way into its galleries were finally thrown back with heavy losses.

Montgomery or Bradley

On October 18, Eisenhower held a conference in Montgomery's headquarters in Brussels. The object of this meeting was to settle the strategic decisions which had to be taken before winter. No one favoured a defensive strategy, but there was disagreement between Montgomery, who still urged a single thrust aimed at the Ruhr, and Bradley, who wanted a simultaneous thrust whereby the 3rd Army would be hurled at Mannheim and Frankfurt and the 9th at Cologne. In support of his thesis, Bradley put forward these arguments which convinced Eisenhower:

"My reasoning on the *double* thrust was quite simple. Were Eisenhower to concentrate his November offensive

△ *Lieutenant-General Courtney Hodges, whose 1st Army took Aix-la-Chapelle (Aachen)—the first city of the Third Reich to fall to the Western Allies.*
▽ *American half-tracks and trucks await orders to move forward into Germany.*

north of the Ardennes, the enemy could also concentrate his defences there the better to meet that single attack. On the other hand, if we were to split our effort into a double thrust with one pincer toward Frankfurt, we might both confound the enemy and make better use of the superior mobility of our Armies. Patton had the most at stake for if Montgomery's views were to prevail, Third Army would be consigned to the defensive south of the Ardennes and there perhaps wait out the war behind the Moselle River. Could not those divisions be better employed against the Saar, I asked S.H.A.E.F.?"

The northern attack got under way on November 16, and met only qualified success, although Generals Hodges (1st Army) and Simpson (9th Army) had engaged 14, and subsequently 17 divisions, including four armoured. On October 20, however, the 5th *Panzerarmee*

took up position between Brandenberger's right and Student's left. Consequently the defence gave ground, but held seven miles further back.

On December 10, a S.H.A.E.F. communiqué announced that between Düren and Linnich all resistance on the left bank of the Roer had stopped: this put the Americans within 25 miles of Cologne, but the communiqué failed to mention that the crossing of the Roer depended on a condition that had not been fulfilled. The American V Corps, attacking upstream, had not, in spite of repeated efforts, succeeded in taking the Roer and Erft dams. And, according to calculations made at General Bradley's headquarters, if the Germans were to breach these dams, an expanse of water, approximately 1½ miles wide with a maximum depth of more than 25 feet, would form for a few days near Düren, effectively halting the Allied advance.

▽ *French M5 General Stuart light tanks during the liberation of Huningue on the Franco-Swiss frontier. The white cross on the water tower in the background indicates that it is in neutral Switzerland.*

The German Pzkw VI Tiger II heavy tank

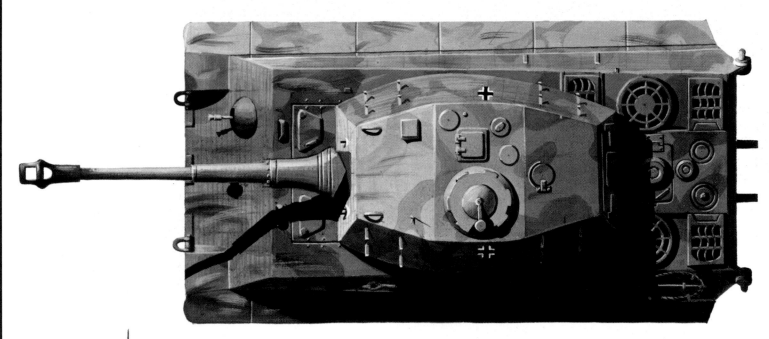

Weight: 68.65 tons.
Crew: 5.
Armament: one 8.8-cm KwK 43 gun with 80 rounds, plus one 7.92-mm MG 42 and two 7.92-mm MG 34 machine guns with 5,850 rounds.
Armour: hull front 100-mm, sides and rear 80-mm, and belly 40-mm; superstructure front 150-mm, sides and rear 80-mm, and decking 40-mm; turret front 185-mm, sides and rear 80-mm and roof 40-mm.
Engine: one Maybach HL 230 P30 inline, 600-hp.
Speed: 25.7 mph on roads and 12 mph cross-country.
Range: 106 miles on roads and 75 miles cross-country.
Length: 33 feet 8 inches.
Width: 12 feet 3⅝ inches with battle tracks, 10 feet 8¾ inches with narrow tracks.
Height: 10 feet 1⅝ inches.

This is America..

...where men have left their peacetime jobs to defend the liberties that are their birthright, where the might of a free people is marching toward victory ★ This is your America

...Keep it Free!

The internees: ordeal of the civilians

Many factors made World War II a total war. There was the very *extent* of the conflict – from the Volga to the Channel, from the Sahara to the North Cape, from India to Hawaii, and from the Aleutian Islands to Australia. There was the tremendous impact of aerial bombardment. And there was the unholy partnership between modern technology and primeval hatreds which produced the Nazi genocide programme. All this was on an unprecedented scale and out of all proportion to anything seen in previous wars. But one aspect of World War II was not new. This was the fate of the age-old victims of any war: the civilians betrayed by the failure of politicians in peacetime and caught up by the clash of armies in war.

Until World War I the fate of civilians in war had not varied much. There was conscription and rising prices and falling amounts of food and other

supplies. Civilians in occupied territory would get plundered by the armies of both sides whenever they marched through, and made to suffer for the work of compatriot resistance groups. But in general the civilians remained essentially localised in the countries of their birth until the floodgates of emigration were lifted in the 19th Century – and the first major sifting of the population of the world began.

There were German and Russian Jews in Britain and France, and British and French governesses in Germany and Russia. The United States, with a ravenous labour market, took in practically every nationality in Europe like a parched sponge. But at the same time the new emergent nations were creating a fierce new awareness of national patriotism which was poles apart from this new intermingling. As the 20th Century began, and international tension built up

towards the explosion of 1914, the "foreigner within the gate" took on a new and more ominous significance. And during World War I the inevitable results occurred. Deliberately-inspired hate campaigns ended up with completely innocent foreigners being beaten up and having their shop windows smashed by loyalist mobs.

The Armistice of 1918 did not lay the ghost of nationalist hatred. Far from it. The story of the territorial grievances outstanding from the end of World War I have already been told, together with the grim events in the 1920s and 1930s, from the French occupation of the Ruhr to the end of the Spanish Civil War. Germany, spared from war by Anglo-French inertia, buckled down to the task of expelling or incarcerating her Jewish population. Millions died in Russia during Stalin's purges. In the Far East the

1. *A promise not always kept. Thousands of loyal Americans were rounded up and interned on account of their original nationality.*
2. *Japanese fishermen and cotton planters put behind bars as soon as the news of Pearl Harbor came in.*

decades-old Sino-Japanese conflict broke out again and the martyrdom of the Chinese people began. By the outbreak of the European conflict in September 1939 the nationalist tensions of 1914 had been not only intensified but enlarged onto a far wider canvas.

To start with the tempo of civilian internment was slow. The tensions of August 1939 had been obvious to all and the number of German, French,

3. *The phobia of "the enemy within."*
4. *Japanese aliens in California.*
5. *and* 6. *Internment camp for aliens at Fort Meade, Maryland – complete with watch-towers and sentinels.*

LOOK WHO'S Listening

THIS POSTER IS PUBLISHED BY THE HOUSE OF SEAGRAM AS PART OF ITS CONTRIBUTION TO THE NATIONAL VICTORY EFFORT

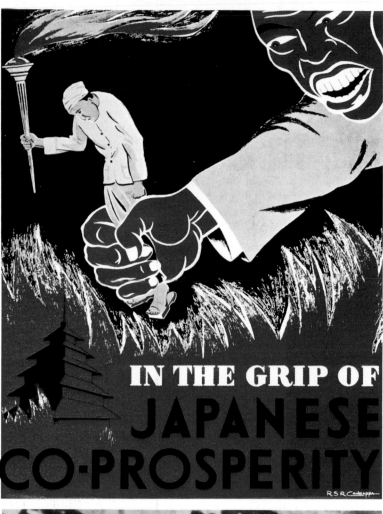

IN THE GRIP OF JAPANESE CO-PROSPERITY

7 and British civilians caught on what had suddenly become enemy territory was vestigial. Formalities were duly observed and diplomats handed in their passports. Defeated Poland was the first to suffer: not merely the Jews, who had long been marked down for elimination, but the "intelligentsia" of the country— prominent civilians, writers, artists, and politicians, who had at all costs to be prevented from keeping alive Poland's will to

7-10. The other side of the coin: American and British internees in Japanese hands.
8. Early days. A holiday look prevails in the Santo Tomas camp, Manila, in the Philippines.
9. Japanese soldiers pause at a stall in the Santo Tomas camp.
10. Primitive huts in Santo Tomas.

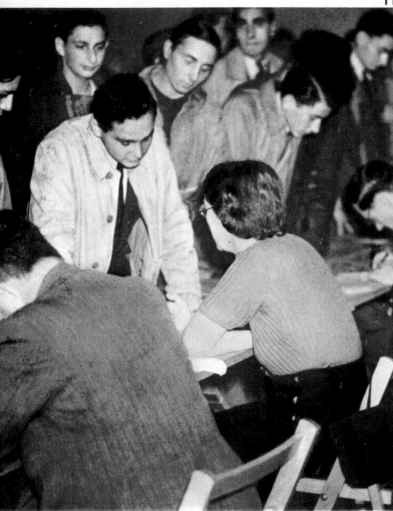

resist.

The first big change came with the runaway German victories of May-June 1940 which ended up with the French armistice and the German occupation of the Channel Islands. For the first time appreciable numbers of British civilians were rounded up in the conquered countries and shipped off to internment camps in Germany. Here their treatment was austere but conducted according to the Geneva Convention–after initial hardships in "sorting" camps in Belgium and France before the deportations began. The lot of the Channel Islanders was harder. They were an occupied part of the United Kingdom. They were forced to submit to repeated drafts of manpower for labour in Germany, and by 1944-45 the problem of food supplies was rapidly approaching starvation level. Total disaster was only averted by Red Cross intervention and the end of the war in Europe.

Italy's entry into the war in June 1940 witnessed the large-scale internment of civilians in Britain. The problem of housing them was solved mainly by shipping them off to Canada, running the threat of U-boat attacks, but with spacious camps and fair treatment at the far end of the route.

Across the Atlantic the problem of what to do with enemy civilians did not arise until December 1941–but there the targets were far more defined. For a start there was the American German *Bund,* a well-knit Nazi network with official headquarters and public rallies hailing the Führer's latest victories and pledging support to him. The Italian population of the United States was far higher than in Britain–but it had put down deep roots. The Duce's new Empire was far away, and there was a general tendency for Italians in the United States to consider themselves American citizens–epitomised by the Order of the Sons of Italy in America, which solemnly pledged allegiance to the Stars and Stripes.

When America was plunged into war by Pearl Harbor the situation, as far as Germans and Italians were concerned, was therefore comparatively straightforward. *Bund* members and leaders were rounded up and headquarters closed down, and the crews of Italian ships in American ports duly interned.

Matters were far more complicated–and heartbreaking–for the Japanese in America. They were branded as the villains of the piece for the shock of Pearl

11. *Aliens register in Britain.*
12. *On the way to internment.*
13. *A solemn profession of loyalty: the Supreme Council of the Order of the Sons of Italy in America pledge their allegiance to the United States in front of the Liberty Bell.*

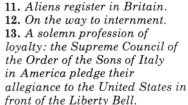

4

15

16

14. *A tagged collection of guns, cameras, and radios surrendered by aliens in New York City.*

15. *Allegiance to the other side. German-Americans give the Nazi salute at the German Day Rally, October 4, 1940, in Madison Square Garden.*

16. *Federal officers point to the huge swastika on the ceiling of the American Bund Camp at Andover, New Jersey.*

Harbor. Official whitewash for the attack hinted at widespread "fifth-column" activity, not only on Oahu but in the homeland itself. Familiar scenes of nationalist hostility took place in America as mass Japanese internment began. It was an agonising and uphill fight for the second-generation Japanese-Americans to gain recognition. When they did they won renown in no uncertain manner — particularly the Japanese-American "Mo' Bettah" battalion in the bloody attacks across the Rapido river during the Battle of Cassino.

The big internment camps set up by the Americans were clean, well-ordered, and humane – but across the Pacific the scene was totally different. Immediately

after the sweeping Japanese victories in South-East Asia and the Pacific there was a definite distinction drawn between military and civilian prisoners. To the Japanese a surrendered soldier was disgraceful, human filth, a betrayer of his country, to whom no Western concept of humanity or justice should apply. But to start with the civilians were deluged with clumsy propaganda blandishments of the brave new world awaiting them in Japan's "Co-Prosperity Sphere". It did not take long for the Japanese to realise that European civilians in their charge were not reacting according to plan; and the ordeal of the civilians began.

It is a story best kept short – of the civilian prisoners given rations hopelessly inadequate for Western metabolisms and doomed to slow starvation, forbidden to resort to barter to supplement their scanty food supplies. In the main internment camps on Sumatra and Java – Tjideng and Kramat, Struisweg and Brastagi – conditions rapidly slumped to create all the horrors discovered by the Allies in concentration camps such as Belsen, Buchenwald, and Ravensbrück, with all the hideous refinements of tropical diseases thrown in. Hunger-strikes, demonstrations, and break-out attempts were put down with the utmost cruelty by the sadists of the *Kempetai* – Imperial Japan's Gestapo.

Thus the ordeal of the civilians was one of the oldest aspects of war, brought up to date and refined by the processes of 20th Century war. The ultimate victims of the conflict, they could not escape the sufferings – both mental and physical – of the fighting men.

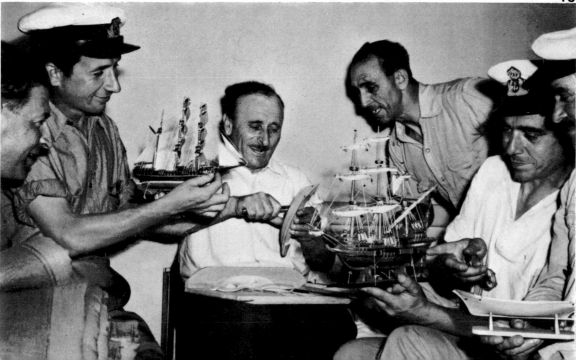

17. *When all seemed set fair for Italian victory: Italian seamen cheerfully give the Fascist salute aboard the liner* Conte Biancamano *as they are interned at Brooklyn.*
18. *Whiling away the months of captivity: Italian seamen, interned at Fort Missoula, Montana, make ship models.*

CHAPTER 132
Into the Siegfried Line

Whilst Bradley's offensive in the north was at a standstill again, south of the Ardennes, Patton was preparing to force the *Westwall* in the region of Saarlouis, and had already chosen the date December 19 to do so. The transfer of the 5th *Panzerarmee* had left the defence of Lorraine to the German 1st Army alone. In spite of the addition of LXXXIX Corps (General Hoehn), this was reduced to nine divisions (each numbering on average fewer than 10,000 men) spread across a 125-mile front. Facing it, the American 3rd Army, reinforced to three corps (nine divisions, three of them armoured), numbered 250,000 men. Furthermore, Patton had the advantage of surprise, because, on November 8, the rain was so heavy that any important action seemed unlikely.

Sure enough, that evening, XII Corps (General M. S. Eddy: 26th, 35th, and 80th Infantry, 4th and 6th Armoured Divisions) threw aside the three feeble divisions which LXXXIX and XIII S.S. Corps (the latter under General Priess) put in its path and captured Moyenvic and Nomény. Eddy rapidly exploited this success: to the right along the line Château Salins – Morhange – Rohrbach (4th Armoured Division, 35th Infantry Division); to the left by Han-sur-Nied – Faulquemont – Saint Avold (6th Armoured Division, 80th Infantry Division) in spite of counter-attacks by the 17th S.S. *Panzergrenadier* Division *"Götz von Ber-*

Hanging out the washing - five years late

1. *The promise at last carried out: a member of the R.A.F. hangs out his washing on the Siegfried Line.*
2. *Anti-tank defences in the Siegfried Line.*
3. *Warrant Officer Millard Grary, an American of Scots extraction, practises the bagpipes amid the dragon's teeth of the Siegfried Line.*
4. *Last view of the vaunted Westwall for a group of German prisoners passing through it en route to a P.O.W. camp.*
5. *An innocent-looking barn disguises a concrete pillbox in the Westwall.*

lichingen", then by the 21st Panzer Division. Within XX Corps, the 5th Infantry Division set about outflanking Metz to the south and east of the fortress. The 95th Infantry Division (Major-General Twaddle) crossed the Moselle above Thionville during the night of November 8-9, then turning south met up with the 5th Infantry Division on November 19 on the Metz-Saarlouis road. This was the division's first experience under fire. Meanwhile, the 90th Infantry Division, which had forced a crossing of the Moselle below Thionville and which was followed by the 10th Armoured Division (Major-General W. H. H. Morriss), reached the Franco-German frontier on November 20.

Metz falls

The mopping up of Metz was entrusted to III Corps under Major-General J. Millikin. The fortress works mounted only 30 guns, and the 462nd *Volksgrenadier* Division which constituted its garrison numbered barely 7,000 men. On November 25, fighting in the centre of the town ceased and the Americans found Lieutenant-General Kittel, the fortress commander, severely wounded in hospital. The western fortifications fell one after the other. The "Jeanne d'Arc" Fort, which covered the district round Gravelotte, was the last to capitulate (December 13).

Patton into the *Westwall*

LXXXII Corps (General Sinnhuber) had no better success than XC and XIII S.S. Corps. Furthermore, the reserves which Army Group "G" and O.K.W. made available to give support to the 1st Army were in too poor shape to remedy the situation. So it was that Major-General Walker and his XX Corps were able to bite into the *Westwall*. On December 3, the 95th Infantry Division managed to secure by surprise the bridge over the Saar between Saarlouis and Fraulautern, on the right bank of the river, then secure the right bank area after reducing 50 pillboxes. On December 18, the 5th Infantry Division joined it in this bridgehead, while slightly downstream the 90th Infantry Division, overcoming two concrete positions, secured a second bridgehead occupying half of Dillingen.

Patton's optimism with regard to the offensive he was preparing for December 19, with the help of 3,000 planes from the Tactical Air Force, appeared to be well grounded. Events would prove otherwise. Even so, between November 7 and December 21, at the cost of 4,530 dead, 21,300 wounded, and 3,725 missing, his army in Patton's own reckoning accounted for 21,300 Germans killed and 37,000 taken prisoner. At O.K.W. Hitler reacted to the 1st Army's defeat by dismissing General Schmidt von Knobelsdorff. On December 4 he was ordered to hand over his command to General Obstfelder.

Allied forces in Alsace reshuffled

If for the 12th Army Group victory on the Saar was to some extent compensation for failure on the Roer, the 6th Army Group won so convincing a victory in the Saverne gap and to the south of the Vosges that for a time it seemed likely it would reach positions along the left bank of the Rhine between Lauterbourg and Huningue. Fortunately for the Germans this did not occur, and the opportunity did not come about again.

It has been mentioned above that the American 7th Army had earlier been reinforced by XV Corps (79th Infantry Division and French 2nd Armoured Division). During October it also received the 44th, 100th, and 103rd Infantry Divisions, then after its breakthrough into lower Alsace, the 14th Armoured Division. And the French 1st Army, still responsible for the Mont Blanc–Barcelonnette sector, in addition to keeping its 2nd Moroccan Division (General Carpentier), received the 5th Armoured Division (General de Vernejoul), transferred from North Africa. At the end of November, the 4th Moroccan Mountain Division was relieved of its duties on the French-Italian border by the newly-constituted 27th (Alpine) Division and was transferred to the French 1st Army.

When he established his H.Q. at Vittel, General Devers had seven divisions under his command between Epinal and the Swiss frontier. At the start of the new offensive, his army group numbered 14 divisions, three of them armoured.

Outlining his new mission to General Balck on September 19, Hitler had conveyed to him the paramount necessity, for political reasons, of holding Alsace and Lorraine at all costs. The transfer of the 5th *Panzerarmee* to the Roer sector was not compensated for, however, by new reinforcements, and the German 1st Army had to extend its left flank to block the way to Strasbourg between Château Salins and Raon-l'Etape. Meanwhile the 19th Army had taken up defensive positions on a line linking Saint Dié, Gérardmer, and the western spurs of the Vosges, and ending to the west of Montbéliard in front of the Belfort gap.

The French press on to the Vosges

The first plan conceived by General de Lattre de Tassigny, whose left flank reached Rupt-sur-Moselle at the end of September, was to force a way across the Vosges by the Col de la Schlucht. He was forced to change his mind, however, and accept Guebwiller as the initial objective for II Corps, which in a later phase of the battle thrust forward vigorously to reach the Rhine at Chalampé, thus pinning the left flank of the German 19th Army back on the Swiss frontier. With this aim, he reinforced General de Monsabert with three further divisions and the support of two others. Nevertheless the plan came to nothing, for two reasons. Firstly, while the French II Corps was struggling to reach the crest of the Vosges, the American 7th Army found itself drawn off in the divergent direction of the Saverne gap, and de Lattre was most reluctantly forced to use some of the troops he wanted to throw into attack for purposes of consolidation. Patch and Devers above him had simply acted in conformity with the instructions they received from S.H.A.E.F., namely to provide cover for the 12th Army Group (3rd Army) in its advance north-eastwards.

Secondly, the very heavy rains of autumn 1944 slowed down infantry, and blinded artillery and aircraft, with the added effect that as winter closed in and the men of II Corps scaled the long slopes of the Vosges, cases of frostbite grew numerous. The leather ankle-boot with its rubber sole was not the most successful article of American equipment.

Previous page: *French Moroccan* goums *move up behind the Colmar front.*
◁ ◁ *Infantry shelter in a depression in a wood before moving off into the attack.*
◁ *A Sherman covers a column of infantry moving up a country lane towards Metz.*
▽ *French* spahis *on forward reconnaissance. While two of them report by radio, the other two keep watch, fingers on the triggers of their machine guns.*

▷ *A German soldier loads a ten-barrelled field rocket launcher.*
▽ *Victims of superior Allied firepower: a knocked out German Pzkw Mk IV and, behind, a Mk V.*

1940

CHAPTER 133
The fight for Alsace

△ *General Béthouart commanded I Corps in de Lattre's army.*
◁ *A column halts during the push into the snowy forests of the Jura.*

▽ *General Guillaume. His Algerians kept up the pressure on the front of II Corps.*

On October 17, after a fortnight's sustained drive which took the 3rd Algerian Division up the Moselotte as far as Cornimont, General de Lattre decided to change his plans and make a surprise attack on the Belfort gap. But it was important nevertheless that II Corps should not lessen its pressure and allow the enemy to redeploy his forces. The offensive forged ahead, and on November 5 the 3rd Algerian Division (General Guillaume) reached the outskirts of the Col d'Oderen, more than 3,000 feet high; the opposing enemy forces here included as many as 15 infantry battalions as well as the 169th Division, which had been refitted after its return from Finland.

Such deployment of force was combined with a piece of trickery, whose aim (in de Lattre's own words) was "to give the enemy the impression of total security in Vosges sector. Counterfeit troop movements and the setting up of fictitious H.Q.s were made conspicuous in the area of Remiremont. At Plombières a detachment of the 5th Armoured Division set up roadsigns, signposted routes and made full use of radio. All this activity drew the attention of enemy spies and if by chance it escaped them the Intelligence agents were there to open their eyes to what was going on." All these indications were corroborated, in General Wiese's mind, by bogus orders and letters, bearing General de Lattre's personal signature, which reached him from reliable

sources. The supreme instance of planned deception being "General Directive No. 4", in which the French 1st Army commander announced his intention of simulating troop concentrations in the region of the Doubs to encourage the enemy to withdraw troops from the Vosges.

The attack goes in

At any event the Swiss 2nd Division, in the Porrentruy area, using sound detection apparatus, was able to follow the progressive deployment of powerful artillery on the slopes of the Lomont, for all the discretion the French used in their registration shoots. It is not known whether these indications escaped the notice of the Germans.

De Lattre decided on his plan on October 24: I Corps (General Béthouart) was given the objective of capturing the roads eastwards out of the Belfort gap and simultaneously storming the fortress town. In the event of success, II Corps would join battle, its objective being the Rhine between Huningue and Neuf-Brisach and the line linking Neuf-Brisach–Colmar–Ribeauville. General Devers, whose intention was to push his 7th Army onwards from Saverne to Strasbourg, fully approved the plan drawn up by his immediate subordinate, and allocated him a battalion each of 203-mm guns and

240-mm howitzers, in addition to other weapons.

General Béthouart's first line troops consisted of the 9th Colonial Division (General Magnan) which, reinforced by a Combat Command of the 1st Armoured Division, was to attack between the Swiss frontier and the Doubs (it should be remarked that his Senegalese troops were relieved by Zouaves and Moroccan light infantry, and F.F.I. [French Resistance forces] recruited in the area); also, of the 2nd Moroccan Division, which was given Montbéliard, Héricourt, and Belfort as objectives. The main action would devolve on this latter division, so it was given two Combat Commands, from the 5th Armoured Division.

On the enemy side, LXIV Corps (General Schalk) was deployed on a 30-mile front. On the left was the 338th Division with its back to the Swiss frontier; on the right the 159th, barring the Belfort direction. These were divisions of poor-quality infantry, mainly composed from heterogeneous elements and of differing morale (there was even one deaf battalion).

They were covered by deep, dense anti-tank minefields whose clearance proved to be particularly hazardous, as they were protected by a fearsome array of anti-personnel devices and explosive traps. Requisitioned workers from occupied France–from the Delle district of Belfort–completed the main construc-

△ *American infantrymen prepare to attack from trench positions on the outskirts of Colmar. A French-manned tank stands by to give support.*

▶ How the Allies cleared
Alsace and Lorraine. By the
last week of 1944 they had
closed up to the Franco-German
frontier but the Germans, on
Hitler's orders, continued to hold
on in the Colmar pocket.

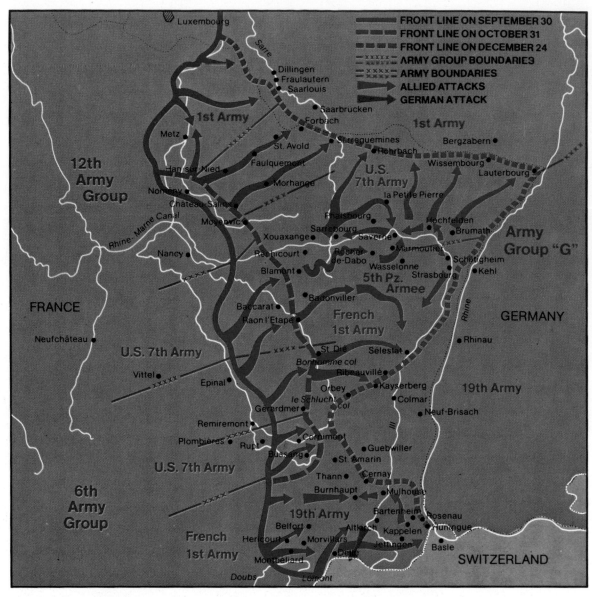

tion of a 12-mile anti-tank ditch; this
would have constituted a formidable
obstacle to the French 1st Army if
General de Lattre had deferred the date
of his offensive, giving the enemy time to
mine it and man its defensive positions.

The attack got under way on November
14 in conditions of sleet, and serious
losses were sustained in the minefields. I
Corps got a foothold in the enemy positions, but was unable to break through.
Two factors favoured the French, however: Lieutenant-General Oschmann,
commanding the 338th Division, was
killed by a patrol from the 2nd Moroccan
Division near the Besançon–Montbéliard road, and his aide-de-camp's brief-
case yielded a plan of the division's
positions, in addition to copies of several
orders. Also, it would appear that for
48 hours, General Wiese's H.Q. minimised
the gravity of the French offensive.

At all events, on November 16, the 19th
Army received order from Army Group

"G" to fall back on to the Belfort–Delle
positions. But its LXIV Corps was so
enfeebled that its rearguard was overtaken and mauled by the enemy. The
main action took place the following day.
On the evening of November 17, the 4th
Combat Command (Colonel Schlesser),
having adroitly managed to conceal its
movement forward from the enemy, took
the bridges over the Luzine at Montbéliard by surprise and opened the way
for the 2nd Moroccan Division. Near the
Swiss frontier, the 9th Division broke
through the scanty line of the German
338th Division, enabling Béthouart to
unleash the 1st Armoured Division
(General du Vigier).

Leaping at the chance, de Lattre the
same evening issued a "general order to
exploit the situation in full": he issued
simultaneous orders to I Corps to head
for the Rhine (1st Armoured Division),
to reduce the fortress of Belfort (2nd
Moroccan Division), and to reincorporate

Hitler and Colmar

In fact, this view was quite mistaken. On the contrary, in the middle of all this, Hitler dismissed General Balck and put General Wiese and his 19th Army under a new command known as *"Oberrhein"*, which he entrusted to *Reichsführer*-S.S. Heinrich Himmler; and far from proceeding to evacuate the Colmar bridgehead he set about reconstituting its defence, which he did with great success.

Carrying out the orders that had come from the 6th Army Group, General de Lattre incorporated the two divisions he had been allotted as well as the 3rd Algerian Division, the Moroccan troops, and the 4th Combat Command (5th Armoured Division) in II Corps and ordered it to attack the north-west front of the pocket, from a line linking the Col du Bonhomme, Ribeauville, Sélestat, and Rhinau. At the same time, I Corps had orders to attack from a line between Mulhouse and Thann, both corps being given Neuf-Brisach as their objective. We drew attention earlier to the reasons for the reverse suffered by Béthouart around December 10. And Monsabert, for all his dash, had troops that were too few and too battle-weary to bring him greater success. The energy he displayed enabled him to batter the enemy front but not break it, as his orders required; in arctic conditions, he managed to capture Orbey and Kayserberg, taking 5,568 prisoners, but his own losses were heavy and on December 19 he was ordered to take up a defensive position on the line he had reached.

In this battle, the French 1st Army, as General de Lattre de Tassigny remarks, was at a disadvantage in that the Wehrmacht's Panthers and *Jagdpanthers* outclassed the Shermans and Allied tank destroyers with disastrous consequences. But apart from this, morale on the German side had been greatly strengthened.

The diminished success of the Colmar offensive caused some friction between de

▽ *Algerian troops dug in, with M10s at the ready in the background.*

The American/British Sherman M4A4/VC Firefly tank

Weight: 34.8 tons.
Crew: 5.
Armament: one 76.2-mm (17-pounder) Mk. IV gun with 78 rounds, one .5-inch Browning machine gun with 500 rounds, and one .3-inch Browning machine gun with 5,000 rounds.
Armour: hull front 51-mm, sides and rear 38-mm, belly 25-mm, and decking 19-mm; turret front 76-mm, sides and rear 51-mm, and roof 25-mm.
Engine: one Chrysler A-57 inline, 430-hp.
Speed: 25 mph on roads and 10 mph cross-country.
Range: 125 miles on roads and 50 miles cross-country.
Length: 25 feet 6 inches.
Width: 9 feet 6 inches.
Height: 9 feet 4 inches.

surrendered to a detachment of the 2nd Armoured Division. So ended General Leclerc's amazing exploit.

Eighty-two days' misery: that, in General de Langlade's words, was to be the lot of the 2nd Armoured Division on the morrow of its brilliant victory. Without necessarily disagreeing with this opinion, it should, however, be observed that the same run of bad luck afflicted the American 7th Army, indeed the whole of the 6th Army Group.

After cutting through the solid front formed by the enemy 1st and 19th Armies, General Patch threw his VI and XV Corps forward towards the German fron-

◁ ◁ *A farm building blazes near Sarrebourg.*
◁ *A bag of German officers captured at Saverne.*
▽ *The tricolour flies in a Belfort street as the French march in—hugging the walls against possible ambush.*

△ Lieutenant-General
Vaterrodt, who surrendered
Strasbourg to Leclerc.
▷ French gunners in
Strasbourg.

tier in accordance with his orders to provide support for the 3rd Army in its attack on the *Westwall*. On his right, VI Corps, now commanded by Major-General Edward H. Brooks, following General Truscott's appointment as commander of the American 5th Army in Italy, got its 79th Division to Lauterbourg on December 6, while the 45th was attacking the Siegfried Line parallel to Bergzabern, both of them biting deep into the German defensive system. On his left, XV Corps was hammering away at the fortifications in the area of Bitche, the only section of the Maginot Line to play a rôle in 1944. It had reduced them when the Ardennes offensive forced it to let go its hold.

At Strasbourg, the American 3rd Division (VI Corps) had relieved the French 2nd Armoured Division which, in company with the American 36th and 103rd Divisions, tried to prevent the enemy establishing new positions round Colmar. Here General Patch was endeavouring to do two things at the same time: effect a break-through in the *Westwall* between the Rhine and the Saar, and clear the enemy from the left bank of the Rhine above Strasbourg. This double assign-

ment was given him by General Devers who, in calling for two divergent operations, was doing no more than conform to instructions from S.H.A.E.F. where the enemy's capacity for resistance was not fully realised.

However, on December 2 H.Q. 6th Army Group took the American 7th Army off the Colmar assignment and gave it to the French 1st Army, at the same time allocating the 36th Division and the 2nd Armoured Division. This was indeed a logical decision, but one that resolved nothing, since the switch produced no reinforcements. And de Lattre, as we know, had been reluctantly obliged to part with his 1st Free French Division and was further expecting, according to orders received from Paris, to lose his 1st Armoured Division, which was to be sent to Royan.

Then again, at Vittel, General Devers's Intelligence staff took an optimistic view: the stiffening of enemy resistance in Alsace was recognised, but attributed to O.K.W.'s concern not to pull its troops back from the left bank of the Rhine until it had had ample time to provide for the defence of the right bank of the river.

The American/British Sherman M4A4/VC Firefly tank

Weight: 34.8 tons.
Crew: 5.
Armament: one 76.2-mm (17-pounder) Mk. IV gun with 78 rounds, one .5-inch Browning machine gun with 500 rounds, and one .3-inch Browning machine gun with 5,000 rounds.
Armour: hull front 51-mm, sides and rear 38-mm, belly 25-mm, and decking 19-mm; turret front 76-mm, sides and rear 51-mm, and roof 25-mm.
Engine: one Chrysler A-57 inline, 430-hp.
Speed: 25 mph on roads and 10 mph cross-country.
Range: 125 miles on roads and 50 miles cross-country.
Length: 25 feet 6 inches.
Width: 9 feet 6 inches.
Height: 9 feet 4 inches.

Hitler and Colmar

In fact, this view was quite mistaken. On the contrary, in the middle of all this, Hitler dismissed General Balck and put General Wiese and his 19th Army under a new command known as *"Oberrhein"*, which he entrusted to *Reichsführer*-S.S. Heinrich Himmler; and far from proceeding to evacuate the Colmar bridgehead he set about reconstituting its defence, which he did with great success.

Carrying out the orders that had come from the 6th Army Group, General de Lattre incorporated the two divisions he had been allotted as well as the 3rd Algerian Division, the Moroccan troops, and the 4th Combat Command (5th Armoured Division) in II Corps and ordered it to attack the north-west front of the pocket, from a line linking the Col du Bonhomme, Ribeauville, Sélestat, and Rhinau. At the same time, I Corps had orders to attack from a line between Mulhouse and Thann, both corps being given Neuf-Brisach as their objective. We drew attention earlier to the reasons for the reverse suffered by Béthouart around December 10. And Monsabert, for all his dash, had troops that were too few and too battle-weary to bring him greater success. The energy he displayed enabled him to batter the enemy front but not break it, as his orders required; in arctic conditions, he managed to capture Orbey and Kayserberg, taking 5,568 prisoners, but his own losses were heavy and on December 19 he was ordered to take up a defensive position on the line he had reached.

In this battle, the French 1st Army, as General de Lattre de Tassigny remarks, was at a disadvantage in that the Wehrmacht's Panthers and *Jagdpanthers* outclassed the Shermans and Allied tank destroyers with disastrous consequences. But apart from this, morale on the German side had been greatly strengthened.

The diminished success of the Colmar offensive caused some friction between de

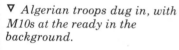

▽ *Algerian troops dug in, with M10s at the ready in the background.*

Lattre and Devers, the first asking the second for two further divisions and the second replying that the other Allied armies were managing well enough without receiving reinforcements. It would seem that in drawing this comparison, General Devers quite failed to appreciate the factor of air cover, which operated very much to the advantage of Simpson, Hodges, Patton, and even Patch, while his French subordinate was cruelly deprived. Apart from that, neither Devers nor General Eisenhower even had the two divisions requested by de Lattre available to give him. The supply of reinforcements from across the Atlantic had been speeded up, but in early December 1944 S.H.A.E.F. had only 66 divisions immediately available, so that its main reserves were barely sufficient.

Not enough manpower

And this leads us to draw the following conclusion on the whole episode. In every army in the world, before the appearance of atomic weapons, it was an article of faith that the commander-in-chief's power of decision depends on the number of men at his disposal. Thus, on the eve of the German counter-attack of March 21, 1918, behind the 119 divisions at the front, Haig and Pétain had 62 in reserve. In the present instance, this was far from the case. So Eisenhower should not be blamed, as so often he is, for not exercising greater authority over his immediate subordinates, since he lacked the means that would have enabled him to enforce his decisions.

This situation led to defeat at Arnhem, and qualified success or failure on the Roer. As for the victories won on fronts which Montgomery would have preferred to leave inactive, they were not exploited for want of the ten or so divisions that would have allowed Patton, Patch, and de Lattre to attack the *Westwall* between the Moselle and the Rhine, before Hitler moved in the Ardennes.

▽ *General de Lattre de Tassigny salutes his tank crews.*

▷ *By the end of 1944 de Lattre's troops had cleared Alsace, but the Colmar pocket was still holding out.*

▽ *A French Stuart passes a rank of recently-captured Germans, waiting with their hands up to be marched off to the P.O.W. pen.*